LEADERSHIP
AND STRATEGY

UNDERSTANDING, PLANNING
AND IMPLEMENTING

LEADERSHIP
AND STRATEGY

UNDERSTANDING, PLANNING
AND IMPLEMENTING

EDWARD A. MERRITT, PhD

Day Press

Published by Day Press

ISBN: 978-1-59330-920-6

Library of Congress Control Number: 2017901409
Library of Congress Cataloging-in-Publication Data
Leadership and Strategy/Edward A. Merritt
Printed in the United States of America

For Margaret

Contents

Chapter 01

Current Theories Of Leadership

Introduction

The purpose of this chapter is to introduce current theories concerning the subject of Leadership and provide a working definition for the topic. I present several models to help provide a useful framework for conceptualizing leadership. You will notice that leadership revolves around involvement with people, as leadership is a social process. How we relate to others in groups is central to understanding key elements of leadership. I review familiar concepts of leadership style as well as theories that relate to followers' ability to follow and the leaders' ability to adopt behavioral styles that maximize the potential for effective leader-follower relations.

Situational Leadership uses four classifications, which range across a spectrum from a high degree of direction to a high degree of delegation. Situational leadership suggests that leaders have a preferred (default) style and there is one style is most appropriate to a given situation. This given situation varies widely based on the capabilities of the followers.

The Grid Model provides a way of looking at behavior and leadership effectiveness with certain leadership styles. The Situation Model relates follower readiness for a task to the leader's ability to modify his or her style to the follower's readiness. I introduce the concept of power to show how power enhances the effectiveness of leaders. Theories X, Y, and Z reveal how an individual's view of others can affect leadership style. Again, all of these theories attempt to frame how people relate to each other. Indeed, leadership is a social process.

I cover the idea of effectiveness in this chapter to introduce how we evaluate leaders. This is often a difficult task. However, one must have a measure of how leaders are performing in order to judge their worth to the organization.

The goal of this chapter is to present various ways of thinking about leadership. You will study several theories and concepts that relate to leadership to help you become familiar with this important element of management.

Background

The study of leadership is difficult. The primary reasons are that it covers many disciplines and it is vague to the point of being open to a variety of interpretations concerning its meaning. There have been a host of definitions offered for the concept of leadership. The most used definitions in vogue revolve around statements including terms like: influence, induce, group, goals, behavior, effectiveness, environment, leader personality traits, leadership style, follower maturity, situation, and others. These terms help to construct frameworks in identifying primary interacting leadership elements. The aim of developing these frameworks is to identify the essence of leadership. After developing a framework, we form a definition of leadership. Although many definitions exist in the literature, the definition used to describe leadership in this text is most similar to the one proposed by James Burns:

Leadership is the action of inducing, influencing followers to accomplish certain goals that represent the values, wants and needs, the aspirations and expectations of both leader and follower.

While Burns' definition works well, I would add emphasis that *effective leadership* is a *process of social influence* that employs the tools of management in a manner that yields superior results. After all, what organizations strive for is effective leadership and not mere leadership. While some would consider effectiveness implicit in the term leadership, it is worthwhile emphasizing. Effective leadership is what makes good organizations great. If leadership is a plain pizza, effective leadership is a pizza with all of your favorite toppings and cooked to perfection. As Emeril Lagasse might say, effective leadership is leadership kicked up a notch.

After developing a working definition of leadership, it is logical to try to develop concepts that apply to it. Many theories have attempted to capture the nature of leadership but all seem to have fallen short. Most leadership concepts seek to provide a comprehensive explanation of how and why some leaders perform more effectively than others do.

Theory development in this area has not been entirely successful. However, the next few pages will be devoted to presenting an overview of leadership theories and how they may be practically applied.

Framework

The manner in which one obtains a leadership position begins to build a leadership *framework*, which is a basic structure underlying a system, context, or text. Such structures include follower expectations, skills required of the leader, group maturity, and other circumstances. Because of the complexity these variables, some authors tend to oversimplify leadership. For example, researchers often classify leadership into either an autocratic or a democratic framework, or describe the leader as the one in control. These terms have categorized the leader and placed a framework around the concept so that specific labels apply to both leaders and followers. By framing leadership, a particular view develops so that leader and follower relations become clear. Concepts and terms become a descriptive device to help develop an understanding of leadership as a concept.

For example, one term often used to describe a leader is *control*. It is a common notion that the leader is the one in control of followers and the environment. To investigate this concept it is important to provide an idea of the meaning of the term control within a leadership context. One way to look at this is to understand how a leader gains control. Does the method of gaining control affect the leadership environment? What is control? How does control help influence a group? These questions will need addressing in understanding how control affects the leadership environment. For example, the leader may gain control as the result of tradition. If this is the case, followers will have little to say about who has group control. The follower may accept the tradition without questioning its authority.

Followers may blindly accept all consequences of leader actions without questioning the circumstances. Under these circumstances, followers are subjects under the leader's control. Control may coerce followers and force the will of the leader.

At the other end of the spectrum, we have followers electing their leader. While this leader will also have control, it will be of a much different nature. In this case, the leader becomes authorized, within certain parameters, to control the group. If followers are not willingly controlled, they may have a voice in changing the control factor, if desired. If followers decide not to be controlled by a particular leader, they may change leaders. It should be obvious that the element of control within these two environments is different.

From this example, the context and framework from which one is working are extremely important in developing a concept of leadership. The reason for showing how one variable, such as control, may be viewed is to reveal how a wide variety of elements affect leadership. The general environment becomes a mixed bag of factors that affects how group members and leaders interact. Understanding how leaders and followers interact is very important in understanding leadership.

It is important to identify various facets of leadership to gain an understanding of the leadership environment. It is apparent that creating an exhaustive review of all leadership elements and cause and effect relationships cannot be identified as there are just too many. However, the primary goal of this chapter remains one of identifying essential leadership elements and investigating how they interact. The underlying factor in conducting preliminary work is to isolate those primary elements. The question then becomes: Do leadership elements exist which interact in certain ways to produce leader effectiveness? If these elements exist, can they be identified from situation to situation? If there is some consistency to how these elements interact to produce effective leadership, then we may be able to develop predictive models for effective leadership behavior.

The example of control is only one element, which affects the concept of leadership. Frameworks should identify several key leadership elements to provide a solid base for theory development. If cause and effect relationships can be identified, this is a basis for predicting leader success and effectiveness. The next few pages include some theories and concepts that have been used to explain leadership and to isolate cause/effect relationships in the leadership environment.

Personalized Theories

Armchair Theories

Armchair theories are those that are based on personal experience, conjecture, and personal feelings and do not include collecting new information. Instead, armchair theories develop after a comprehensive analysis and/or synthesis of current research. This is not to imply that these theories do-not have valid use and benefits, they may, but the purpose in explaining their origins is to identify the foundations of their claims. One such theory is the *Great Man Theory*, which might be referred to more appropriately as the Great Person Theory. The Great Man is viewed as one who is above the group; is superhuman, and can handle any situation for which the group may need him. This is a throwback to medieval thinking—men were expected to take charge and rescue damsels in distress. The Great Man possesses the attributes of a hero in which courageous traits are the basis of group support. There have been many examples of the Great Man Theory in history: Hercules, King Arthur, etc.

Another armchair theory is the *Follower Theory*. This theory proposes that the way to become a leader is to be an effective follower. The smart follower becomes a leader because he/she has learned through on-the-job training all the necessary skills to lead the group effectively. This concept places primary importance on the experience of the leader and the leader's ability to relate to group members. This leader's skills have been learned through years of experience and experience is the only manner in which he/she can become qualified and accepted by the group. Examples of this model exist in factories, in corporations that rely on corporate experience, and in work environments where skills must be handed from group member to group member.

The Genius Theory, another armchair theory, promotes a person to a position of leadership and separates the person from the rest of the group members because of his/her innate talents and/or knowledge. This person is a leader by virtue of his/her special talents. Einstein and Babe Ruth are two examples of special talents that exemplify this concept.

These concepts or theories present a line of reasoning that describes how leaders obtain their position of leadership and why they are viewed with esteem, but offers little to identify systematic interactions of leadership elements. There are other concepts that could be classified in the category as Armchair, all having the quality of personal perception based on experience. The *value* of these concepts is that they do help explain elements of the leadership environment. The *fallacy* or failing of these concepts is that they do not formulate a sound basis for theory development and consequently a body of reliable information to study the subject. Recently, however, there have been major improvements in developing a sound and meaningful body of leadership information.

Leadership Theories and Models

The Grid Model

The *Grid Model* helps in determining a leader's tendencies toward a high concern for both people and production. The Grid Model was originally conceptualized by a University of Ohio research team in the 1950s using terms to describe task-oriented and person-oriented behavior. At about the same time, a group of researchers from Japan established a similar model describing an effective leader as one who is high in both performance behavior and maintenance behavior. They referred to their model as the PM Leadership Theory (Peterson and Misumi). However, it is generally believed that Blake and Moulton propelled it into gaining popularity under terms that described a High High leader. This behavioral system applies to leaders and not to groups. It attempts to identify a leader's behavioral patterns on an X and Y coordinate plane, using two basic variables. These variables were identified as systems-oriented behavior on the Y-axis, and person-oriented behavior on the X-axis. Simply stated, the person-oriented behavior is action directed toward satisfying the needs and preferences of individuals, and systems-oriented behavior is behavior directed toward structuring the work environment to accomplish group goals. The coordinate plane and the variables are depicted in the upcoming figure 1.

Paula Silver described her understanding of the systems/person-oriented scheme as having six categories of specified behavior. Again, the purpose for these classifications is to identify leader behavior (applies to leaders and not to groups).

Systems variables

(Also referred to by others as *production* and/or *task* axis variables.)

1. Production Emphasis—increased production of the group.

2. Initiating Structure—establishment and clarification of rules and policies to govern group actions.

3. Role Assumption—active exercise of the leader's position.

4. Representation—acting as the group's spokesperson, furthering the group's interaction with higher authority.

5. Persuasiveness—refers to having firm convictions, convincing others of one's point of view.

6. Superior Orientation—actions that serve to maintain the group, actions that maintain or increase the leader's position within the group.

These six categories provide a comprehensive view of Y-axis variables. A composite score of systems axis variables is obtained to provide a score for the Y-axis. This score represents a leader's systems-oriented behavior.

Relations

(Also referred to by others as *person* and/or *social relationship* axis variables.)

1. Tolerance of Uncertainty—refers to actions that show the leader has the ability to accept postponement and indefiniteness without becoming upset or anxious.

2. Tolerance of Freedom—allows followers latitude in making their own decisions, actions, etc.

3. Consideration—expressing friendliness and interest, consulting with group members and attending to their suggestions.

4. Demand Reconciliation—dealing with conflicting demands without becoming upset.

5. Integration—action that serves to maintain a closely-knit group and to resolve conflicts among group participants.

6. Predictive Accuracy—set of behaviors that exhibit the leader's foresight and ability to anticipate outcomes.

A composite score for the relationship axis variables yields the value of the leader's tendency to exhibit person-oriented behavior along the X-axis. When the X and Y variables are plotted against one another, patterns may be identified to classify a leader's behavioral style.

Figure 01: The Grid Model

Systems Oriented. The Y-axis moves vertically from bottom (low) to top (high) from 0-9

Person Oriented. The X-axis moves horizontally from left (low) to right (high) from 0-9

	0X-	1X-	2X-	3X-	4X-	5X-	6X-	7X-	8X-	9X-
9Y-										
8Y-										
7Y-										
6Y-										
5Y-										
4Y-										
3Y-										
2Y-										
1Y-										
0Y-										

In the *Managerial Grid*, Robert Blake and Jane Moulton applied elements from the Grid Model to develop another, but similar, behavioral approach to leadership, the Managerial Grid. Their Managerial Grid matrix utilizes the intersection of the grid model, coordinate (O,O), forming a matrix with an axis maximum, and uses what Blake and Moulton refer to as *relationship* and *task* variables instead of the *systems* and *person* variables.

The matrix is formed in a slightly different arrangement than the Grid Model, but still indicates specific areas identifying certain behavioral tendencies. Coordinates are used on specific areas of the grid to identify the type of leader who would display high/low, low/high task/ relationship behavior.

For example, the (1,1) leader is said to exert minimum effort to sustain the group; they are low-task and low-relationship. The leader with a rating of (9,1) is high-task and low-relationship oriented. This person would be classified as emphasizing efficiency, order, and results, with minimum concern of human relations. The (5,5) category reveals a leader that has an orientation toward adequate performance through the balance of work requirements in maintaining satisfactory morale. The (9,9) leader exhibits high-relationship and high-task behavior and is usually a person that allows people a great deal of freedom and independence in their work. The (1,9) leader pays particular attention to the people in the group but is not oriented toward getting things done. These labels are helpful because they allow one to think in specific terms about a leader's behavioral patterns.

There have been various labels used to describe the two dimensional variables, task and relationship. This text will use the terms, task-oriented (TO) and relationship-oriented (RO), when referring to this theory.

For most, the Grid Model is seen as *a more intuitive and understandable model* than the Managerial Grid in depicting the task-oriented focus on work and relationship-oriented focus on people.

Situational Leadership Contingency Theory (Hersey and Blanchard)

Situational Leadership Contingency Theory is a contingency approach (no one best way) to leadership developed by Paul Hersey and Kenneth Blanchard and applies to both individuals and groups. Essentially, their theory specifies an appropriate leadership style based on the capabilities of the subordinate and/or group. A high capability subordinate has the ability and willingness to complete a task successfully. A low capability subordinate lacks both ability and self-confidence to attempt a task.

The model variables are labeled relationship and task and are shown in the figure. The contingency model considers both the follower and the leader. It posits that the leader must assess the follower's task readiness before choosing the appropriate relationship behavior. The accurate assessment of the right mix of these two behaviors will yield the most effective leadership style. This assumes that the leader can change his/her behavior (style) and that a change in leadership style will have a maturing effect on the follower. Maturity, at its extremes, means that the follower moves from almost total reliance on the leader for direction and support to the follower developing self-reliance and freedom in performing a task. This model also assumes that the follower's behavior can be changed and that the follower desires his or her behavior to be changed. The essence of the model is that the leader recognizes follower maturity (readiness), and correspondingly chooses an effective leader style.

Hersey and Blanchard characterized leadership style in terms of the amount of direction and support that a leader gives to his or her followers under the classifications: Directing (the highest amount of supervision and control), Coaching, Supporting, and Delegating (the lowest amount of supervision and control).

- **Directing.** In directing, the leaders define the tasks to be accomplished and supervise the process closely. Decisions are made by the leader and communication with followers is mostly one-way from leader to follower or group. Directing is also referred to as autocratic and militaristic.

  The true nature of this concept is not as simple as it seems. What most people usually mean when they say autocratic leadership is that the leader dominates by force, power, coercion, threats, etc. While directing can have a sometimes-negative reputation, there are times when this style is appropriate. An appropriate time to use a directing style would be in an emergency, such as an emergency department physician providing trauma care. Another less dramatic situation where directing would be an appropriate style would be if a dining room captain was having places set by entry level servers for a banquet of 100 guests.

- **Coaching.** In the coaching style, leaders continue to define tasks and supervise closely. However, leaders begin to seek ideas, input, and suggestions from followers. Communication is far more two-way in that there is an expected give and take between leader and follower. Coaching is also referred to as consultative.

  An application appropriate for a coaching style would include followers who have some relevant experience performing a related task, but might not be fully capable of performing the particular task. More specifically, we may have a group of machinists who have a great deal of experience cutting precision automobile pistons from steel who are now asked to cut a specialized connector using titanium.

- **Supporting.** In a supporting style, it is appropriate for leaders to pass day-to-day decision making along to followers. Here, the leader facilitates work processes and an outcome, but control of goal achievement lies with the followers, as their responsibility. Communication is very much oriented from followers to the leader. Supporting is often referred to as participative or democratic.

Applications for a supporting leadership style are many. By definition, we have a situation whereby a follower is capable (high commitment) but may lack the confidence to take charge and go it alone. Specifically, think about a situation such as a long time supervisor of a hotel front desk is offered the position as front desk manager. A supporting style helps allay the follower's doubts in him or herself.

• **Delegating.** In delegating, the leader is involved in major decisions and problem solving, but otherwise followers are in control. Because followers are in control of work processes and outcomes, the followers invite the leader in when they want his or her involvement. Delegating is often referred to as laissez-faire.

Delegating style works quite successfully when the follower is an experienced professional doing an excellent job in his or her position. One example would include an experienced golf professional being encouraged to run his or her day-to-day business within a hotel resort. The General Manager is a specialist in business management but not in golf management.

Lessons for consideration

This theory of Situational Leadership suggests several important lessons and points for consideration.

1. **Versatility.** Effective leaders are versatile and should be able to provide variable amounts of control and support to their followers based on follower ability.

2. **Direction.** Less experienced followers need more direction. Followers who are more capable need to be encouraged, but do not need or appreciate constant micro-managing from their leaders.

3. **Cannot do everything.** Leaders are physically limited. Leaders, especially in large organizations, cannot possibly (and should not attempt to) run their day-to-day organizations—at some point it becomes physically impossible to do so. Therefore, using situational leadership allows a leader to focus his or her attention where it is needed, which makes leadership manageable.

4. **Involve others.** The supporting leader involves others. Fellow workers and constituents assist in the process of making important decisions. This does not mean that the leader acquiesces to the

responsibility of making decisions, instead it means that followers aide in making decisions—they have expected and binding input.

5. **Delegation.** Make decision-making at the lowest level. The coaching, supporting, and delegating environments foster decision-making by lower level management by degree because task and authority have been delegated.

6. **Direction of information.** Information flows laterally and downward in the coaching, supporting, and delegating organizational structure, whereas the directing leader typically keeps followers in the dark and makes his or her own decisions.

7. **Common pitfalls.** Over-managing and trying to do too much is a very common pitfall of less experienced leaders. They typically believe that they must try to do it all and do not know how to delegate effectively. Left unchanged, this behavior leads to inefficient management and possibly burnout.

8. **Move toward delegating where possible.** While there are situations that favor a directing style over the more participative styles, current trends seem to favor a style, which ideally moves along the continuum toward delegating where possible and/or practical.

9. **Ideal.** In an ideal, established, and effective work environment, all followers would be trained and educated with high competence and high ability in their jobs, which would allow the leader to use a delegating leadership style.

Assessment and Motivation

Assessment and motivation are integral to the contingency model; thus, according to this model the leader must possess skills in these areas to be effective. To move a person or a group from low maturity (beginner) to high maturity (expert) takes leader time, perseverance, and talent. The leader must continuously motivate followers toward established goals, and be able to assess the follower's skill level. Skill levels are viewed relative to where the follower *is* to where the follower *needs to be* when the desired competency level is reached.

This model is limited in that it should only be employed with one skill at a time. The starting point on the curve corresponds to the follower's maturity, and this point suggests the leadership style to be adopted.

For example, a leader's style may be low-task, low-relationship on a particular skill for a follower, and high-task, low-relationship style on another skill. Individual skills are emphasized. Using this model, the leader must be able to demonstrate a mix of two behaviors to institute the appropriate style for followers' maturity levels. In short, a leader must be able to adapt and adjust his or her behavior to react to follower readiness levels.

It is assumed the contingency model may also be used for group behavior as well as individual behavior. The group's maturity level would be assessed in much the same manner as individuals, and change in leadership style would be dictated by group maturity level changes. The problem is that individuals mature at different rates; thus, the leader must assess maturity in an aggregate manner for groups. This could lead to problems that this model does not address. Therefore, care must be used if this model is applied to group behavior.

LPC Contingency Model (Fiedler)

Fred Fiedler's basic theory is that the leader's effectiveness depends on a match between the personality of the leader and the complexities of the particular situation.

Fiedler developed the *LPC (Least Preferred Co-worker)* questionnaire to measure whether a person is task- or relationship-oriented. This situational model includes what Fiedler refers to as the group, task, situation (GTS). The group, task, situation includes three elements.

Fielder's GTS

1. **Leader/Member Relations**—the loyalty, friendliness, and cooperativeness of subordinates toward the leader. It describes the quality of feelings that the group members and the leader have.

2. **Position Power**—the extent to which the leader's position enables the leader to evaluate and thereby exercise influence over the group in the form of rewards and punishment.

3. **Task Structure**—the degree to which the group's task, goals, and objectives and other operating procedures are in place and expectations for outcomes are well defined along with an objective plan for assessing goal attainment.

Fiedler ordered these variables by degree of importance by identifying relations as first (the most important), task as second, and the leader's power position as third. The combination of these factors influences the environment to the point of determining the most effective style of leadership that the leader should exhibit. Fiedler concluded that the degree to which these factors are present in the environment affects another concept he introduced—situational favorableness.

The favorableness of the situation prescribes the most effective leadership style. Fiedler displayed the favorableness concept along three ranges.

a) Favorable.

b) Moderately favorable.

c) Unfavorable.

Quadrants are used to correspond to groupings with the appropriate leadership style identified. The LPC Contingency Model is diagrammed in figure 2.

Favorableness is a composite of the three factors. Each variable is considered on a scale (high, low) and then grouped to determine the degree of situation favorableness. By grouping all combinations of the variables, Fiedler categorized the groups into classifications of favorable, moderately favorable, and unfavorable. Fiedler further prescribed a leadership style for each category, which includes two styles in the designated positions within the eight categories:

- Task-oriented style for categories (octaves) 1, 2, 3, and 8.
- Relationship-oriented style for categories 4, 5, 6, and 7.

Fiedler's assumptions

1. **Favorable situation**. The group would complete more tasks, or reach their goals more efficiently with a task-oriented leader. For example, in a favorable situation, the leader/follower relationships are assumed positive and consequently, followers would expect the leader to take charge.

2. **Moderately favorable situation.** The relations-oriented leader would be most effective. In a moderately favorable situation, the

leader should apply the principles of relationship behavior because relations are poor in three of the four categories. Further, in the category where relations are strong, that category is not supported by the other two categories.

3. **Unfavorable situation**. The group would (as in the favorable situation) complete more tasks or reach their goals more efficiently with a task-oriented leader. Because all categories rate low, the effective leader would apply task behavior to clarify expectations for the group.

With a leader structuring his or her behavior along these lines, the group may be able to realize success and that success may help improve the group/leader relations. While relations (as a category) is the most important variable, it must be supported by the other two variables or the right combination of the other two variables.

As the factors either improve or deteriorate, the variables will change. These changes will likely indicate a change in leadership style. Like the situational model, this model suggests leader adaptability and flexibility. The model indicates that a person may be a successful leader in one situation but not in another. Research supports Fiedler's contention that a leadership style may be indicated; however, one must be cautious of relying on this as a formula for quick leader effectiveness. Since many leaders have a preferred style and therefore often apply their preferred style instead of an indicated/appropriate style, there is a possibility that some leaders will not freely adapt different styles. The degree of leadership effectiveness may be found in the leaders' flexibility in assessing situations, prescribing behaviors, and adapting styles.

Figure 02: LPC Contingency Model

Note: LPC indicates least preferred coworker

	Favorable 1-3			Moderately Favorable 4-7				Unfav
Octant	1	2	3	4	5	6	7	8
Relations	good	good	good	good	poor	poor	poor	poor
Structure	high	high	low	low	high	high	low	low
Power	strong	weak	strong	weak	strong	weak	strong	weak

Bases of Power and Leadership

Webster defines *power* as possession of control, authority, or influence over others. This definition takes on additional meaning when combined with the concept of leadership. *Leadership power* is based to a great degree of the follower's willingness to be influenced, induced, controlled, and guided by a particular person. One commonly held but mistaken belief, is that a leader is necessarily the person within a group setting who holds the highest degree of power and/or authority. A person may have power and/or authority by virtue of his or her position, but still not be a leader. Also, people are considered leaders because of their rank or title within an organization. However, positions (titles and/or ranks) do not possess leadership characteristics, only people possess leadership characteristics. One may expect certain leadership characteristics to be exhibited by people in certain positions, and that a position calls for some expected style of leadership to be anticipated, but a position (title and/or rank) itself, of course, does not exhibit leadership.

Leadership power is derived from a follower's willingness to be led. That is not to say that individuals in administrative and managerial positions do not have power, because they do have power. Position power is derived from vested authority and responsibilities and is different from power bestowed by willingness to follow. A person may possess both position power and personal power, maximizing his or her influence. Leadership power is derived from the fact that followers allow themselves to be influenced; thus, merely possessing position power does not make one a leader. Furthermore, power does not create a leader; power is derived from someone being—in action and behavior—a leader.

We will identify and examine several types of power within two main categories: organizational power, which is granted formally by administrative edict and personal power, which derives informally from the leader's personality:

Organizational Power Forms

Administrative Power Elements

Position Power

Chester Barnard developed the Zone of Indifference theory, which posits that followers may allow supervisors, managers, and administrators to exercise control over them as a condition of organizational rank. According to this concept, the follower is willing to be influenced or controlled by the authority vested within a position's bounds, but may or may not be willing to be influenced beyond the position's vested authority. The amount of position power that a person inherits, because of the power vested in the position, influences how much control the person has over a group.

Representation Power

The leader is usually given the power to *represent* a group internally and/or externally. The leader may be the representative for the missions, goals, and operations of the group and may communicate the purpose and intent of group actions to entities external to the group. Internally, the leader may occupy any position; the consistent factor is that group members look to the leader to represent their interests.

Purpose Power

The concept of *purpose power* suggests that mission or purpose of the group takes priority over the desires of any single individual or individuals. Therefore, leader actions that are perceived as group goal directed and actions that perpetuate group purpose are considered more important than special interests that arise. Group purpose is apparent in the leader, so the group, as long as they represent the group's purpose and intent, accepts his or her actions.

Legitimate Power

Legitimate power is granted by virtue of one's position in an organization. A legitimate power base can be exercised through the acquisition of formal authority, title, and/or position. Legitimate power is also enforced by organizational edict, the existence of an organizational chart delineating reporting relationships, and a willingness of others to recognize and accept that source.

Reward Power

The extent to which one person controls *rewards* that are valued by another. Influencing the behavior of another by the benefit of a reward can result in power for the benefactor. The reward must be perceived to be of value to the recipient in order to alter performance. In addition to pay, promotion, and prestige, rewards may include praise, publicity, respect, favorable working conditions or scheduling, and other such considerations perceived as desirable by the recipient.

Coercive Power

Coercive power is the opposite of reward power. Exists when somebody has the ability to physically or psychologically punish someone. One possesses power in this mode if the leader has the ability to punish or withhold rewards for non-performance in a prescribed manner. Punishment or withholding rewards includes denial of raises, demotion, unfavorable transfer, or other actions that are deemed undesirable by the recipient. Coercive power is not always as overt as other forms of power. However, a person under the influence of another must perceive that the supervisor has the capability and authority to use coercive power. Current leadership concepts do not recognize *brute force* as a leadership element, but rather that leadership power is a form of influence and inducement. If brute force were to be considered, it is more accurately categorized as coercive power.

Personal Power Elements

Beyond power being granted to a leader administratively, effective leaders use their personalities to help influence subordinates. Leaders may have magnetic personalities; people are naturally and positively drawn to them. This is not always true, however, as some leaders may not be liked, but are still perceived as having personal qualities that are worth emulating. Leaders can use this personality attraction as a power of presence to influence the group. Minimally, a leader is perceived as one who has the qualities to get the job accomplished. The group's collective feelings concerning the leader's positive qualities (whether they like the leader or not) give the leader personality power.

Influence Power

If a group perceives a person as their leader, this person has inherent *influence power* within the group. The leader usually has the power to influence policy, operations, and the general group climate. The leader is usually a key person in establishing important work relationships and how people interact to accomplish group missions.

Expert Power

Control over information or knowledge gives one *expert power*. If one is judged as possessing more knowledge or skill, he or she may influence others who have correspondingly less knowledge or skill. The importance of this form of power is easily discernible in a superior-subordinate relationship and either person can enhance his position of power by using it.

Referent Power

A leader's power is gained through identification, association or imitation. *Referent power* may exist when a person is liked, admired, or respected because of personality traits or skills that another finds desirable. The person who holds this power over another may or may not be conscious of such influence. People like to identify with those they perceive as winners.

Administrative and personal power elements comingle

Power may be used in many ways, but it is important to realize that *position power* is limited by the boundaries of the position's authority. Leadership power, by definition, is power the group gives the leader. Followers perceive the leader will use the power to move the group in a desired direction. On occasion, the leader may be allowed to go beyond position bounds because leadership power expands the zone of influence of the leader. Leadership power is accepted as goal directed and it is not likely that a group would continue to support a leader who is perceived as detrimental to that group's purpose. Therefore, *leadership power* is bestowed on the leader, and perceived by group members as being goal oriented.

Therefore, the difference between position power and leadership power is one of follower perception. Position power is accepted by followers because it is perceived as the authority in a position. Leadership power is accepted because followers perceive the use of power as promoting group goals, purpose, and values. There is willingness of followers to submit to leadership power because of an overriding commitment to group values. The difference in these types of power may be subtle, but substantial.

Power is recognized as a leadership element, but it can easily be misinterpreted. *Power is not leadership, but leaders have power.* Power is manifest in the leader's actions to achieve group goals. Position power may be easily misinterpreted as leadership power because people frequently use their positions in an influential manner. However, not all types of influence are necessarily leadership influence. The test to determine if power is vested in leadership can be determined by answers to the following questions.

Test whether power is vested in leadership

1. **Willingness.** Do followers express a willingness to recognize power beyond influence inherent in a position?

2. **Goal achievement.** Is the leader's power used to influence action to realize group goals?

Group Behavior

Becoming familiar with group dynamics is important in understanding the nature of leadership. A group, in a context of leadership, has a special meaning; it is not simply a gathering of people, but rather a gathering of people who have come together for a specific reason, intent, or purpose and are bound by certain moral and/or philosophical beliefs and/or values. In studying leadership, it is important to note and understand some group characteristics and the manner in which groups take action.

Categorizing groups

Group actions can be categorized in three fundamental ways:

1. **Interacting.** *Interacting* groups are those in which the product outcome involves a group effort and the individual members working interdependently with one another.

2. **Co-acting.** *Co-acting* groups are those in which the members work independently of one another.

3. **Counteracting.** *Counteracting* groups are those in which members compete with one another.

Relationship to leadership theory

When these three classifications are applied to leadership theory, we discover the following relationships:

- The Fiedler Situational Model applies to groups in which individuals within the groups are interacting and not to groups in which members either work independently or compete within the group.

- Hersey and Blanchard's Contingency model applies to all three classifications of groups and is often applied to individuals.

- The Grid Approach is geared to individual leader behavior. Therefore, groups and their corresponding work would not be considered within the boundaries of this approach.

The study of group dynamics is necessary for serious students of leadership, because leadership, by definition, takes place within a group setting. Group dynamics goes beyond mere group classifications and delves into the inter-workings of various group types.

Time: A Leadership Variable

Likert's Time-Lag Concept

Rensis Likert's (pronounced LIK-ərt'). Time-Lag concept stresses group performance and environmental climate as the primary forces that produce results (outcomes). The importance of this concept lies within its recognition that leader actions do not directly affect results. Instead, leader actions affect results indirectly. Likert suggests that there is a time lapse between leader action and results.

Likert's three concepts to support his hypothesis

1. Causal variables. Causal variables are elements that are under the control of the leader and include issues such as philosophy, structure of the organization, policies, rules, regulations, leader behavior, and the like.

2. Intervening variables. Intervening variables are those elements that are affected by causal variables. They include issues such as climate of the organization, attitudes of the employees, perceptions, and politics among group members, etc.

3. End-result variables. End-result variables can also be described as the product or outcome. Likert posits that end-results are the product of the first two variables (causal and intervening variables) and that the cause/effect relationship between the first two variables creates a natural flow to produce the third variable referred to as end-results. For example, in a school setting, end-result variables might include test scores, rate of attendance, percentage of college-bound students as compared to the total school population, teacher turnover rate, etc.

This model is referred to as time lag, because, in most cases results are not immediately realized when leader action is taken and time becomes a variable that effects realization of goals and objectives. Most complex organizations have goals that are realized longitudinally across time. Consequently, the benefit of a leader's action taken today may take years to be fully realized. The Likert model takes into consideration the time element involved in fully realizing the effect of leader actions. That is, the effect that leader actions have on causal and intervening variables on end-result variables.

An example of the time lag concept: A college dean maintains relatively high morale and good relations with professors, but the college's student test scores fall far below the national average. The university president is concerned about the test scores and eventually terminates the dean. The president hires a hard-nosed dean to get the test scores in this particular college back up to the national average.

The new dean raises the test scores but is so tough on the professors that he/she has caused half of the faculty to leave the college. The test scores are up, but the morale of the faculty is down. In the end, faculty production will drop, which will cause declining test scores.

Between the time of the test scores going up for the hard-nosed dean and then going down again, pressure has been placed on the president, and as a result the hard-nosed dean is fired, and the president hires another dean who can get along with the college faculty. This cycle may continue indefinitely, revealing the president's actions and over time, affects the college climate. This ultimately affects the end-results sought by the university. This example provides a clear picture of the time lag effect. One cannot always accurately judge the effect of a leader's actions at the time that they occur. The proper criterion for judging a leader's actions is the long-term effect that actions have on end-results.

Figure 03: Time Lag Model

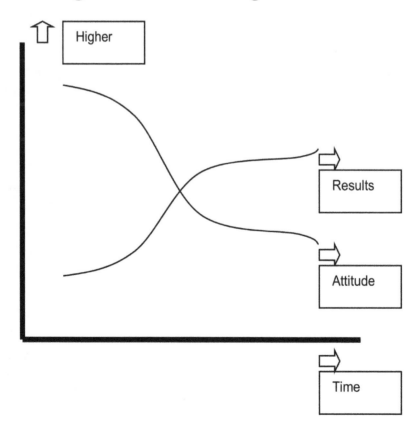

Theory X and Theory Y

Douglas McGregor of MIT's School of Management developed Theory X and Theory Y in the 1960s. Rather than a theory on leadership, Theory X and Theory Y are both anchored in philosophies as to how people view other human beings. This is significant because how leaders relate to others is a critical element in predicting leader behavior. The value of Theory X and Theory Y comes in realizing that it places emphasis on the particular leader's attitudes. A leader's attitude about people in general, is a key in the development of leader-follower relations. Theory X stresses the importance of strict supervision while Theory Y focuses on the motivating role of satisfying workers without direct supervision.

Theory X assumptions

1. Dislikes work. The average person has an inherent dislike for work and will avoid it if possible;

2. Need direction. Most people must be coerced, controlled, directed, or threatened with punishment to get them to exert adequate effort toward the achievement of organizational objectives; and

3. Want direction. The average person prefers direction, wishes to avoid responsibility, has relatively little ambition, and wants security above all else.

Theory Y assumptions

1. Satisfying work is natural. The expenditure of physical and mental effort in work is as natural as play, as long as it is satisfying;

2. Goal commitment. People will exercise self-direction and self-control toward an organization's goals if they are committed to the goals;

3. Rewards. Commitment to objectives is a function of rewards associated with their achievement; The most effective rewards are satisfaction of ego and self-actualization;

4. Avoidance. The average person learns, given favorable conditions, to not accept and seek responsibility. Avoidance of responsibility and emphasis on security are learned and not inherited characteristics; and

5. Creativity, ingenuity, and imagination are widespread among people.

All people like to be treated with dignity and respect. Effective leaders should review Theory X and Theory Y assumptions and ensure that they have or develop Theory Y philosophies. For Theory X leaders, especially in a setting that deals directly with people, time has come and gone. It is likely that leaders with this predominate style will not be successful in people-oriented environments.

Theory Z

Abraham Maslow first conceptualized Theory Z in the 1960s. William Ouchi and W. Edwards Deming continued Theory Z's development into the 1970s and '80s. W.J. Reddin followed from the 1980's and into the '90s. Theory Z built upon Theory X and Theory Y. Theory Z is the direct opposite of a bureaucratic philosophy of management and counters the view that leadership must be a behavioral continuum. Theory Z's philosophy implies trust in the judgment and goodness of people and embraces group members' opinions to help influence group actions.

Application of Theory Z stresses upward mobility for all group members with skill specialization so that group members can become competent in specific areas. However, after becoming a competent specialist in one area, group members are encouraged to progress to other tasks, which will challenge their existing skills and intellect, thereby encouraging group members to view education and training as a never-ending and key element of career and personal development.

Position security is another mainstay of Theory Z; providing group members with the opportunity to work in confidence while knowing their positions will not be threatened. Theory Z also encourages an attitude of greater cooperative effort between and among group members and group leaders, allowing leaders to obtain firsthand information about group activities and making followers feel they are part of the leadership team.

The leadership philosophy in many organizations during the 1900s in the United States was the opposite of Theory Z. One of the main influences in the United States was the work of Max Weber and the development of *bureaucratic structure*. Weber's philosophy of management can be observed throughout federal, state, and local government, the military, and other organizations. The bureaucratic philosophy stresses chain of command, span of control, policies, regulations, and rank. It is obvious that organizational structures have influenced how leaders have developed and expressed their leadership styles. *Current trends* appear to have shifted toward Theory Z, as reflected in the manner in which organizations are operated.

Evaluation

Success and Effectiveness

There is a difference between being an effective leader and being a successful leader. Leadership that produces desired results may be termed successful, but not necessarily effective. A leader can be successful without being effective, but cannot be effective without being successful.

Successful leadership results in intended group behavior, but in the long run success alone may not produce the desired results. One could achieve all the goals set forth for a group and still not be considered effective. The effective leader will motivate the follower toward continued success and instill in the follower the desire to strive for future goals. The non-effective leader may accomplish immediate goals, but not motivate the followers for future activity. The effective leader will take into consideration follower feelings and desires, and attempt to satisfy the followers' personal needs as well as accomplishing group goals. Effectiveness is a process; the result is success and motivated followers.

Addressing follower satisfaction is a primary element in developing an effective leadership style. Knowing what satisfies a particular follower may vary from group to group, but the astute leader will learn the satisfying environmental elements as well as the dissatisfying environmental elements. The effective leader will seek to minimize the latter while maximizing the former. The desired result for the leader is successful accomplishment of goals, as well as a satisfied and motivated work group.

A leader's behavior is particularly difficult to assess since, to be considered effective, the leader must be both able and willing to lead; the followers must be both able and willing to follow. An explanation of willing and able is illustrated in the following discussion. There are four combinations (of leader and follower) for failure and only one combination (of leader and follower) for success. This being illustrated, is it reasonable to conclude that it is four times as easy to fail as to succeed when leading people? Or for that matter, is it four times as easy to fail anytime one deals with people? Perhaps that is not the discrete conclusion to draw from this line of reasoning, but almost anyone who has been in a position of dealing with groups will admit that it is difficult to be successful. The leader's responsibility when dealing with people is to turn the failure situations into the success situations by creating willing and able scenarios for all involved.

Three criteria of leader effectiveness

1. Group satisfaction.

2. Group productivity.

3. Group performance.

In many cases, these criteria are judged by questionnaires administered to the group under study. However, there are several different ways by which to judge effectiveness. The concept of effectiveness in leadership has much to do with motivation of followers. The concept of effectiveness is central to the study of leadership.

Five Leadership Effectiveness Combinations

Just one effectiveness combination results in success.

- Follower is *willing* to be led and *able* to be lead. Leader is *willing* to lead, but *unable* to lead. *Failure* occurs.

- Follower is *willing* to be led and *able* to be lead. Leader is *unwilling* to lead, but *able* to lead. *Failure* occurs.

- Follower is un*willing* to be led, but *able* to be lead. Leader is *willing* to lead and *able* to lead. *Failure* occurs.

- Follower is *willing* to be led, but un*able* to be lead. Leader is *willing* to lead and *able* to lead. *Failure* occurs.

- Follower is *willing* to be led and *able* to be lead. Leader is *willing* to lead and *able* to lead. *Success* occurs.

Leadership Skill

Many of the current approaches to leadership have focused on behavioral elements. Studies of leader behavior have been thought to reveal and/or suggest success and effectiveness patterns. Analysis of specific situations has provided insight to the type of leader behavior, which is thought to be most effective for a particular situation. Another approach to leadership has been to identify skills that when executed successfully, yield effective leadership. With this approach, the leader exhibits certain skills, and is rated on his or her successful execution. The major emphasis of this line of thought is on teaching skills of how to become a leader. It is assumed that if someone can be taught appropriate skills that he or she will become an effective leader.

This approach highlights a philosophical argument: Is leadership an art or a science? The answer to this question is probably both. The answer lies somewhere in a gray area, as leadership is both an art and a science. The degree of whether art or science depends on personal interpretation and, perhaps, application. It is important to note that the skills approach is not all-inclusive. Competence in certain skills does not necessarily guarantee leadership success. Necessary skills in one situation may not be a requirement in another situation. Thus, to determine the skills necessary for success, one needs to analyze carefully the specific leadership situation in question.

Certainly, some group of skills is necessary for one to become a competent, successful, and effective leader. However, the type of skills and degree of expertise depends on the environment—often referred to as the situation. Assessing skills required for effective leadership without analyzing the environment is tricky. For example, an engineering environment would require demonstration of different skills than a social-work environment. There may be leadership skills common to both environments, such as effective communication. However, there are skills unique to both environments, which require their own type and degree of competency. The student of leadership should be careful not to view execution of skills as leadership itself. The act of executing skills does not equate to leadership, but execution of skills may be necessary to be a leader in a particular situation.

Execution of skills involves a process that affects the perception of leader effectiveness. Therefore, it would be easy to confuse the process of executing a skill with leadership when really it is the effectiveness of executing the skill, which is being judged. There is a difference between executing a skill and effective leadership. Although the two may be related, short-term execution should not be judged as effective leadership. Effective leadership and execution of skills should be judged across different parameters.

The skills approach typically describes the necessary skills a person must competently demonstrate to be a successful leader. On the other hand, behavioral approaches typically prescribe behaviors the leader must exhibit to be effective. Many of the theories covered in this chapter are related either directly or indirectly to behavioral theories. Some theories have considered follower readiness and the general climate that exists between leader and follower.

In review, all of the topics that have been covered are important to the study of leadership and all impact leadership. It is advisable to become familiar with several approaches to leadership to obtain a broad understanding of this concept.

Chapter 02:

Motivation

Introduction

This chapter examines motivation. Motivation is an integral element of leadership, and is included as a major section in the majority of leadership texts. This chapter provides a descriptive narrative of the subject and provides insight into many of the current theories of motivation. Here is a brief rundown of the theories of motivation that are covered:

Expectancy Theory is the first to be covered in this chapter. It presents a process model of how people are motivated. The drive of Expectancy Theory is that people have choices to make, and for their effort expended, people expect results.

Expectancy Theory questions

- Pay-off. What do we perceive as the pay-off for our efforts?
- Drive. What is it that drives us?
- Goals. Why do we choose the goals we choose?

These are some of the questions that Expectancy Theory explores. Expectancy Theory is a psychological theory that places the individual in the position of choosing between or among values.

Path Goal Theory emphasizes the leader and stresses how a leader must recognize the needs of the follower while recognizing the elements in the environment that may keep the follower from accomplishing established goals. Path Goal Theory posits that it is the responsibility of the leader to remove external obstacles that would hinder the follower in accomplishing his or her goals.

Maslow's Hierarchy of Needs delineates personal needs and orders them sequentially into priorities of likely fulfillment. This theory provides a framework in which a continuum of motivational factors is considered in the priority of how they may be satisfied.

Herzberg's Two-Factor Theory considers two sets of factors—maintenance factors and motivation factors. Maintenance factors do not motivate, but they help keep employees from being dissatisfied. This theory proposes that if a person is dissatisfied then he or she is not capable of being motivated.

Background

Motivation in organizations and institutions over the past 100 years has been handled predominantly from a negative perspective.

Followers have been largely motivated with negative words similar to these:

If you do not show up for work on time then I will suspend you for a week.

Some refer to this method as motivation by fear, intimidation, or coercion. Whatever the case, it is certainly an example of negatively oriented motivation. Negative motivation may be the most often-used method, but it is not always the case and is rarely the preferred method. For the past several years, leaders have changed toward using positive forms of motivation.

In many instances, effective leaders instinctively know that each follower is different and that not all individuals are motivated in the same manners. Moreover, they realize that not all people can be treated effectively in exactly the same manner. However, all people should always be treated with both dignity and respect. Leaders who hold this view tend to make an effort to know their followers and know why and how each person is different. These leaders do not stress the *sameness* of followers; instead, leaders notice *individual* qualities. Astute leaders use these differences to their advantage in dealing with followers. Many theories stress the importance of an individual in motivation and thereby address factors that cause people to take certain actions over others.

The term *drive* is often used in psychological circles to describe the amount of energy focused and channeled toward accomplishment of a particular objective. The direction and intensity of a person's motivation are influenced by two factors:

1. A person's perceptions of him or her self (intrinsic) and

2. A person's perception of the world external to him or her self (extrinsic).

A person's perception of how well he or she can perform and the external forces acting on the individual to either aid or hinder performance will influence:

1. Whether the individual will or will not take action and

2. The amount of energy that will be exerted toward the action.

In considering motivation, one should realize that any environment involving people deals with varying degrees of uncertainty. One cannot always accurately assess how others will react to particular leader behaviors.

For example, an administrator praises John for a job well done. Afterward, Rachel demonstrates a 10 percent increase in work output. The leader uses the same technique with Ken only to observe a corresponding decline in Ken's work. Identical leader behavior resulted in two distinctly different responses. Later, the same leader praises Rachel and gets another increase in performance. Now the leader criticizes Ken and observes a corresponding increase in Ken's work. A reverse effect is observed. This illustrates that individual followers may react in the same manner to very different leader behavior. This may be due to differences in individual preferences or it may be due to differences in perception by the individuals themselves.

This chapter covers several theories on the subject of motivation. These theories attempt to explain why people act as they do. Some of these theories address issues that motivate others and some address the process of motivating others. Inferences are made concerning group behavior from conclusions drawn about individual behavior.

These inferences are used to help explain how motivational factors affect groups. Trying to draw inferences from individual behavior and to predict or prescribe group behavior can be problematic. To think that motivational factors of individuals are also descriptive of a particular group's motivational climate is not valid reasoning. The approach that we will present in this chapter is primarily focused on individuals, with the hope that one can gain some understanding about group actions, as well. The study of these motivation theories will provide insight into the nature of motivation and allow one to use this information to gain an understanding of peoples' actions.

One of the primary tasks of any leader is to try to help motivate followers, both individually and collectively. Knowing what prompts a follower to action can help provide the leader with the tools necessary to accomplish group tasks and goals.

Many current theories treat motivation as *a process* that begins with some unsatisfied need. A need produces tension, which in turn stimulates a level of drive within the individual. Drive leads to a search for appropriate behavior to achieve the goal and thereby to satisfy the need. If the need is satisfied, then the tension is thereby relieved.

Expectancy Theory

Expectancy theory suggests that work motivation is determined by an individual's belief in making decisions and producing effort toward results and outcomes—performance, relationships, and work outcomes. Developed by Victor H. Vroom in 1964, expectancy theory proposes an individual will behave or act in a certain way because he or she is motivated to select a specific behavior over other behaviors due to what he or she expects the result of that selected behavior will become. Essentially, the motivation of the behavior selected is determined by the desirability of the outcome. Because expectancy theory is about the mental processes regarding choice, or choosing, the core of the theory is the process of how an individual processes various motivational elements. This is done before making the ultimate choice. The outcome is not the sole determining factor in making the decision of how to behave.

Three assumptions

1. Anticipation. People do not just respond to events after they occur; they anticipate or expect that things will occur and that certain

behaviors in response to those events will probably produce predictable consequences;

2. Confront alternatives. People usually confront possible alternative behaviors in rational manners, and

3. Predict. Over time, people learn to predict likely consequences and therefore modify their behavior in a way that desired results could possibly be achieved.

Expectation motivation concepts

The constructs that follow help provide an understanding of motivation in terms of expectancy:

- Valence. Valence refers to the degree of preference that one has for a potential outcome. Valence may be described as the amount of care one assigns to a potential outcome: How much does one care about the outcome? Valence can be either positive or negative. Different people will assign different values to items and issues such as income, working conditions, status, or security. Valence helps define the parameters of what an individual wants and/or expects from a job.

- Outcome. Outcome is the consequence, product, or result of one's behavior. Outcome may be described as goal achievement.

- Action. Action is open, observable, and obvious behavior. Action entails physical movement as well as cognitive content and emotional tone. Expectancy theory assumes a range of behavior is available to and applicable by each individual.

- Expectancy. Expectancy is the belief that some particular behavior will likely result in a predictable, first-level outcome.

- First level outcome. First level outcome is the direct or immediate consequence of one's behavior.

- Second level outcome. Second level outcome refers to the personal impact that the first level outcome has on a particular individual. A first level outcome may affect something else in the life of the individual. For example, more productive work on the job (action) may produce better pay (first level outcome), which may yield a better lifestyle for the worker (second level outcome). Better lifestyle is a second level outcome that occurred directly because of the first level outcome.

- Instrumental Effect. Instrumental effect refers to a correlation between the first level outcome and the second level outcome. It is an individual's perception as to how strongly the initial outcome (first level outcome) will affect other outcomes (second level and subsequent outcomes).

A direct outcome is desirable or undesirable to the extent that it is perceived to relate to indirect outcomes that are desirable or undesirable. A direct outcome takes on valence, as it is perceived to be instrumental in attaining desired indirect outcomes and/or avoiding unpleasant indirect outcomes.

Expectancy theory is a *psychological* theory that places the individual in the position of choosing among values. It is based on the assumption that all human behavior can be regarded as the result of a state of internal tension which serves as a drive for action. It is drive that produces the energy to act. Expectancy theory is a descriptive model of how individuals act relative to their perception of *environmental* (external) stimuli.

One major force within an individual is his or her perception concerning their ability to act. A second major force is the perceived consequence of action taken. These two forces are major factors in determining whether an individual will take action, and the degree of energy the individual will exert toward the action. Expectancy theory helps explain the process of how individuals are motivated and the factors present when an individual is motivated.

Understanding the motivational process will help leaders identify ways to motivate individuals. It is incumbent on the leader to recognize what followers value, which are the elements that cause internal tension. It is also important for the leader to recognize how followers perceive their ability to act. Confidence is a major factor in successful completion of activities.

Path-Goal Theory

R.J. House's Path-Goal Theory is one example of Expectancy Theory. *Path-Goal Theory* focuses on appropriate leader behavior for various situations. Directive-, participative- or achievement-oriented leader behavior may be appropriate depending on the characteristics of the person and the situation.

This theory hypothesizes that if a follower clearly understands the path to take to reach a desired goal, and explicitly understands the rewards that will be received if he or she is successful, then that person will be motivated to choose the appropriate path that leads to the rewards that best suit his or her wants and needs. An individual can expect certain outcomes from actions because the various paths to those outcomes have been clearly identified. The individual is motivated by clearly understanding the amount of energy (drive) needed to achieve a particular outcome. An individual is also motivated to achieve a particular outcome if the path has been cleared of as many possible obstacles as can be anticipated.

According to Path-Goal Theory, the primary function of the leader then becomes one of a facilitator in removing obstacles from the path of followers so that desired outcomes may become realized. The leader should provide skill training for the follower to accomplish desired goals, and identify the necessary amount of effort that will be required to accomplish an outcome. The leader should point out the reward for successful accomplishment, and help show the follower the way to go about successful accomplishment. House is quick to make leaders and followers aware that there is no guarantee of success even if the follower is aware of the means of reaching his or her goals and even if most obstacles are removed from the follower's path. A major portion of responsibility for success lies with the follower. The follower must value (have valence for) the goal enough to take the necessary action (drive) to fulfill the goal.

House and Dressler's suggestions for implementing Path-Goal Theory

1. Recognize and arouse the follower's need for outcomes over which the leader has some control.

2. Increase personal payoffs to followers for successful goal attainment.

3. Make the path to payoff easier to obtain by offering coaching, directing, and other forms of mentoring.

4. Help followers clarify expectations in terms of objective terms (discrete metrics which can either be timed and/or counted);

5. Reduce frustrating barriers.

6. Increase the opportunity for personal satisfaction contingent upon effective performance as evaluated in terms of objective measures.

If these guidelines are implemented, the result should be a significantly higher percentage of followers who are motivated and directed. Path-Goal Theory places the follower at the front of the focus—the follower successfully completes tasks to achieve goals, while the leader provides the guidance and direction.

It is necessary for the leader to understand the individual follower's wants and needs and also the group's wants and needs. The leader must know the task accomplishments that are necessary for the follower to realize success. This implies that the leader must understand the environment and have empathy for the follower's goals.

Leaders using any leadership style need to know and understand these variables:

1. Know and understand themselves.

2. Know and understand the external environment in which they are working.

3. Know and understand their followers.

Knowledge of one's strengths and limitations, and knowing the followers' characteristics are basic issues for practical application of Motivation Theory.

When the path (means for accomplishing a goal) is clear to followers, research shows that some followers do not respond well to further path clarification. This may help explain why many people resent close monitoring and/or micromanaging. These types of people believe that they are professional, know their jobs, know what is expected of them, and can operate independently. They prefer a style whereby a leader provides the structure for getting the goal achieved and then allows the follower to execute the plan. Research efforts in the area of motivation have been contradictory in its findings. However, this can be expected since motivation deals with prescribing, predicting, and explaining human behavior.

The follower will choose among the paths that they perceive fulfill their needs. This process helps explain some of the issues that motivate people. It does not attempt to either define or otherwise explain the nature of motivation, it simply attempts to identify some elements that cause a person to take action. If given a choice, which would you choose, peer recognition or financial security? Of course, it is not always a matter of simply choosing, it is often a matter of simultaneously working on several paths to achieve desired goals.

The House approach suggests that there is a more or less general pattern to one's actions. These patterns provide insight into a follower's behavior and can help a leader establish a meaningful leadership plan (rewards, task, goals, and expectations). It is difficult to judge how much value (utility) a person may place on any specific goal, especially when involved in complex environments. However, one primary leader task is to assess what motivates followers and to use this information to achieve optimal follower performance.

Maslow's Hierarchy of Needs

Abraham Maslow's theory from the 1940s is one that delineates personal needs and orders them in priorities of likely fulfillment. In this theory, Maslow posited that each person has an innate hierarchy of five needs that include physiological, safety, belongingness & love, esteem, and self-actualization; they are one-directional and progressive (moving from low to high). A brief description of each level from lowest order to highest order:

- Level 1 Physiological. Represented by food, water, warmth, and rest.

- Level 2 Safety. Represented by feelings of security and safety.

- Level 3 Belongingness and love. Represented by friends and intimate relationships.

- Level 4 Esteem. Represented by prestige and feelings of accomplishment.

- Level 5 Self-actualization. Represented by achieving one's full potential.

Maslow's four assumptions

1. A need that has already been satisfied is not a motivational factor.

2. Needs of an individual are complex; nothing is as neat as a hierarchy is and one is subject to a variety of needs.

3. One will tend to be motivated toward higher order needs once the lower-level needs are met.

4. Higher-level needs may be met in a variety of different manners. However, there are relatively few ways in which to satisfy lower-level needs.

The United States typically assumes that most followers' basic needs are being met, which allows us to concentrate effort on higher order needs, such as self-actualization. In reality, basic needs being met may or may not be a valid assumption.

Herzberg's Two-Factor Theory

Another motivation theory is the Herzberg's Two-Factor Theory. The Two-Factor Theory is different from the Maslow Theory in that Herzberg posits that motivation cannot be sufficiently explained in terms of a hierarchy alone. Instead, he theorized that motivation is composed of two distinct factors, which he referred to as being either motivational or maintenance.

Herzberg's primary assumptions

1. Maintenance factors (external)

   a. Must be sufficiently present in order for motivational factors to come into play.

   b. When not sufficiently present, conditions can be created that can block motivation and lead to dissatisfaction.

   c. Originate from the outside (extrinsic).

1. Motivational factors (internal)

   a. Lead to satisfaction.

   b.Originate from within (intrinsic).

Maintenance factors are not motivational. Instead, they help keep individuals from being dissatisfied. In order for one to be motivated, a follower must derive a certain degree of satisfaction from his or her effort.

According to Herzberg, it is the task of the leader to eliminate or mitigate sources of dissatisfaction for individuals. For example, if a group of workers is to be motivated, then that group must perceive that their environment is significantly free of conditions that Herzberg labeled as *dissatisfiers*.

Maintenance factors include salary, benefits, working conditions, and other such elements. Herzberg concluded that motivation does not appear to come from maintenance factors, but from other factors. He concluded the factors that incubate motivation include recognition, job challenge, achievement, responsibility, advancement, and promotion.

Historically, researchers had suggested that the opposite of job satisfaction was job dissatisfaction, which sounded logical. And, further, that if the dissatisfaction could be eliminated from work, the job would become both satisfying and motivational. Herzberg disagreed, writing that the opposite of dissatisfaction is not satisfaction. By eliminating sources of dissatisfaction one might reduce the dissatisfaction of a worker, but this does not mean that the worker will somehow become motivated or find job satisfaction.

Herzberg's suppositions

1. Proactive. Individuals do not simply respond to events after they occur. Instead, they are highly proactive in trying to shape their events and influence situations, and are thereby proactive.

2. Alternatives. Individuals usually consider alternative behaviors and their possible consequences in a more-or-less rational manner.

3. Anticipate. Through experience, individuals learn to anticipate (forecast) likely outcomes of alternative behaviors in dealing with events and, because of this learning, modify their responses toward positive outcomes.

Motivating Factors

There are a limited number of actions that a leader can take to motivate followers. The first action, however, should be for the leader to examine the work environment to identify dissatisfiers. This analysis should then be operationalized with a goal of reducing or eliminating dissatisfiers where possible. It is likely that not all dissatisfiers can be effectively eliminated. However, the demonstration of willingness on the leader's part to act on behalf of the group members typically will positively enhance the leader's image among group members. If the leader evidences a caring attitude, an atmosphere of confidence typically develops toward the leader.

After eliminating elements from the environment that keep people from being motivated, the leader must address the notion of actually motivating followers. To attain this, the leader must determine what it is that his or her followers value and/or otherwise care about. In order to do this the leader needs to understand the wants and desires of each group member. This can be quite difficult, but the leader should make a concerted effort to determine wants and needs to help ensure that each individual is being accommodated in such a way as to allow followers to realize their maximum potential.

Examples of motivating (internal) factors at work

- Achievement.
- Growth potential.
- Responsibility.
- Advancement and job promotion.
- Job recognition.
- Job status.

Maintenance Factors

Application of Herzberg's theory suggests that overall group feelings are a critical element in analyzing the efficacy of maintenance factors. The leader should ensure that dissatisfiers in this category are significantly reduced so that followers will feel compelled to participate in-group goals. To the extent possible, group members should share positive feelings overall about interpersonal relations, working relations, salaries, benefits, the environmental climate, and their collective job security.

Examples of maintenance factors (external) at work

- Working relationships.

- Salary.

- Interpersonal relationships.

- Work benefits.

- Working environmental climate.

- Job security.

Alderfer's ERG Theory

In 1969, Clayton Alderfer, a psychologist, further developed Maslow's Hierarchy of Needs theory by categorizing Maslow's hierarchy into *ERG*—Existence, Relatedness, and Growth. Alderfer essentially added additional detail to Maslow's theory.

Material. The Existence group is concerned with providing the basic material existence requirements of humans and include Maslow's physiological and safety needs. Relatedness.

Relatedness. Alderfer's second group of needs is those of relatedness, which is the desire people have for maintaining important interpersonal relationships. These social and status desires require interaction with others if they are to be satisfied, and they align with Maslow's social need and the external component of Maslow's esteem classification.

Growth. Alderfer's third group isolated growth needs: an intrinsic desire for personal development. These include the intrinsic component from Maslow's esteem category and the characteristics included under self-actualization.

Alderfer said that when needs in a higher category are not met then individuals redouble the efforts invested in a lower category need. For example, if self-actualization or self-esteem is not met then individuals will invest more effort in the relatedness category in the hopes of achieving the higher need.

Equity Theory

J. Stacy Adams developed equity theory (one of the *justice theories*), in 1969. Equity Theory focuses on determining whether the distribution of resources is fair to both relational partners. Equity is measured by comparing the ratio of contributions (or costs) and benefits (or rewards) for each person.

Adams, a workplace and behavioral psychologist, asserted that employees seek to maintain equity between the inputs that they bring to a job and the outcomes that they receive from it against the perceived inputs and outcomes of others. When an inequity is perceived, individuals can change their input (effort) or outputs (production), choose a different referent for comparison, do nothing, and/or leave the field.

Example: Mary has the same experience and education as John. They do the same work at a resort. Mary finds out that John earns 20 percent more in wages than Mary. Equity theory suggests that Mary, because she has become aware of this inequity, can and may react in one or a combination of several manners:

- Reduce her effort.
- Reduce her production.
- Re-focus her comparison to another individual.
- Leave the job.
- Do nothing.
- Perhaps do some combination of those options.

Goal-Setting Theory

Cecil Alec Mace began the first studies related to goal setting in the 1930s. Later, in the mid 19602, Edwin A. Locke reignited the interest in goal setting and pursued goal setting as a research subject for the next 30 years. Initially, the idea of goal setting goes back to Aristotle's time when he speculated that the establishment of a purpose can cause one to take action, which was the impetuous for Locke. Specific and difficult goals lead to higher performance.

Goal setting involves the development of an action plan designed to motivate and guide an individual or group toward a goal. Goal setting can be guided by goal-setting criteria (rules) such as SMART criteria. Goal setting is well developed and typically recognized and used as a major component in both personal development and management literature.

Components of SMART criteria in goal setting

- S = Specific. Goals must be specific (not general) and target a precise area for improvement. Regarding specificity, detail and precision written and expressed in clear and unambiguous terms are valued over broader measures.

- M = Measurable. Goals must be quantified in order to determine both interim and ultimate goal achievement. If we have a goal of achieving an ultimate goal in 12 months, the interim goals (sometime referred to as objectives) are those milestones that occur along the way—perhaps expressed in terms of months or quarters. As you will read when you get to the T, measurable is closely tied to time-related. Typical means of measurement include using *objective* terms. An objective measure is one that is expressed in terms of times and/or counts.

- A = Acceptable. Goals must be tolerable before one will take responsibility for committing to and achieving such goals. Think about a boss that tells a department head that he or she needs to achieve a 55 percent improvement in quality over a 30-day period. If that goal is not acceptable (in this case reasonable or perhaps possible) to the department head, he or she will not commit full effort toward achieving such a goal.

- R = Realistic. Goals must be realistic. Realistic refers to results that, given the available resources, can be achieved. Often, realistic is similar to acceptable because they work together closely. If our goal, for example, is to buy a used luxury car in like new condition, less than two years old, and with fewer than 10,000 miles for less than $5,000, that goal is (obviously) not credible.

- T = Timely or time-related. Goals must be written in a way that recognizes some ultimate outcome by some date. Additionally and when appropriate, interim goal dates should be established, as well. As you discovered when you read the M, time-related is closely tied to measurable because time is one of the key elements used in measuring. The interim dates allow measuring goal progress on the way to the ultimate goal achievement. In the example used with the word, measurable, we discussed achieving an ultimate goal in 12 months and the interim goals (sometime referred to as objectives) being those milestones that occur along the way—perhaps expressed in terms of months or quarters.

Organizational Behavior Modification

Organizational Behavior Modification theory (also referred to as Reinforcement theory) deals with changing behavior through rewards or punishments that are essentially contingent on performance. Management identifies performance-related employee behaviors and then implements an intervention strategy to strengthen desirable behaviors and weaken undesirable behaviors.

Organizational behavior's two principles

1. A behavior that leads to a positive consequence (reward) tends to be repeated, while a behavior that leads to a negative consequence (punishment) tends not to be repeated.

2. Managers can influence and change an employee's behavior through properly scheduled rewards or punishment.

Five-Step Model for organizational behavior modification

1. Identify performance-related behaviors needing improvement.

2. Measure behavior to allow a comparative assessment after training.

3. Identify behavioral contingencies in terms of rewards for positive improvements and punishment for negative results or no change.

4. Develop and implement a training intervention strategy.

5. Evaluate performance improvement in terms of measurement. It is often beneficial to have interim goals along with an ultimate goal to allow measurement along the way.

Management By Objectives (MBO)

Management by objectives (MBO) also known as management by results (MBR), was first popularized by Peter Drucker as early as 1954. MBO is a management model that aims to improve performance of an organization by clearly defining objectives that are agreed to by both management and employees. In this sense, an objective connotes an interim goal leading to some stated ultimate goal (so, not to be confused with objective measures, which use times and/or counts).

The MBO process allows management to take work that needs to be done one step at a time to allow for a systemized and productive work environment. This process also helps organizational workers see their accomplishments as they achieve each objective. An important part of MBO is the measurement and comparison of the employee's actual performance (performance feedback) with the standards set. Ideally, when employees themselves have been involved with the goal setting and choosing the course of action to be followed by them, they are more likely to fulfill their responsibilities.

While MBO is included in this chapter, it is also re-addressed in the Management Chapter because of the orderly structure by which it is operationalized in the work place.

Chapter 03:

Leader Values, Behavior, and Culture

Introduction

The fundamental idea presented in this chapter is that a leader's values affect his or her enacted behavior, which in turn greatly influences the organization at a level that the leader exerts influence. Therefore, a department head's behavior will affect the culture of individuals, groups, and teams within that particular department. As a leader moves up within an organization, his or her behavior naturally affects an increasing number of individuals', groups', and teams' culture.

Values are attitudes about what is correct and incorrect, fair and unfair, honorable and dishonorable (Yukl). Examples of values include fairness, integrity, trustworthiness, courtesy, and support. Values are salient because they influence leader choices, awareness, and behavior, which, in turn influence and shape the work place culture. Leader values and their consequential behavior play an important part in shaping organizations.

The concept of leader behavior suggests that managers may use certain behavior in order to contend with the varying demands of their positions.

Organizational culture (also referred to as corporate culture) has received varying degrees of attention over the years. It first became popular in Barnard's (1938) research into the functions of executives setting the tone for the organization. It underwent resurgence in popularity in the '90s as organizations began to search for cultures that foster an environment for teams, particularly self-managed teams (Mohrman & Mohrman).

Background

The Relationship Between Values and Behavior

Values are important because they influence leader preferences, perceptions, and behavior, which, in turn influence and shape the work place.

Values are fundamental convictions that a certain mode of behavior or end result state is preferable to a converse mode or end result existence (Rokeach). Values have nested within them an element of judgment in that they are a reflection of an individual's or group's belief about what is right, desirable, or good. Values have attributes regarding content and attributes that regulate intensity. The content attribute states that some behavior or end result is desirable. The intensity attribute states the importance of such behavior or end state. By ranking values by intensity, an idea of a person's individual or work group's value system can be obtained (Bales & Cohen).

Values are important to the study of leadership and organizational culture because they help establish a foundation for the understanding of attitudes and motivation and because they influence perceptions, attitudes, and behavior (Connor & Becker). Individuals enter organizations with interpretations and ideas of what should and should not be. Furthermore, such interpretations imply that some behavior or end states are preferable to others. As a result, individuals' value systems may be incongruent with those of the organization. With an increasing demand by consumers for a higher level and quality of service (Cline; Coyle & Dale; Zeithaml, Parasuraman, & Berry), the effect of values on employee organizational culture become a key issue to help ensure that individual value systems are aligned with those of the employing organization's staff, in order to meet such demand.

A review of the literature substantiates Bales' work in integrating interpersonal behavior and values. Many researchers treat behavior as phenomena characteristic of developing lists of traits. Others, such as McDougall, and Lewin, theorize that behavior is part of a higher-order system. In this higher-order system, values are considered more complex than behavior and the product of multiple filters and therefore not easily determined.

McClelland attests that values guide interpersonal behavior, and states that they are best obtained from questionnaires and non-obtrusive observational methods. Triandis believes that values are a critical determinant of social behavior. Elizur et al. assert that values motivate goal-directed behavior. Hofstede suggests that values determine the meanings of people's behavior.

Kluckhohn and Strodtbeck offer, from an anthropological (the study of humankind) perspective, their definition of value orientations as being complex, rank-ordered principles developing from cognitive (relating to thought), affective (of emotional expression), and directive (guided) elements. And, such influences provide order and direction for the ever-changing situations.

Feather contends that individual values, as they relate to behavior and social interaction, were largely ignored by psychologists who seemed to have more interest in studying behaviorism, personality theories, and group dynamics.

Bales suggested that behavior is something that can be observed. And, that once observed, certain evaluations are placed on such behavior. The evaluations inform a behavioral response to the original initiated act. These evaluations can be treated as sets of values held by both the observer and the person being observed. Moreover, Bales contends that values' primary focus is the evaluation tool for the behavior of the self and others in interaction. Thus, values and behavior are closely intertwined.

Values and Culture

Shared values are a vital component of organizational culture. Shared values are not easily observable, even though most organizational members are aware of and can describe them (Nahavandi & Malekzadeh). They include values and beliefs that are shared among an organization's members about what is important, such as what the organization stands for, what the organization is about, and what the organization values in their employees.

Organizational Culture

A third concept of leadership inquiry examined was that of organizational culture (also referred to as corporate culture). Organizational culture has received varying degrees of attention over the years. It became popular in Barnard's research into the functions of executives—that of setting the tone for the organization, and again in the 1990s as organizations began to search for cultures that support and integrate self-managed teams (Mohrman & Mohrman).

According to Smircich, *organizational culture* can be defined as a fairly stable set of assumptions, shared meanings, and values that form a framework for action. Ott offers another conception of culture as shared values, beliefs, assumptions, perceptions, norms, artifacts, and patterns of behavior. Culture includes jargon and slang, humor and jokes, and other such forms (Trice & Beyer). It can also include strong ideologies (Hyde). Strong ideologies make an organization conservative, since actions and decisions are made within a particular ideological framework. Schein defines organizational culture as shared assumptions and beliefs about the world, the nature of time and space, human nature, and relationships. Schein distinguishes between underlying beliefs (which may be unconscious) and espoused values, which may or may not be consistent with these beliefs. However, Schein found that espoused values do not accurately reflect the culture when they are inconsistent with underlying beliefs.

Hall states that underlying beliefs representing the culture of an organization are responses to problems of adaptation to the environment and internal integration. The primary external problems are the vision and mission, goals and objectives, and evaluation methods. Solving problems of internal integration include determining organization membership, issues of status and power, rewards and punishment, and agreement about the meaning of buzzwords and symbols (Hall).

A major function of organizational culture, therefore, is to help people understand each other and the organization environment, thereby reducing anxiety and confusion. As solutions to internal and external problems are developed, they become shared assumptions. Over time, the assumptions may become so familiar that organizational members are no longer consciously aware of them.

Leader Influence on Culture

By changing or strengthening the culture of an organization, a manager influences the motivation and behavior of its members (Yukl).

Leaders can influence the culture of an organization in a variety of ways. According to Schein, there are five primary devices that offer the greatest potential for embedding and reinforcing culture.

Devices for embedding and reinforcing culture

- Attention. Leaders communicate their priorities, values, and concerns by their choice of things to ask about and measure.

- Reactions to crises. A leader's response to a crisis can send a strong message about values and assumptions. A manager who faithfully supports espoused values during difficult times communicates the importance of the values.

- Role modeling. Leaders communicate values by their own actions. A leader who walks the walk and talks the talk helps reinforce value importance.

- Allocation of rewards. The criteria used for allocating rewards signal what is valued by the organization. Formal recognition in ceremonies and informal praise communicate a leader's priorities.

- Selection and dismissal. Leaders can influence organizational culture by their choice of criteria for recruiting, promoting, and firing people.

Culture and Organizational Stage

The influence of a leader on the culture of an organization varies depending on the developmental stage of the organization. For example, the founding manager of a new organization has a strong influence on imbedding its culture. This is due mainly to the founder's position of influence in molding new culture. However, creating culture may involve considerable conflict if the founding manager's ideas are not successful or if there are other powerful members of the organization with competing ideas. To succeed, the founder needs an appropriate vision and the ability and persistence to influence others to accept it (Kets de Vries & Miller).

The culture in young, successful organizations is likely to be strong because it is fundamental to the organization's success, the assumptions have been adopted by members, and the founding manager is still available for reinforcement of founding principles (Trice & Beyer). Eventually, as the organization matures and the founding manager moves on, the culture becomes less distinctive. Subcultures develop in different departments that may lead to conflicts and power struggles.

In general, it is more difficult to change the culture of an organization than to create culture in a new organization (Trice & Beyer). There are several reasons for this difficulty. Many of the underlying beliefs and assumptions shared by people in an organization are not consciously acknowledged. These cultural assumptions usually help explain the past and serve as fundamental tenets of the organization. In a mature, relatively prosperous organization, culture influences leaders more than leaders influence culture. Drastic changes are unlikely unless there is a major crisis (Yukl).

Maintenance of Culture

Trice and Beyer suggest that the literature on a leader's influence on culture emphasizes situations in which a manager either makes changes in culture or establishes a new organization with a different culture. The way in which managers maintain existing culture in an organization has been largely ignored (Yukl). Although less dramatic than cultural change, cultural maintenance is important for the continued effectiveness of an organization.

In a period of stability and prosperity, it is appropriate to strengthen the existing culture to keep it consistent with the strategy (Schlit & Locke). The culture of an organization naturally evolves over time, and without strong cultural leadership, it can change in undesirable ways. Key values in the culture may slowly erode if top management ignores them.

Trice and Beyer formulated a model comparing cultural change and maintenance management. For both types of cultural leadership, the manager creates an impression of competence, articulates ideology, communicates strong convictions, communicates high expectations and confidence in followers, serves as a role model, and otherwise motivates follower commitment to the organization's objectives and strategies. However, there are also some important differences between the two types of cultural leadership, whether maintenance or innovator.

Cultural maintenance leaders make only incremental changes in strategies, and they affirm existing values and traditions. In contrast, cultural innovators advocate new strategies and changes in culture. These managers may need to be more influential in convincing their reports and in dealing with their opponents.

Use of Symbols, Slogans, and Rituals

A change in organizational ideology usually requires modification of organization culture. One way to influence the culture is to change forms such as symbols, slogans, and rituals (Trice & Beyer).

Rituals, ceremonies, and rites of passage can be used to strengthen identification with the organization as well as to emphasize core values. Orientation programs can be used to socialize new employees. Training programs can be used to teach the ideology of the organization. However, one study by Ardichvili, Cardozo, & Gasparishvili found that entrepreneurs are using work design and performance management programs more often than training and development to change organizational culture. Other approaches to change include mentors who model and teach key values and special assignments to work areas of the organization where the new culture is strong (Fisher).

Distinguishing Organizational Culture From Societal Culture

Some researchers, such as Erez & Earley, suggest that organizational cultures are formed as a function of the societal culture present within them. However, Hofstede, suggests that the concepts of organizational and societal culture are different. Organizational culture is comprised of members who most likely exercised some influence in their decision to join the organization, and could also decide to leave it. On the other hand, members are born into their societal culture without choice.

Summary

Individual values as a person's established, enduring beliefs and preferences about what is worthwhile and desirable, will differ to some degree across managers (Rokeach). Behavior is the manner of acting in a given circumstance—what a person says and how he or she says it—as observed by both that person and others. Behavior is influenced by a person's values and their particular circumstances (Bales). Understanding that values tend to reflect important events and influences can be helpful in gaining insight into and predicting behavior. The argument was made (Merritt) that leader values influence behavior. And, that these independent variables influence employee organizational culture.

Values have become a central topic in the study of leadership. As you read in the first chapter, there have been a number of attempts to explain leadership in terms of models.

Several current studies focus on values as a central component of leadership. Others integrate values into a larger framework of variables that influences leadership. This chapter emphasizes the elements of meaning and direction as the key functions of leadership.

Meaning is a concept that conceptualizes the leader as the person who represents the value system of the group he or she is leading. Direction is a concept that represents group direction, such as where the group is headed. The Functional Approach is comprehensive in that it can help integrate several theories within its framework. It is not necessarily a unified theory. However, it is a theory that can accommodate other approaches to values.

One should attempt to read widely about the concept of values. Perception and philosophy are two areas of study that help explain how values play a part in shaping a group and how values guide one's actions and behavior.

As you read, try to imagine yourself in a present or past work situation and refer to that (or those) leadership environment(s). Close investigation should shed light on how values affect purpose and how purpose affects operations.

Approaches to Leadership

Some researchers have taken the view that the appropriate approach to understanding leadership is to study leaders' behaviors, traits and characteristics. However, over time this method has not revealed either the depth or breadth of significant data, as researchers had hoped. After considerable study, there are no consistent characteristics or behavior patterns, which define an effective leader.

A somewhat more convenient approach to understanding leaders was in analyzing the conditions and situations under which leadership takes place. While this approach to studying leadership showed promise, it also turned out to be less than acceptable, primarily because leadership takes place under a wide array of circumstances with an almost infinite number of micro conditions present in defining a discrete situation. Therefore, it is almost impossible, certainly impractical to try to list every circumstance and condition that could define a situation.

There have also been attempts to correlate certain leadership characteristics with environmental characteristics in an attempt to help discover the most effective leadership style given specific environmental variables. However, as was the case with the conditions and situation approach, the variables that interacted to determine an effective leadership style are enormous. It became an extremely difficult exercise to develop algorithms that could accurately determine relationships among traits, environmental characteristics, and effectiveness.

All of these approaches have been less than acceptable because they have not identified reliable elements that constitute a consistent leadership framework. In order for a leadership element to be considered reliable, it must satisfy one condition: the element produces factors that are consistent from one leadership situation to another. Even if consistent leadership elements are identified, it is obvious that no concept of leadership could be considered all-inclusive. The very nature of leadership is conceptual. We probably will never develop an algorithm for each situation that would guarantee leadership effectiveness.

One element that does seem to relate consistently to leadership is the values of a leader and those of his or her followers. The values of leaders and followers do affect leadership environments with reliability.

Values

Group values can seem abstract. However, values become operational and thereby identifiable through the vision, mission, goals, and objectives that are established by groups.

If group members adopt and conform to a set of values, it is almost certain that group members want and expect their leaders to conform to a similar set of values. The reality that rational followers perceive is the same reality that they want for their leaders to perceive, as well. It is reasonable to assume that if followers in a group setting are free to choose their leaders, they will choose and promote leaders who perpetuate the particular group's values. This is true whether the group is the American public electing a president, a school district electing a board member, or a quality assurance group at an automobile plant electing a team leader and spokesperson. Group members logically prefer a leader who represents most closely the group's value perceptions. The important message for the leader in this discussion is that leader values and his or her consequential behavior (the operationalization of values) must be perceived by the followers to mirror a value system of the followers, which becomes the culture of that group. The effective leader must support and otherwise champion goals and objectives that reflect the group's values in order to maintain long-term group support.

Meaning and Direction

As groups change in size and makeup, their values and goals evolve over time. As part of this natural evolution, polarizing elements will develop that challenge the group's original purpose and intent. Conflict and confrontation occur, which evidence one of the primary forces behind leadership: That the leadership environment is constantly changing. Effective leaders must remain cognizant of and responsive to such change in order to maintain their leadership status. Leaders must effectively forecast and lead appropriate change. Hence the use of the term, *leader*.

The effects of change may be as far reaching as to alter group values. The concept of meaning is introduced to help demonstrate how group values relate to leadership. Meaning in this context represents the essence of a group. It is the ethical foundation (as in group ethic), which makes the group what it is. It is important to note that the term ethical foundation in this context is not intended to include religious or moral overtones, unless the leader is leading a religious group. Instead, ethical foundation is used to represent the group's basic beliefs, such as group ethic.

On the surface, it appears that the most important leader action is to achieve the group's goals and objectives. However, real leadership action leads to realizing group meaning. Although the successful accomplishment of goals and objectives is important, it is the realization of the values that speak to the key purpose of leadership. Ideally, accomplishment of goals and objectives will yield realization of values but that is not necessarily correct.

For leader action to be of substance, the group's goals and objectives must reflect the group's values. Because of the vague nature of values, there is not always an obvious link between goals and values. The accomplishment of goals should be the tangible evidence of fulfilling values, if the two are significantly related. It is a group's values from which real group purpose is formulated, and it is values that provide the leader with substance for providing leadership. Thus, the first primary function of leadership resides in the concept of meaning. It is the leader's responsibility to communicate values that are important to the group, and this can only be done through action—his or her behavior. Action to realize group meaning implies direction. The second primary function of leadership is direction.

Direction as a concept is the course of action (behavior) that the leader uses to realize group meaning. Direction should relate directly to tasks, goals and objectives, and mission, just as meaning should be linked to group values. The saying applies: *If you do not know where you are going, then any path will work nicely.* An effective leader must have a clear sense of direction in order to accomplish group goals. Without clear direction, goals will not be realized and the meaning of the group's very existence will not be realized.

A leader's effectiveness will be evaluated by group members' perception of the leader's support in realizing group values. The ideal leader should exemplify the values of the leader and follower environment, and provide acceptable direction to realize those values. Bernard Bass expresses the manner in which group values affect group members:

Anyone born into a culture conforms to the same value orientation in order to be accepted and remain in the same social order. Deviation is likely to result in rejection and loss of esteem among the rest of the members sharing the cultural values.

Functional Approach

Although groups may require leaders to demonstrate certain skills and behaviors under certain conditions, not all behavior of a person in a leadership position can be accurately referred to as leadership behavior. Leadership's basic nature can be lost if skills, circumstances, and conditions are not taken into consideration as being a function of values.

Leader behavior, leadership environment, goals, objectives, etc. are symptomatic conditions of the essence of leadership. Using the functional model, all leader and follower behavior, conditions, and situations surrounding the leadership environment are accurately viewed within the context of how meaning and direction relate to group values. The major question becomes: How effectively does the leader portray group values, and will the direction that the leader prescribes move the group toward realization of its basic value system?

This does not imply that the study of leader behavior—analyzing the leadership environment, scrutinizing follower perceptions, and the like—is not important, because it is important. However, meaning and direction are the core elements that can be found in all effective leadership.

A leader's actions must include the following three dimensions or the actions should not be considered acts of leadership:

1. The group consists of rational people.

2. Specific group ethical and directional elements (which may change over time) can be identified.

3. A leader or leaders can be identified within the group.

If values vary from group to group and situation to situation, then values are relative. A group's ethical (as in group ethic) foundation (value structure) affects the group's collective perception of reality. The cause and effect interactions between values and environmental factors affect perception of reality and determine the mix of variables that the group uses as criteria for group membership. Therefore, for any particular group, reality is a function of value perceptions. Hence, a group's collective view of reality is the ultimate criterion for choosing, following, and evaluating who is to lead and who will be members of the group.

The functional approach is rooted in the group's beliefs, values, and principles—the group's ethical foundation. The concept of meaning may be thought of as the leader being the role model who characteristically reflects the principles, values, beliefs, and dogmas. The concept of direction may be thought of as the course a leader plots to achieve and/or realize group meaning. Direction is not so much the act of directing people, as it is the overall course of action that moves the group toward realizing its essence. The primary functions of a leader are to exemplify group values, and to communicate meaning to the group so that the group has a clear understanding of group purpose, intent, and direction.

The functional approach gives purpose to the leader's action and behavior, and provides substance for the group's mission.

Leadership Propositions

There are several assumptions that concluded from the study of theories and concepts that affect leadership. These statements take the form of propositions that encourage further inquiry.

Leadership propositions:

1. Leadership is universal. Leadership occurs in every situation where people come together with common goals and missions.

2. Leadership usually takes place in a group setting. Leadership is typically defined in terms of some group function.

3. Leadership is not a position or a set of characteristics that exists within an organizational structure. Positions do not lead others. People lead others. Leadership characteristics are exhibited only by people. One may have expectations of leadership from people in positions that require leadership, but a position (per se) cannot lead.

4. Two skills are essential for effective leadership: Motivation and assessment. The leader must get followers to act (motivation) toward group goals and the leader must be able to recognize (assessment) when the goals are being reached. Motivation and assessment skills may also be supported by other skills of varying degrees. However, whatever other skills are necessary, the end-result is that they must be used effectively to motivate the group and assess the group's progress toward its goals.

5. The skills necessary to be an effective leader depend upon the circumstances and conditions under which the leader is acting. The type of skills may depend on group size and purpose, and where the leader fits into the group's formal structure (This is particularly true in today's corporate structures).

6. The primary leadership functions include meaning and direction. This is a functional approach to defining the nature of leadership.

7. Leaders should exemplify the ethical foundation of the group. The leader should unify group goals, values, principles, beliefs, and dogmas and provide a direction of action so that these goals can be realized.

8. Leadership is situational. A leader may be successful in some situations and unsuccessful in others.

9. More than one leader may emerge from within a group. Leadership is not confined to one person.

10. A follower's readiness and skill level determine the effective style for a leader to adopt.

11. Certain leadership styles in particular situations are desirable over other styles. The adoption of an effective leadership style is dependent on the particular situation in the leadership environment.

12. A leader's actions have an effect on group attitude. A leader's actions influence general interactions of group members as they work toward realizing the group's purpose and intent.

13. In many cases, it takes time for a leader's actions to manifest into group conscience. It also takes time for the leader's actions to have bearing on results.

14. A leader's general attitude toward people will affect how the particular leader relates to people. Attitudes permeate one's actions whether they are leaders or followers.

15. Organizational structure and a group's managerial philosophies affect a leader's preferred leadership style. The group climate affects leadership style.

16. Leaders can be successful without being effective. To be effective, followers must have positive feelings about success.

17. Leaders' actions that are not group-goal-directed cannot be referred to as leader actions.

18. The nature of the contact (such as, daily, weekly, formal, informal) that the leader has with followers will determine, to a large extent, the leadership style that is most effective for that group.

The purpose of presenting these preceding propositions is to initiate discussion and thought concerning leadership. Exploring some of the propositions may lead to new thinking about leadership, and may one day provide the information for a more detailed and scientific investigation of the subject.

By-products of the preceding leadership propositions

1. Accessibility to a leader by the followers affects the followers' perceptions of leader behavior. The more direct access a follower has to the leader; the better a follower is able to assess the leader's behavior.

2. Leadership is a function of meaning and direction. Leadership's primary function is to provide a group with a consolidated view of the group's values and provide direction to realize these values.

3. Group diversity increases difficulty in consolidating group meaning. This seems reasonable since there would be various values, principles and beliefs to encounter.

4. Group size affects a leader's role in providing group direction.

5. As groups increase in size, administrative and managerial functions necessary to accomplish group goals, increase.

6. Complexity of a group's vision, mission, goals, and objectives has bearing on the functions of meaning and direction.

Although it is not possible to develop a neat formula for successful leadership, it is important to know as much about the elements that affect leadership as possible. If elements can be identified and put together in such a manner that it helps explain leadership conditions and interacting forces, it will help the student of leadership to understand the nature of effective leadership.

General Review

Leaders exist to help fulfill the purpose and intent of the groups that they lead. This may seem to be an elementary statement, but the implications are far-reaching.

Leadership implications

*   Group purpose and intent is a reflection of why a group exists, and is more deeply a statement directly related to ethic—the group's bonding element. This bonding element will be termed the ethical foundation of a group.

*   The ethical foundation is the cornerstone of group values.

- A group's values become the foundation for the philosophy of the group.

- Philosophy will dictate the group purpose.

- Purpose is directly accessible through group policies, objectives and goals.

Thus, one may determine a group's ethical foundation by analyzing its policies, goals and objectives. Admittedly, other sources of information would need to be included in order to gain an understanding of a group's values, but goals, objectives, and policies seem to be a logical starting place.

Leadership is universal; it takes place within all group settings. Group, in this context, is a collection of people who are brought together for common goals and purposes and bound by certain philosophical ideas, beliefs, and moral persuasions. Therefore, a group could be a nation, social club, school, society, marriage, or any other situation in which two or more people bind themselves for specific purposes. Using this line of reasoning, purpose relates directly to the group's ethical foundation; thus, the core of leadership revolves around values.

A group's ethical foundation affects the perception of leader performance. It is apparent that groups operate and develop expectations of their leaders based on the group's particular beliefs, values, and principles. Since group ethical foundations may vary from group to group, groups will develop particular leader expectations. And, these groups will develop their own unique criteria for evaluating their leadership.

It is clear that expectations are linked to beliefs. Beliefs, in this sense, relate to the ambiance of group beliefs and are a reflection of the group's ethical system. It is also clear that people group themselves according to their beliefs and values.

Environmental factors, such as catastrophes, economic conditions, political conditions, and the like will affect the leadership style preferred by and appropriate for a group. Unexpected and/or other major events occur, which affect a group's value structure. When this occurs, the values of the group will shift, quite possibly affecting the group's perception of the leadership role.

Chapter 04:

The Leadership Environment

Introduction

This chapter revisits the term leader and presents questions about the leader. Over time, you have developed ideas about leadership from past experience and the text. So, these questions should encourage you to think critically about elements that go into helping mold and shape leaders in their organizational environments.

Environment is a term used conceptually to represent the ambient surroundings—the workplace—of the leader and followers. What are some of the symbols we use to communicate more effectively? Why are they important? What part does our society play in shaping our ideas about how things should be? Is it important for us to know about symbols in our environments and society at large in studying leadership? Does the way in which we communicate affect how others perceive us? All of these questions are obviously important to the leader and the leadership environment. However, an even more overriding question for a student of leadership might be to ask, how do we frame these and other important topics in order to develop a coherent field of study?

This chapter attempts to present some of these concepts with the hope of bringing closure to the text. Knitting these concepts together is a difficult task. You should be at a point in your study that you should be able to analyze this chapter and understand the importance of each topic both as it relates to other concepts and to the larger concept of leadership itself. Your readings and writings on the topic of leadership should enable you to initiate and synthesize thought on the topic and formulate original ideas for response during discussion.

Background

The theories that have been discussed in the preceding chapters involve three foci:

1. The leader.

2. The followers.

3. The environment

Almost anything that can be written about leadership involves one or some combination of these three areas. Gaining knowledge of leadership preferences and styles, identifying wants and needs of followers, and becoming familiar with the organizational environment becomes a fundamental analysis to anyone who finds him or herself in a leadership situation. Upon reviewing the definition of leadership, it is obvious that these three areas are conceptually related. The definition restated:

> Leadership is the action of inducing and/or influencing followers to accomplish certain goals that represent the values, wants and needs, aspirations and expectations of both leader and follower.

While reference to both leader and follower appear in this definition, the leadership environment is clearly implied.

By stating that it is necessary to understand group goals, we emphasize that effective leaders and followers must understand where the group is heading. One prerequisite for reaching a goal is effective communication. In order for the group to move toward common objectives, an understanding of the leadership environment must encompass the values of the leader, followers, and those of the general environment. The leader must understand and adapt to the style in order to be effective. The followers must perceive the leader as a person who represents group values and also perceive the direction being proposed as one that will effectively achieve group goals.

That is not to say that persons who gain knowledge about their leadership environment will become successful leaders. The essence of this proposition is that knowledge in these three areas is a prerequisite for a successful and efficient group and leader situation.

The question then becomes one of how do we choose an appropriate leadership style, and how do we recognize when we are becoming effective leaders. For many, this knowledge is gained through experience—trial and error. People learn about life by living. As indicated earlier, there is no specific formula for understanding leadership. Therefore, one may have to experience leadership situations one at a time to enable him- or herself to establish and categorize general propositions about leadership. Ideally, these categories are filed away in a leader's memory to be called upon when a similar situation occurs; whereupon the leader considers and then either 1) acts or 2) adds new information, modifies the category, and then acts.

The Leader

Are you a leader? What type leader are you? What are some of the characteristics that help make a person capable of being a leader? Is leadership training necessary? What personal attributes must a leader possess? What skills must a leader know? These are questions that many people want to answer when they take a leadership course.

By studying theories in preceding chapters, we discovered that one might label leaders by their behavior, personality, and/or situational circumstances. Some theories promote a leader as being born with certain characteristics that allow him or her to assume roles of leadership. Other theories promote education and training as the necessary ingredient for obtaining leadership qualities. Leaders' actions have been used to identify style and terms have been adopted to describe the relationships between leaders and followers.

The terms directing, coaching, supporting, delegating, and others were used to describe a leader. Other theories attempted to describe the leader in terms of their character traits. For example, the leader is intelligent, brave, fair-minded, loyal, trustworthy, friendly, true, etc. Through the course of studying leadership, it should have become evident that there are neither behavior styles nor established traits that can automatically make a leader effective. Effective leadership depends on style, traits, environmental conditions, maturity of the group, and other variables in specific circumstances.

Some leadership courses administer personality tests to identify personality traits of the subjects. The purpose for this is to identify individuals' behavioral preferences when dealing with people and situations. There is some usefulness to this approach, but one should not rely on this type of analysis as providing necessarily reliable data. Personality tests of this type provide generalized descriptions and may not consider changes in behavior that occur after training or education. Personality is an important area to investigate in learning more about how a person may view followers and the leadership situation.

Theory X, Theory Y, and Theory Z attempt to categorize how people view one another, especially in terms of leaders' viewing of followers. By identifying how a person views others, an attempt is made to reveal how that person may react to others. These theories provide ways of predicting how one may generally behave or react in the face of certain events.

Evidence gained from the results of personality tests and knowing one's general attitudes toward others may be helpful in understanding actions taken in the leadership environment. If we know why people may behave as they do, we may be able to change behavior that does not produce desirable results. If people can be taught to change behaviors, then they may be taught to be leaders. This is a key assumption behind the question: Are leaders born or can one be trained to lead? A similar question that seeks leadership information: Is leadership more an art or a science? The answers to these questions are not conclusive.

Leadership observations

- Leadership is part art and part science, suggesting that it is both an art and a science.

- Some may be born with or grow up influenced by external variables (taught) which foster tendencies toward and an interest in and leadership.

- It is reasonable to assume that education and training may be the tools through which one learns or enhances leadership behavior.

It is not easy to determine which components interact in varying proportions to yield an effective leader.

It would be helpful for the prospective leader to gain insight into how he or she may be perceived by others. Knowing one's self and knowing how others perceive us is one of the first rules for becoming an effective leader. However, this is no easy task. At times, it is difficult to know our true selves because we fail to do (or may be incapable of doing) honest self-appraisals. Similarly, it is no easy task to know how others perceive us because we may not really want to know or others may be afraid to tell us.

Understanding how others perceive us

- Ask. The leader may solicit information from individual followers concerning their perception of the leader. This approach may have several drawbacks, the obvious one being that a follower may be unwilling to provide a true assessment to someone who may have an influence over rewarding or punishing them.

- Survey. An indirect approach to gain the same information may also be taken. One way is by conducting a survey, asking followers how they would evaluate areas for which the leader has control. Areas such as morale, communications, and productivity are within the purview of most leaders. These general areas are probably good assessment points to obtain a picture of how the leader is viewed by followers.

Note that if followers are negative about much of the work environment, such as poor facilities, unsafe working conditions, and negative human resource policies, it is unlikely the leader will be perceived as being highly effective. One drawback to surveying is that followers may not have a complete picture of the leader and may not understand the global view that affects the leadership environment.

In knowing one's self, it may be helpful for leaders to know their predominate personality traits. It may be surprising to realize that followers do not rate leaders the same that leaders would rate themselves. It is convenient to overestimate one's abilities and effectiveness when self-interests are involved. Thus, self-evaluations often fall to personal bias and thereby do not produce accurate assessments.

Evaluating leader behavior, personality, and ability will probably be somewhat biased, depending on the source of information. However, it is important for a leader to know how he or she is viewed and it is important to possess an accurate assessment of his or her abilities.

A personality test, a survey of follower opinions, a self-evaluation, and an assessment of the leader effectiveness would provide data useful in understanding the effectiveness of a leader. Overall, perhaps none is more accurate than any other, as they all have their strengths and drawbacks. Therefore, effective leaders are wise to use a combination of methods. Leaders must maintain a constant assessment of the perceptions of followers in order to determine the most effective leadership style to adopt.

Knowing One's Self

Over time, theorists, researchers, and effective leaders have stressed the importance of leaders understanding themselves more thoroughly before they can become effective leaders of others. We introduced the concept of situational leadership (Hersey & Blanchard) earlier in the text. We have also discussed several types of behavioral tests and surveys designed to assist leaders in learning more about themselves. We will present several diagnostic tools in the form of exercises to assist you in learning more about yourself as a leader. As you complete these exercises, it is helpful to reflect on how they affect who you are as a leader. Note that these exercises may be available as assignments, handouts, and/or worksheets from your professor.

Environment

The leadership environment encompasses all variables external to the leader that affect leader efficiency and success. In order to examine the leadership environment it is necessary to examine how people interact within this environment.

Symbols

Knowing how people interact is very important, especially when cooperation among people is necessary. One method of communication is by using symbols. Symbols are often subtle and it takes understanding the undertones of an environment to realize their full meaning.

Warren Bennis, one of the major researchers of leadership over the past many years states that the extent to which leadership is truly effective is based on the extent to which individuals place symbolic value on leader intentions. Most environments are loaded with symbolism. Their use helps communicate real and deep feelings that people have about values and issues. Picture for a moment some of the major symbols used throughout the world: A corner office with a view, the American Flag (or any other country's flag), the skull and crossbones on a pirate ship, a gold star in class, etc. Symbols are usually subtle (picture a successful businessperson wearing an Armani suit), while others are blatantly obvious (picture a hate group burning a cross in someone's front yard). Whether subtle or obvious, people communicate with symbols. Symbols represent a way for people to communicate and/or otherwise help reinforce their beliefs, values, and traditions. Effective leaders should understand how their followers interpret and value symbols. Some symbols come and go in a culture, while others are more long lasting. Whatever their duration, symbols communicate meaning. How we use and view symbols is important in interpretation of the reality they represent. Earlier in the text, we covered the concept of perception. Symbols, most certainly, play an important role in forming and supporting the perceptions of both leaders and followers. Effective leaders look for the undertones in symbols in order to understand their broader meaning.

Society

Society, as a whole, plays a major role in the formation of groups as well as their interaction. Thus, society plays an important role in the concept of leadership. Within this context, society represents the big picture values, principles, and traditions that are accepted and practiced by the mainstream of people within a particular culture.

The Encarta dictionary defines society in terms of relationships among groups as the sum of social relationships among groups of humans or animals. Similarly, it defines society in terms of a structured community of people as a community bound together by similar traditions, institutions, or nationality.

One often-used cultural comparison is between the United States and Japan. This interest is perhaps due to the economic competition between the two countries. I will use these two countries as examples of how different cultures view elements that influence leadership.

Many articles have been written about how leadership styles are affected by cultural characteristics. Several studies have compared and contrasted cultures, and found that the differences have a major influence on preferred leadership styles. One study (Bass and Burgher) discovered a cultural propensity in the U.S. toward entrepreneurship and resourcefulness. Japanese people, on the other hand, seem to prefer to use intuition. The Japanese think in long-term perspectives while the U.S. is culturally geared toward shorter-term perspectives.

Communication

As the world becomes an instantaneous communication system, the societies of the world have become more accessible and available. As a result, information moves very quickly among localities, states, nations, and continents. What happens in Russia one morning can affect western economic markets, such as those of the U.S., before noon. Effective leaders must be aware of the impact—both positive and negative—of swift communication. Leaders must consider public opinion and its consequential effect on organizations, groups, and institutions. Warren Bennis notes the importance of leaders in effectively managing public relations. Leaders, in their decision-making roles, are becoming increasingly involved in the managing of external constituencies in order to provide thoroughness of leadership.

Cultures are becoming entwined and intermingled and there seems to be no set of rules in dealing with cultural interaction. At times, it appears that the strong survive or at least the strongest hand rules the day. Leadership, whether it is within a group that has minor involvement or whether it is leading a multinational corporation, is affected by the availability of instantaneous communication. Communication has become a power that influences leadership.

Followers

Groups

The term *followers* can be used contextually in this text to describe individuals, groups, or teams. Studying group behavior and group characteristics are important conceptual components of leadership. Leadership involves actions taken (by a person), which are centered on a particular group. A group comes together for specific reasons in a manner that their collective actions assist in accomplishing group goals. Since groups are goal directed, a major function of the leader is to accomplish group goals in the most effective way possible. Therefore, to be effective the leader must have an understanding of the people in the group, their reasons for being group members, and group dynamics in the way that they interact.

If group goals are simple, there may be little emphasis placed on planning and development. If group goals are complex and the organization is complex, planning and development may be key factors in the structure of the organization. If group goals are complex, then communication may become a critical element to the success of the entire organization. Group interaction and the complexity for each set of circumstances must be identified in order to understand the dynamics of any particular group. Understanding these dynamics is not as simple as learning how to conduct a successful meeting. Understanding group dynamics means knowing why and how people within groups interact. This is a far more complicated scenario than following rules for group meetings.

At times people become confused when the subject of group dynamics is addressed. They tend to think of group meetings and the things that go on in meetings. This may be an element of group dynamics, but the term implies much more. A group may be defined as the entire body of people who work for an organization or it may be a small work group that consists of just two people. The group dynamics include all of the interactions that take place, whether in meetings or between or among individuals.

Variables influencing groups

- Size.
- Complexity.
- Task.
- Relations.
- Working conditions.

An understanding of motivational theories and organizational behavior are two areas of study that are necessary components for leaders of large organizations.

There are some helpful hints about meeting dynamics that leaders need to know. Research has found that groups are usually more willing to take risk (than individuals), and that if the group leader does not commit to a specific course of action, the group will develop alternative courses of action with greater creativity. Group unity and morale is of constant concern to the leader. All groups must feel single minded in their purpose in order to realize true success. To understand how groups function, there have been several codification systems developed.

Classifying Groups

Robert Owens developed a classification system to help describe group characteristics. He conceived that an effective group could be defined and differentiated by at least three characteristics:

- Interdependence. Members of a group are interdependent when they share with others certain values, beliefs, attitudes, knowledge and fears. This interdependence is expressed through interaction between and among members of the group in communicating, sharing, and engaging in rituals.

- Part of the group. Members of a group derive satisfaction of individual needs from being part of the group. These needs include issues such as safety, security, belonging, and esteem. The satisfaction of these needs is not readily observable in the behavior of individuals but must be inferred from their patterns of behavior.

- Share goals. A group seeks to achieve specific objectives or goals. To achieve these goals, the members of the group must interact and must derive satisfaction from the interaction processes, as well as from goal achievement itself.

There are several important implications in the above listed three characteristics. Satisfying individual needs as well as group goals is the balancing act that makes or breaks the group. If an individual's needs are not being met by group membership, it is likely the person will not remain a group member. If group goals are not being met, it is likely the group will falter. Therefore, harmony must exist between satisfying individual needs and accomplishing group goals.

One example of individual needs and group goal conflict can be illustrated by examining the labor union movement in America. Unions have traditionally represented concerns of employees, while management has represented company interests. In many cases, these two factions have been in conflict over employee concerns and company concerns. To survive, companies must be competitive in their respective markets. On the other hand, in order for families to survive, employees must earn adequate salaries and benefits. It is clear that needs exist for both individuals and the company. World economies are in a state of flux and it is evident in the U.S. that many organizations are having trouble. Some companies have not survived. Unions have lost strength, as organizations are cutting back on permanent work forces and outsourcing in many areas.

The point of this example is to illustrate that groups exist side-by-side with conflicting interests. This is an example of how group dynamics are affected by variables of conflicting interest. Groups may have common goals but there may be internal conflict about how things will operate. This illustration does not typify all groups. One could examine another type of group where conflict of this nature does not exist. One thing is certain, groups differ in their wants and needs.

Group Climate

Successful groups may be identified by how they accomplish goals. Leaders of effective groups seem to stand out in the crowd. In a survey of followers over a two-year period, specific adjectives were commonly used to identify the effective leader. These terms have been used to describe the effective leader and the climate in which effective leadership takes place. The most common of these terms are listed below.

The terms themselves are not surprising. However, the interpretation of these terms varies greatly

Positive leader terms

- Strong

- Warm

- Friendly

- Smart

- Helpful

- Fair

- Supportive

- Confident

- Effective Communicator

- Admired

Positive group terms

- Proud
- Efficient
- Successful
- Elite
- Unique
- Friends
- Positive Attitude
- Dependable

Positive climate terms

- Enjoyable
- Rewarding
- Good Morale
- Success Oriented
- Competitive
- Friendly
- Responsibility
- Clear Direction
- Goals Identified
- Rewards Identified

These terms may aid in explaining how people feel about a successful and effective group setting. Others respond with similar language, which can roughly be classified under the aforementioned terms into the three areas. The overarching message to leaders is that they should strive to create a positive group climate, forge interpersonal relationships, and develop skills that group members perceive as being success oriented. These terms help formulate perceptions of group members that produce group reality.

Follower perception of leader action is the driving force behind group success. How a particular leader acts may not have as much impact on the group as a follower's perception of those actions. Thomas Sergiovanni points out that real meaning in leadership rests with the meanings, which become more important than the actions themselves. He emphasizes the long-term by stating that leaders must move beyond the obvious and focus on the subtleties of long-term effort to bring about effective leadership. The real value of leadership rests with the effects of actions on others rather than the actions themselves. The implication is that the perception a follower derives from a leader's action is the essence of leadership behavior.

If a leader intends one thing by certain actions but followers perceive another, then the leader's action does not serve the leader's intended purpose. The perception a group gets from a leader's behavior has more bearing on the ultimate fate of the group than what the leader perceives. Many times we see the clarity of situations and wonder why others do not or cannot see it the same way. However, some of the most severe difficulties between leaders and followers come from simple miscommunication and misperception of one sort or another. It is apparent that leaders must consistently be mindful as to how their actions are being perceived by others.

Chapter 05:

Leadership Skills

Introduction

The purpose of this chapter is to begin to consolidate many of the concepts, ideas, constructs, and theories covered in preceding chapters and present them in a *best practices* format of behavior and application that effective leaders can use in the workplace. The first concept goes back to the strategic concept of establishing a strong vision. Then, recognizing and working from that vision, go about the business of leading others in a steady and predictable manner—during both good times and challenging times. Here then is a collection of those best practices for application.

From the beginning, we must understand the fundamental precept that effective managers must be or become visionary leaders. Their roles in today's work environment vary across the management practices of recruiting, training, retaining, coaching, and helping motivate employees while meeting the needs of the organization to compete successfully in the market place. Without effective leadership skills and an understanding of human behavior, managers will find it difficult to meet workplace demands. Effective leadership greatly affects increased employee performance, efficiency and effectiveness, resulting in payoffs and profits for everyone largely through the use of effective social interaction. If management could be envisioned as a cupcake, leadership is the icing on that cupcake. It is the icing that distinguishes a cupcake from being just a small and boring piece of cake.

Visionary leadership elements:

- Establishing vision. Establishing a strong and clear vision, while obvious, is step one. Leaders who do not have a strong and clear picture as to where the organization or department is heading cannot share that vision with those with whom they interact and work. That vision creates a kind of map that can be followed.

- Establishing goals and objectives. Once vision is established and communicated, leaders must reinforce that vision by establishing goals and objectives that complement where it is that the organization is headed.

- Focusing on people and work. Once goals and objectives are established, it is the job of the leader to provide focus on two key skills: people (social) skills and work (goal achievement) skills. Focusing on a high degree of care for and genuine interest in people and in getting a high degree of work accomplished on time and on budget. In the end, the two most important duties of an effective leader are approximately evenly split between care and concern for people (social) and dedication and capability in achieving goals and objectives (work).

- Providing meaning and direction. Whether focusing on people or goal achievement skills, leaders must provide two functions: meaning and direction. The definition of meaning includes that the goals and objectives that others will work toward contributing to the success of the organization—that their work effort matters. Direction includes that leaders will provide guidance, clarification, and understanding at an appropriate leadership style—refraining from micromanaging (over directing) those who are capable and not relying on (delegating to) those who are untrained and therefore not yet capable.

- Maintaining predictable behavior. Utilizing creative and thoughtful leadership skills that inspire others in a positive and predictable manner. In this sense, predictable refers to no personality surprises. Employees should know and understand a leader's hot buttons, cold buttons, and over time, almost all buttons in between. Similarly, a leader should not vary from that behavior in leading and managing effectively.

- Appreciating and valuing uniqueness. Understanding human behavior and the inter-relatedness of management and staff.

Diverse backgrounds and opinions provide richness of discussion and ideas. The outcome of such richness is increased creativity, efficiency, and consequential productivity. Everyone should be valued for his or her unique contributions.

- Building cohesive high performance work teams.

- Seeking to understand and be understood. Working through problems at the project (big picture), task (specific), and interpersonal (social) levels. Effective leaders sense questions, confusion in terms of big picture (the overall plan), tasks (down to minute adjustments in processes), and conflict (either personal of interactive) and are able to drill down or up in advice and coaching without wasting time and effort at an inappropriate level. As Covey urged, seek first to understand and then to be understood.

- Negotiating and producing positive outcomes from conflict resolution. Effective leaders allow conflict to play out—but only to a certain level before interceding. While clearing the air is important, there is a major difference between allowing venting of frustration (getting it all out there) and conflict becoming insulting or worse (harassment).

- Serving as a role model for the organization. We all know of leaders who are advantage takers. Yet, somehow, those same leaders think no one knows. Effective leaders run their work lives in a manner that assumes that their behaviors would not be embarrassing (or worse) if they were on camera.

- Developing and implementing positive attitudes toward authority. Knowing how to be fair, not just tough. I wrote in an earlier bullet about predictability and want to clarify and reinforce the importance of employees knowing what to expect in terms of a leader's behavior in a given situation. This predictability over time—both in good times and in challenging times—is a key to mutual trust and respect in the work place.

- Planning, problem solving, and making decisions in a timely manner. We have all experienced the frustration from the manager who cannot (or will not) assist in these functions. Earlier we covered the two primary responsibilities of every leader—providing meaning and direction. Meaning, in this sense, helps ensure that the work is important, valued, and meaningful both to the organization and to the individual (or group). Direction, in this sense, refers to the importance of the leader, given a situation and capability of the individual or group, providing the appropriate level of control (situational leadership style) among directing, coaching, supporting, and delegating. Effective leaders sense both capability and urgency and then respond in a manner that neither speaks above or below the capabilities of the group or individual. Speaking above another's capability is confusing and self-indulgent behavior. Speaking below another's capability is micromanaging and wasteful.

Effective Planning

Careful and detailed planning should precede any work actions. Time spent in the planning process helps avoid mistakes, misunderstandings, and wasted time and effort. The process should follow a systematic: *ready (the concept and scope), aim (the planning), and shoot (the implementation)* procedure. Staff members can make important contributions to planning efforts once they become involved in understanding the process. Success will be measured by effective team commitment and results over time.

Effective planning elements:

- Before strategizing actions, interpret all information passed down through management channels to determine implications.

- Develop the big picture of organizational needs into departmental goals and objectives.

- Create implementation plans by going over the available options and alternatives, choosing activities or tasks that best lead to successful results.

- Identify resources needed to achieve the planned goals including people, time, money, materials, and facilities. Make certain resources are available.

- Establish time lines and target completion dates.

- If parsing out work, ensure that those who accept responsibility for achievement also have the corresponding power to get the job done.

- Establish standards of performance, how results will be measured, and what success will look like.

Organizational Skills

Once planning is complete, managers must serve as leaders and role models to create a motivated and productive organization. Staff members need to feel ownership in the organization's success, but they must also receive direction and allocation of resources from their leaders. Often they must be taught to organize and follow through. The following checklist can be used as an aid to train your staff to develop their organizational skills.

Leadership functions

- Dividing work into logical tasks, groupings, and projects.

- Securing and committing resources needed to achieve goals or complete a task or an overall project.

- Possessing knowledge and skills for assigning tasks, resources, and responsibilities to others on the basis of their interests, strengths, and skills. Ensuring that those who accept responsibility for results have the commensurate power to accomplish the job.

- Establishing guidelines to coordinate activities between the staff and other departments and/or work teams involved in a task or project.

- Developing both informal and formal systems for appropriate feedback as the work progresses. Feedback allows improvement in processes and therefore should become a positive feature and used with regularity.

- Establishing communication networks to ensure free flow of information up, down, and across organizational lines. Workplaces should be noisy (but orderly), positive, and dedicated to improving processes.

Building A Climate For Motivation

We dedicate a full chapter to motivation providing a background resource in understanding history, major motivational theories, and other points. In this section, we specifically address methods that effective leaders can use in providing a working environment whereby employees can become self (internally) motivated. Of the two types of motivation, external and internal, the *internal* motivation is the one that produces the highest results over the longest period of time. External motivation, while effective for the short term, is not the lasting motivation experienced in high-performance organizations.

People work for a variety of reasons. Managers must understand personal motivational factors and be sensitive to individual needs. No single technique works for everyone in every situation. Behavior that is rewarded is the behavior you will get. While surprising, many managers do not *really* know what their employees want.

The failure to perceive what people really want is the certainly one of the largest motivational problems faced by managers.

Effective Motivation is based on reality

The more a manager learns about a person's *real* needs, the more effective motivational efforts will be. Only when a manager knows a person's true motivation, will they be able to meet that person's needs. And only when he or she meets these needs will they be able to become the motivating force for that person to become a highly productive and highly valued employee.

Reasons to create a motivational environment

- Helps everyone involved in the organization to have high self-expectations.

- Makes people feel they are important, they have an impact on the organization, and they make a positive difference.

- Ensures that everyone feels a responsibility for the organization's growth and development.

- Makes certain there are ways for each individual to grow, both now and in the future.

- Ensures that each employee knows what is expected and how his or her individual performance is measured.

- Provides training and coaching to assist each person in achieving mutually established goals and objectives.

- Provides resources required for performing the job.

- Recognizes and rewards high performance.

- Helps correct or eliminate poor performance when it occurs (but never in front of customers, other employees or other managers).

Barriers to employee motivation

- Lack of goals or agreement on goals. Not knowing what is expected.

- Unclear about the repercussions if performance does not meet expectations or goals.

- Lack of information, materials, or equipment to complete the job.

- Inconsistency in interpersonal dealings. When people are treated differently, or favoritism is perceived, a lack of trust follows.

- No win situations. Everyone needs to feel that they can succeed.

- No follow-through. Being left in limbo, or continual changes in course, detract from goal attainment.

- Too many people trying to be in charge.

- Lack of support for ideas or performance.

- Lack of recognition. Praise for good work makes a difference.

- Under-utilization of skills. Opportunities for growth are essential.

- Insensitivity to cultural differences.

- Lack of education and training and resources.

Praise and Rewards

Praising staff for work well done is an important concept of external motivation, but it must not be overdone. It must be genuine and specific to the task or responsibility. It also adds value when the praise can be made public. This is best done through employee newsletters, bulletin boards, and public recognition at staff meetings.

Ensure that the praise and rewards are given for achieving agreed upon results. It is not uncommon for a leader to hear from an employee about how hard he or she worked toward the goal. Some have to work harder than others. Create a no-excuses environment. The purpose of setting mutually agreed upon goals and objectives is to allow measuring along the way. When challenges occur, evaluating interim objectives allows leaders to stay up-to-date, see progress or negative indications early, and offer assistance to help get tasks and projects back on track and ensure success.

The real world and workplace is competitive and does keep score. Not everyone deserves snacks and trophies. The message here is to create an environment that praises and rewards achievement and not just effort.

Training Employees

Few would argue the importance of proper training. Yet, in practice, relatively little training is common. Think about the restaurant manager who is often caught short on hiring new servers. Often, the directive goes something like this: *Just follow Becky around and she will show you the ropes.* This is not fair to Becky or the newly hired server.

Training considerations

- It is likely that Becky is not receiving training pay.

- Often there is no agreement between Becky and the manager about training duties.

- Having responsibility for on-the-job training for a new server cuts down on Becky's productivity.

- The new hire may or may not be trained in policies and procedures in a way that the manager would want.

- This type of on-the-job training (considered normative) only covers what actually comes up during a particular shift. Therefore, it is most likely not written down and is not comprehensive.

Best practices for training

- Conduct a survey to assess employee needs or training issues. The assessment results become the baseline comparison.

- Pre- and post-tests are useful tools to assess knowledge at the beginning and end of a training period.

- Treat staff members as adults wanting to learn new ideas, techniques, and strategies.

- Whenever possible, avoid lecturing and use interactive teaching methods. Ensure that new hires know some level of background and then get them into application scenarios as soon as it makes good sense (off-line practice).

- Use training manuals as a jumping off point. Expand on the information presented; ask for questions or ideas about materials presented.

- Over-prepare for each session so that you really know more than the participants.

- Use creativity, such as interesting stories, and/or humor. Keep sessions progressing forward.

- Ask for ongoing feedback. A useful feedback mechanism is to conduct quick start, stop, and change requests. What should we begin doing to make this training more interesting and effective? What should we stop doing to make this training more interesting and effective? What should we change to make this training more interesting and effective? Encourage feedback and, of course, take action on the feedback to demonstrate that you are receptive.

- Use visual aids, such as photos, charts, graphs, and films. Short clips are widely available on the web.

- At the end, summarize each session to clarify ideas and reveal misconceptions or lack of understanding. Discuss and implement changes to make training sessions more interesting and effective.

- If using a key employee to conduct the training, consider a different rate of pay for that time. One idea that may work well when referring back to the restaurant example would be for Becky to have two time cards—one for her regular serving shifts and one where she would be conducting on-the-job training of a newly hired employee. The training time card reinforces that the manager and Becky have an agreement and expectations.

Selecting Qualified People

Making the right hiring choices

- Hiring the right employees can positively or negatively impact the success of any business.

- Overall, too little attention is given to the steps involved in making this critical choice.

- Making good hiring decisions requires training and skills to identify and select the talent needed for each position.

- Two out of every three employees in our labor force are poorly matched to their job. They are either over- or under-qualified.

- Every manager is challenged to identify and hire that one individual out of three who fits the job and organization.

- Even when the right person is hired for the job, it takes from six to twelve months to become cost effective (fully functional) to the organization.

- The loss of, replacing, and training an employee cost including actual costs and costs associated with lowered productivity is estimated to be anywhere from 50 percent to the annual cost of that employee.

- The choice of the right employee who can contribute to the productivity of the organization for an extended period is critical to the success of any business, no matter the size.

Assessing applicants' abilities

- Design a written profile listing the qualities for the ideal employee in terms of must haves (required) and like to haves (preferred).

- Involve employees who will be working with the new employee.

- Identify potential candidates through targeted sources.

- Design and use standardized applications.

- Screen initial applicants.

- Provide a positive environment for interviews.

A hiring plan that is developed, communicated, and focused on the specific needs of the organization helps ensure that the right choice will be made in hiring quality employees. Hiring the right person helps ensure productivity, growth, and profitability. It is essential that everyone be able to do the job and work well within a team structure.

Critical elements for employee selection

- Knowledge of Equal Employment Opportunities Act governing hiring related to gender, age, disabilities, national origin, religious belief, and other preferences and practices.

- Knowledge of appropriate information and laws to help eliminate issues such as using non-discriminatory language for classified ads and discriminatory questions during the interview.

- Analyzing requirements thoroughly before beginning a selection or promotion process. Use criteria from personality and skills of current or past successful employees.

- Probing for objective evidence and assessment of an applicant's skills, knowledge, experience, attitudes and innate ability to learn.

- Ability to estimate teamwork performance.

- Evaluating facts carefully and avoiding premature or prejudiced conclusions when making selection decision.

The interview

The interview is a great venue to go beyond the resume. The interview process is extremely time consuming and therefore should be handled in a manner that produces high and positive results for both the candidate and for the interviewer. The most common errors during the interview process are lack of preparation and focus on the part of the interviewer. These are several of the best practices available in helping ensure that time is not wasted. While considered serviceable by most, check with your legal or HR departments for other issues, requires, or laws.

- Prepare. The interviewer should be completely prepared to conduct the interview.

- Encourage thorough answers. Ask open-ended questions that require examples of past work experiences and skills.

- Probe. Ask probing questions that go beyond *yes* or *no* answers. Get candidates talking beyond their prepared statements and scripts.

- Problem solving. Give applicants problems from your workplace and ask how they would solve them.

- Body language. Watch for body language signals.

- Samples of work. Ask for samples of past work. Note that if you are going to use this practice, ask the candidate in advance to bring a portfolio including the representative items that you would expect to see. It is doubtful that talents, such as twirling the baton or playing the harp will make much of a positive difference in the work place.

- Brief pause. Pause for a very brief silence (perhaps a count of five to seven) after an applicant has answered a question before going on to the next question. It encourages applicants to give you additional information about their strengths and weaknesses. Expanding answers helps provide additional insight beyond what the candidate has practiced.

- Take notes.

- Use consistency. Evaluate all applicants on a consistent rating system to help avoid emotional biases.

- Stick to questions that matter. Do not ask about relatives, spouses, and children during pre-employment interviews.

- Do not ask questions related to credit history or criminal arrests.

- Standardized tests. Do not give personality or intelligence tests unless they have a direct relationship to effectiveness for a specific job. If testing is done and can be validated, make certain it is given to every prospective employee on a consistent basis.

- No maximum age limit. Do not place advertisements indicating age preferences. The Age Discrimination Employment Act prohibits discrimination against people who are 40 years or older.

- Documentation. Make certain that international employees you hire have a permanent immigration visa (green card).

- Use caution. Polygraph tests, in most cases, may not be used.

- Tests. Testing for drugs or alcohol abuse is legal, and many companies have policies requiring these tests.

- Capabilities. When making decisions about hiring, transferring, training or promotions, focus on a person's abilities, not their disabilities.

- Collaborate. Include other team members in the selection process. If you do not have adequate time or resources to select talented people, consider hiring a recruiter who can do the screening for you, or train your staff to do so.

Avoiding Harassment Issues

Sexual harassment issues are not just related to demanding sexual favors. Sexual harassment includes any explicit or implicit behaviors or actions that create an intimidating or hostile work environment. Leaders and managers set the tone across the organization by letting everyone know there is a zero tolerance for any behavior, actions, sarcastic remarks, ethnic, or gender jokes, etc. which can be perceived as discriminatory or threatening.

When reflecting back on avoiding harassment issues, remember the importance of treating everyone fairly:

Treating everyone fairly

- Develop practices that support both the letter and spirit of the law.

- Be aware of and try to avoid stereotypes and biases of your own.

- Develop standards that apply to everyone and administer discipline equitably.

- Human resources departments extol the mantra of treating everyone the same. While treating everyone the same may sound reasonable and sound, it misses the key point that not everyone has the same capabilities. A leader would certainly not give the same basic direction and detailed instruction to a department head that she would give to an entry-level employee. A better and more refined version of this idea is to treat everyone fairly.

- Provide an appropriate level of direction to a person or group based on their capabilities, level of experience, and understanding.

Developing And Evaluating Staff

The attitude, knowledge and approach that managers take in training and coaching their staff will directly influence their performance either positively or negatively. Developing and evaluating staff should be positioned as making an investment in the staff. It occurs over time.

Therefore, for the time, money, and effort involved in developing and evaluating staff it seems logical that conducting both correctly with care and maximizing positive results is far preferable to ill planned and sketchy preparation and procedures.

Best practices in developing and evaluating staff

- Review performance against expectations with each person on a regular basis. For example, I recommend tying goals and objectives in with the budget forecasting/actual reporting system. Using this vehicle for review, leaders are able to receive both a goals and objectives and financial review at the same time in intervals of monthly, quarterly, and annually. Monthly can swing with timing issues that then smooth out with quarterlies, and flow into the annual review.

- Jointly (with the budget forecasting/actual reporting system reviews) identify additional training that will strengthen performance and allow professional growth. Do this often, not just once a year.

- Create non-threatening opportunities to support staff members when they may need assistance or suggestions for improvement.

- Determine how training will be used within the workplace when selecting outside training opportunities. Put in place implementation and follow through opportunities from outside training vendors.

- Develop a plan to cover employees' work when they are in training so they can concentrate on learning.

- Develop action plans to apply training to specific roles and responsibilities. (Assign new tasks and work that allows staff members to apply and use new techniques and methods learned from their training.)

- Compliment staff when they use their new skills effectively.

- Often, developing and evaluating can tie nicely with set goals and objectives.

Terminations

Firing employees is both a sensitive and difficult process. Firing also has legal implications and should be done with careful care and concern for the individual as well as the organization.

While difficult, terminating an employee properly is a necessary skill. Most truly experienced and engaged leaders report that a leader has not been tested properly until he or she has successfully terminated at least eight to 10 employees. Why that many? Again, leaders report that the first few terminations are bound to be clumsy and bungled. If terminations are among the most difficult functions of an effective leader—and they are by most counts—then it seems reasonable that learning from past mistakes and becoming *good* at doing the most difficult tasks *really* brings a leader a combination of valuable experience, knowledge, and good judgment, which is the definition of wisdom. Wisdom manifests itself in terms used to describe effective leaders, such as sagacity, intelligence, common sense, astuteness, circumspection, and sound judgment.

Best practices:

- Keep accurate records of all previous disciplinary actions.

- Review employee records and documentation of employee performance.

- Review the company policy manual or discuss with a human resources professional.

- Invite a third person (preferably someone from human resources) to witness the termination, but not take over the termination.

- Keep the termination time to a minimum. Stay focused on the issue and/or situation and not on the individual.

- Avoid terminating an employee on Friday.

- If it is a layoff or the result of downsizing, consider arranging for outplacement services. It may reduce litigation liabilities.

- Stay calm and do not argue any issue. Make certain the employee realizes this is a final decision.

- Go over your plans with yourself beforehand. Ask yourself if you were the one who was being terminated how would your planned approach be viewed?

- Focus on the fact that what you will be doing will be difficult. As such, do not expect for it to be easy. Conducting a proper termination is among the most difficult functions of a leader. Be extremely well prepared.

- Treat everyone fairly and with a high degree of respect.

Setting Goals And Standards

A goal is a written statement of results that are to be achieved and should be expressed in terms of measurable outcomes. A goal may be referred to as an overall goal, an interim goal, an objective, or an interim objective. While their meaning is essentially the same and the words may be used interchangeably, the word *interim* suggests that it is a milestone accomplishment met along the way as an overall goal is in progress. When the words *goal* and *objective* are used together, the leader is most often using goal to indicate an overall goal and the objective to indicate an interim goal.

A standard is an agreement referring to ongoing written performance criteria that must be followed in providing an agreed upon level of quality and/or service. Standards all have the same basic purpose of setting out agreed principles or criteria, so that people can make reliable assumptions about a particular product, service or practice.

We will cover the finer points of setting goals and standards in the next few sections.

Written goals should include these elements

- Use a checklist that spells the word, SMART: Specific, Measurable, Acceptable, Realistic, and Time bound (timely).

- Conditions that will exist when the desired outcome has been accomplished.

- Create measurable expectations for outcomes. Another word for measurable is quantitative. Another word for quantitative is objective.

- A time frame for the completion of the outcome. A time frame is measurable, quantitative, and objective. I have written an example to demonstrate time frame a few bullets down.

- A count for the completion of the outcome. A count is measurable, quantitative, and objective. I have written an example to demonstrate time frame and count a few bullets down.

- Visualize. Picture (along with the person or team being developed) what success will look like. In other words, ask how will we know when we have achieved our goal? This question prompts a discussion for creating both interim objectives and an overall goal.

- One widely used method for ending up with a comprehensive written set of goals and objectives is to tie them to the budget forecast/ actual reporting system.

- In creating measurable interim objectives and goals, remember to use objective measures as the basis for writing goal assumptions. Objectives are discrete measures that can be timed and/or counted.

- In the following example of a timed and counted objective, assume that the team and the leader have agreed that success will look like this: That we will have sold 350,000 room nights by year-end.

- An example of a timed and counted objective and goal: By the end of the first quarter (March 31, 20XX), we will sell 40,000 room nights (for a cumulative total of 40,000). During the second quarter (by June 30, 20XX), we will sell 90,000 room nights (for a cumulative total of 130,000). By the end of the third quarter (September 30, 20XX), we will sell 140,000 room nights (for a cumulative total of 270,000). By the end of the fourth quarter (year end, December 31, 20XX), we will sell 80,000 room nights (for a cumulative total of 350,000 room nights and therefore meet the overall goal).

- Depending upon the complexity of the organization and its budget forecast/actual reporting system in terms of financial review and budget variance meetings, one can further break the quarters into period or monthly (interim) objectives, which is a normal breakdown for many organizations.

- Detailed assumptions. In any case, ensure that goals and objectives are not only plugged into budget lines as numbers, but their corresponding assumptions are written in enough detail that an out-of-area generalist manager can read and understand them with minimal explanation. So, a food and beverage department head should be able to clearly understand an assumption written by the golf course and grounds maintenance director (and vice versa). When writing assumptions, it is helpful to look them over anticipating obvious questions (in this case, why the dramatic increase in widgets sold during the third quarter?) and document an explanation. The fundamental rule in writing an acceptable assumption is to anticipate questions and answer them inside the written assumption before they are questioned. The reasons for answering obvious questions before they are asked include that the answers help meetings speed along and can serve as handy reminders to those in charge of achieving such goals and objectives.

- Resources that will be used to achieve the desired result. Often, this has already been covered in the assumption. However, unusually high amounts of money, time, and/or effort should be further elucidated in written assumptions.

Create written standards:

- Comparison. At a fundamental level, a standard is more easily understood by comparison.

  1. Performance standard. A bagger in a grocery store may be expected to bag 325 bags of groceries during a work shift. A grocery bagger now performing as a runner may be expected to provide cart delivery service and unloading into a customer's car within 5 minutes. A performance standard is most likely to be expressed in terms of times and counts.

  2. Quality standard. A luxury hotel would likely provide 900 thread count bed linens, down-filled pillows, and luxurious duvets. An economy hotel would likely provide a lower quality standard, such as 200 thread count bed linens, foam pillows, and a simple bed spread with a pattern that resists showing stains. At times, quality standards are expressed in terms of levels.

  3. Luxury standard. A Rolls Royce would understandably be built to a higher luxury standard than a Chevrolet or a Ford. Similar to quality standards, luxury standards are often expressed in terms of levels. Exploring deeper into luxury versus quality might include that a Rolls Royce dealership would typically pick up autos for service at owner's homes and flatbed them to the dealership for service or repair and return and include exterior and interior detailing without charging extra. This level of luxury would not be expected at a Chevy or Ford dealership.

- Written standards. Over time, every leader should work with their staff to develop written standards for the organization (overall), each department, and all the way down to each function. When organizations do have a comprehensive set of standards the staff and the customers understand better both the commitment and the promise.

- Organizational standards. In creating written standards, it is best to begin with those standards that will apply to the entire organization (those that would apply in every department). An example of an organizational standard would be that any ringing phone would be answered within three rings. So, two rings is better and four rings is one too many. Another organization standard would be that every phone message received during a day would be returned before that person leaves for the day. Do these two standards sound too harsh? If your answer is yes, here is a challenge: Suppose that you are a customer phoning in to this organization. Okay, now, do these two standards still sound too harsh? Of course not.

- Departmental standards. Once organizational standards are adopted, departments should begin writing standards for the circumstances that are unique to the particular department. So, while the gift shop and the cafe both conduct a high degree of customer contact and service, both departments will have those standards that are unique to their particular department. The gift shop will focus more on point of sale, such as selling a roll of mints, a hat, or a newspaper. The cafe, on the other hand, will focus more on sequential service elements that depend on a series of interactions that require more coordination, such as meeting, greeting, order taking, order placing, coursing of drinks, appetizers, salads, entrees, desserts, etc.

- Period standards. Period standards vary within the same department based on time of day. For this example, lets re-visit the restaurant. Period standards will vary considerably based on a particular meal period. For breakfast, the expectation will be that from order to table, breakfast will be served within 9-12 minutes. Casual (sandwich-type) lunch might be 11-15 minutes for sit down or as few as two minutes for quick (counter) service. Dinner might vary drastically between fine and casual dining.

- When organizations do not have written standards for performance, they likely fall short of customer expectations.

- Standards are expressed quantitatively (so measurably and objectively) and usually refer to such things as level of service, degree of quality, attendance/punctuality, production rates, and safety standards. Standards may also be set over time based on expectations of customers.

- A standard then becomes a promise or a benchmark that gets everyone working together.

- A properly executed standard suggests that the organization will consistently meet and slightly exceed its standards for both quality and service. An example of a properly executed standard would be that a guest at the Ritz-Carlton hotel ordered room service. The room service operator told the guest that it would arrive by 7:45 PM (within a 30-minute timeframe, which was the service standard). The order actually arrived at 7:42 PM.

Problem Solving Techniques

Problem solving can be used at every organizational level. The process should be simple and performed as required to complete a job.

Useful steps in problem solving:

- Encourage everyone involved to participate in problem solving.

- State what appears to be the problem. The real problem may not surface until facts have been gathered and analyzed. Beginning with a supposition that can later be confirmed or corrected is a positive way to begin.

- Gather facts, feelings and opinions by asking:

  1. What happened?

  2. Where, when, and how did it occur?

  3. What is the scope or severity of the problem?

  4. Who and what is affected?

  5. Is this an ongoing problem?

  6. Does it require time and expense to correct?

- Assign problem solvers or use a team approach to gather the facts.

- Restate the problem. Include supportive information. The problem may change from the earlier supposition.

- Identify alternative solutions. Generate ideas and possible solutions. This is a time to amass ideas. Do not begin to eliminate or refine any until all ideas have been generated and discussed. Eliminating or refining prematurely will disengage, or at least short-circuit the participation and processes.

- Evaluate alternatives.

    1. Which will provide the best solutions? In defining best, the team may start out using the words ideal solution and then work toward most do-able.

    2. What are the risks?

    3. Do the perceived benefits justify the costs?

    4. Will the solution create new problems (unintended consequences)?

- Implement the decision.

    1. Who will be involved and to what extent?

    2. Does the person implementing the decision have not only the responsibility for implementation, but also the commensurate power to help ensure success?

    3. How, when, and where will implementation occur?

    4. Who will the decision impact?

    5. What might go wrong?

    6. How will the results be measured?

    7. How will the results be reported and verified?

- Evaluate the results. Test the solution against the desired results. Modify the solution if better results are needed.

Collaborative Skills

Collaboration leads to commitment and accomplishment of organization goals through personal power.

Benefits of collaboration:

- Efforts are non-threatening when there is an understanding of interdependence (people working together instead of just performing separately).

- When people work together toward common goals they stimulate others to reach for and think in terms of higher levels. New and more creative ideas are generated.

- Collaboration builds and reinforces recognition and mutual support.

Facilitate Open Communication

Leaders use open communication techniques to receive and transmit information. All information that affects the organization should be shared openly and sincerely. The lines of communication must cross many directions and be sensitive to the needs of everyone. The best managers and leaders are also effective communicators. They have learned to give clear instructions, stay responsive to questions and suggestions, and keep everyone appropriately informed.

Enhancing communication efforts:

- Understand and then be understood. In facilitating open communication, a leader makes sure that he or she understands the issue or situation before then providing clear and understandable direction. While I have referred to this concept from Covey elsewhere it is worth repeating: Seek first to understand and then be understood.

- At capability. Messages are best understood when they are sent in language at a level the receiver understands. Do not communicate either over or below a person or team's capabilities.

- Examples. Complex information is more easily understood when expressed along with specific examples and analogies.

- Conciseness. Key concepts are better remembered when expressed with clearness and conciseness.

- Organize. While time consuming, organizing a message before sending, makes it easier to understand.

- Restatements. The leader should determine the level of understanding by asking for a restatement of the message.

- Advance notice. Listening and understanding are more effective when the speaker sends information in advance.

- No early judging. Understanding is easier when judgment is suspended until the entire message is received.

- Paraphrase. Understanding can be improved by periodically paraphrasing the message. However, leaders must be aware of the importance of being both clear and concise. Long stories that do not seem to make a distinctive point are boring and confusing to others.

- Involve others. Encourage questions, comments, and concerns. Get others involved. Good listeners ask questions when they don't understand.

- Eye-to-eye. Sending and receiving a message is enhanced with effective eye contact. Good eye contact includes direct, eye-to-eye connection with those being spoken to, for a count of three (one thousand, two thousand, three thousand). After an internal count of three the leader should make eye contact with another.

Conflict Management

Conflict happens, but should not be approached on a win or lose basis. When animosity occurs, communications break down, trust and support deteriorate, and open hostility results.

When conflict is beneficial

- When it causes everyone to explore new ideas, to test positions and beliefs, and to stretch imaginations.

- When conflict is dealt with constructively, people are stimulated to greater creativity, leading to better results.

Causes of conflict

- Differences in wants, needs, objectives, and values.

- Differences in perceiving motives, words, actions, fairness, and situations.

- Differing expectations of outcomes being thought of in terms of favorable versus unfavorable.

- Unwillingness to work through an issue, collaborate, or compromise.

Coaching

Effective leaders realize they serve the people they lead and are dependent on them to provide resources, information, skills, and experience to make the organization function effectively. Leaders can serve their organizations and their staffs by encouraging growth and development. An important role of the leader is that of a coach.

Enhance the effectiveness of business actions.

Leaders who are committed to coaching see this function not as a luxury, but as a necessity. When coaching is done consistently, it strengthens the organization and empowers all the individuals within it.

Beneficial coaching practices:

- Provide guidance and support in an environment where employees know they are equally responsible for their growth.

- Make sure that staff and department members know they are available to reassure, empathize, listen, reflect, challenge, delegate responsibilities, and allow employees to grow and develop by learning from their own successes and mistakes.

- Constantly create reality checks to evaluate perceptions about performance and goals.

- Emphasize accountability by using action plans.

- Understand how each individual's performance must complement the organizational needs and business climate.

- Ensure that they delegate both responsibility for achievement and the commensurate power to be successful in such achievement.

Coaching for successful outcomes:

- Engage in employee self-assessments. Review sources of self-perceptions.

- List strengths, achievements, and weak areas. Assess their effect on behaviors or performance.

- Discuss effects of behaviors on others in the workplace.

- Analyze behavior. Is it a matter of principle, habit, or preferred work style?

- Determine the organizational need and resources to assist in change.

Equal Employment Opportunity

The laws governing equal employment opportunity effect all of the decisions related to the way leaders hire, supervise, compensate, evaluate and discipline their staff. They constantly change to reflect the latest court decisions. Management must not rely on past knowledge, but must be up to date with these changes, or hire a professional to do so. State laws may have additional requirements. Certain government contractors or organizations receiving federal funds have additional requirements related to affirmative action. Ignorance of the law is not a valid excuse for breaking a law.

Laws affecting equal employment opportunity

- The Civil Rights Act of 1964, as amended, prohibits discrimination on the basis of race, color, sex, religion, or national origin.

- Title VII, the section of law that covers employment, is known as the Equal Employment Opportunity Law and is administered by the Equal Employment Opportunity Commission.

- The Commission also administers the Age Discrimination in Employment Act (ADEA) and the Americans with Disabilities Act (ADA).

- The Equal Pay Act of 1963 requires equal pay for equal work.

Effective time management means

- Learning to use the time one has available more effectively.

- Doing the right things better over time.

Effective time management does not mean

- Wishing for more hours in the day.

- Getting more done in less time (although doing the right things better does take less time in the long run).

Strategies for effective time management

- Creating long-term strategies, planning, and building skills beyond simple to do lists are the goals of effective time management.

- Strategies for taking control and making the tools of technology work for you instead of making you work more involves a conscious effort and commitment of everyone in the workplace. Not all technology is worth the effort.

Concepts and perceptions of time

- Effective leaders recognize that people have varying concepts and perceptions of time. When this aspect of human behavior is understood, leaders adapt goal setting and task completion to each person's strengths and preferences.

- Time is one of the last things most of us would regard as subjective. Clocks and calendars are equally available to everyone and report the same facts to everyone.

- There is growing evidence that not everyone perceives time and its importance in the same way.

- Varying perceptions of time may account for certain behavior patterns that otherwise seem inexplicable.

- An understanding of how individuals regard their time may help the manager use human resources more effectively.

- Using a team approach to setting norms that complement the organization will positively impact the effective use of time.

- To make use of others' time preferences, managers must first understand their own.

- When an organization has a strong and/or precise definition of time and timeliness, it should be stressed and communicated as a key organizational value.

Time saving tips

- Set priorities.

- Run more efficient meetings, using agendas and time limits.

- Set aside time when you will not allow others to interrupt you (either in person or by phone).

- Set time limits for appointments and let others know them.

- Write answers in margins of correspondence requiring responses or use sticky notes.

- Do unpleasant tasks first to avoid procrastination.

- Use your high-energy time based on your natural clock to complete difficult tasks.

- Delegate routine tasks. If you do not have an administrative assistant, train others in the department to assume some of the duties. This can do double duty as a career development tool.

- Use an electronic calendar program to keep organized.

- Don't handle the same paper work more than three times: File it, move it on, or throw it away.

- Develop a time management system that fits your style. There are many planning systems and technology driven aids for time management, but many leaders forget the relevance of the old KISS rule. Keep It Simple Silly. A simple solution that works well is both elegant and effective.

- Ask others for their feedback on your use of time.

- When doing tasks, ask yourself whether this is the best use of your time and energy.

- Let people know how and when you will follow up or decide. Ensure that you meet this agreement on time and with no excuses.

Managers Becoming Leaders

Managers and leaders are most certainly not the same thing. Managers may function as leaders and leaders may function as managers, but they are no the same. Leaders think differently. While managers focus on doing things right, leaders focus on doing the right things. Leaders think strategically. Managers think in terms of to do lists. Leaders orient themselves toward projects. Managers work on tasks.

Here is a list of suggestions for managers who want to develop leadership skills and thought patterns. These are the things that leaders *do* and how they *think*.

Developing a leader's mindset

- Strong sense of vision and mission. Having a clear vision of excellence and a strong sense of your own and the organization's goals.

- Enthusiasm and Commitment. Putting in whatever time it takes to do the job to the highest level of competence.

- Conceptual skills. Being a problem solver. Identifying key themes and patterns underlying complex situations, whether the situations involve understanding specific problems or diagnosing the climate of the team or organization.

- Taking responsibility for actions. Representing yourself and your team, department, and/or organization in distributing generous credit to others while not being afraid to take personal responsibility for failure. Not throwing others under the bus.

- Self-confidence and assertiveness. Feeling comfortable and confident with your own abilities and able to stand up for your own values, beliefs, judgments and intuitions in dealing with problems and other circumstances.

- Communication skills. Able and willing to articulate various situations; explain your role and that of others; ability to express your thoughts.

- Achieving results and commitment to excellence. Having a high standard of performance and accomplishment for yourself and others. Not satisfied with the status quo (much less underachievement). Looking for ways to be challenged and to challenge others. Encouraging creativity and removing obstacles to creativity.

- Seizing Opportunities. Become proactive and creative in approaches to accomplishing goals and solving problems, and in finding innovative ways to get work accomplished.

- Providing Meaning and Direction. Structuring situations and meaningful work for others so the larger goals of the organization can be accomplished. Coaching others to provide guidance, boundaries, and to make decisions that keep things moving.

- Planning Skills. Being a systematic and logical thinker. Setting priorities and developing specific timetables for accomplishing activities. Acknowledging your abilities and confidence in your judgments and intuitions.

Understanding Diversity

In a multicultural workforce, effective leaders must value and manage appropriately with the realities and perceptions of the people with whom they work and supervise. I wrote earlier about the importance of appreciating and valuing uniqueness and that diverse backgrounds and opinions provide richness of discussion and ideas. Everyone should be valued for his or her unique contributions.

Effective leaders should understand preferences as they relate to issues regarding developing a mindset that embraces and promotes diversity.

Critical elements in leading a diverse staff

- Embracing differences. Embracing rather than merely tolerating differences between and among people.

- Understanding attitudes. Understanding attitudes about race, culture, gender, and sexual orientation.

- Resisting prejudice and stereotyping. Creating environments in dealing effectively with prejudice and stereotyping.

- Valuing diversity. Becoming sensitive and responsive to norms, practices, and values of different cultures.

- Valuing style. Recognizing communication differences between and among groups.

- Rewarding. Compensating high achievers appropriately amid diversity.

- Practicing tolerance. Using of nondiscriminatory language and labels.

- Using patience and kindness. Communicating with those for whom English is limited.

- Appealing to importance. Motivating effectively in a diverse environment.

- Resolving cross-cultural conflicts.

- Willing to create strategies for building multicultural work teams.

- Understanding and practicing how to provide feedback in culturally sensitive ways.

- Committing to coaching, grooming, and mentoring diverse employees.

- Recognizing the special needs of different groups.

- Creating an environment where all employees feel included.

- Providing hiring preferences to individuals of underrepresented groups. This is an extremely important element in effectively leading a diverse staff. Unfortunately, its misapplication can become an expensive and time-consuming problem. The common misapplication is weighting a demographic variable over job qualifications. The result of this mistake sets the candidate up for failure, calls into question the judgment of the decision maker, and therefore hurts the organization overall.

Delegating

Leaders need to use a variety of resources to accomplish their goals and objectives. There is no one way that is best, but of all the skills and activities of a manager or supervisor, delegation is among the most indispensable.

Plan the work. Then work the plan

- Employees understand the background and reasoning and become more involved and committed.

- More work can be accomplished and deadlines can be met more easily when everyone knows what they are working toward in terms of outcomes.

- Assignment of specific responsibility and authority (power) makes control easier.

- Employees are given the chance to experience, grow, and develop.

- Compensation and rewards can be more directly related to individual performance.

- Productivity improves.

- A diversity of people and operations can be managed more effectively.

- Proper delegation allows the leader more time for planning, organizing, and motivating.

Delegation dos

- Ensure that the person or team has (or gets) the skills to successfully carry out the assignment.

- Ask the staff person to paraphrase your assignment to ensure they understand their task.

- Set time limits and standards for completion.

- Set a method for evaluation by using elements that can be measured, such as times and/or counts.

- Give the employee the resources, tools and authority to carry out the task.

- Have an open door policy so that ongoing support is available when necessary.

Effective Meetings

Almost nothing discourages motivated staff members more than unnecessary meetings. Although they are important in establishing lines of communication and for problem solving, they often are not worth the time and effort. Each meeting should have a goal set by the person who will lead the meeting. When planning a meeting, first answer the question: *What do we need to accomplish today?*

Leading effective meetings

- Agenda. Create an agenda that includes time limits for discussion of each item.

- Send agenda in advance. Ensure agendas are sent to participants before meetings so everyone will have the relevant information and be prepared to deliver their reports. A draft agenda can be sent to participants to allow for their input prior to preparing the final agenda.

- Relevant. Agendas should contain only information relevant to the people attending the meeting.

- Attendance. Attendance only by those who are affected by the meeting goals.

- Advance notice. Send the announcement for the meeting well in advance.

- Names. Use nametags or table tents if it is likely the attendees have not met.

- Summarize. Summarize action taken and what needs to be done after each agenda item is decided.

- Minutes. Send out a summary of the minutes as soon as possible.

- Time. Start and end all meetings on time.

- Action. Besides reporting meeting minutes it is vital to begin implementation on decisions. Otherwise, meetings are a waste of time.

Chapter 06:

Organizational Behavior

Introduction

Some may wonder why this chapter is not among the first chapters. This book's main focus is on strategic leadership and not on organizational behavior. Organizational behavior (OB) is the broader subject, which includes leadership and therefore helps provide understanding and insight.

The purpose of this chapter is to start toward the historic beginning of management science and review major thinking within organizational behavior that encompasses and influences the study of leadership. *Organizational behavior* can be defined as a systematic study of human behavior within the confines of organization structures. Its foundations can be separated into categorical timeframes including its early history, the behavioral era, and the classical era. From there, we move toward contemporary perspectives including systems theory, contingency theory, and interactional view.

Organizational behavior is not rooted in any one specific discipline. Instead, organizational behavior includes a number of contributing disciplines that are both science and art including management, psychology, sociology, human relations, political science, economics, and cultural anthropology.

Early History

Adam Smith

Adam Smith (1723-1790) was a political economist from Scotland who published *The Wealth of Nations* (1776), in which he proposed that job specialization and a division of labor would increase productivity. The Wealth of Nations has become known as one of the earliest studies of the political economy and is sometimes referred to as the *bible of capitalism*.

Economics of Smith's time were dominated by the idea that a country's wealth was most accurately measured by its physical ownership of gold and silver. Smith suggested that a nation's wealth should be judged not by gold and silver, but by the total amounts of its production and commerce, which has become known as *gross domestic product* (GDP). He also proposed, explored, and tested theories of the division of labor, an idea dating back to the time of Plato, positing that specialization in a particular area (instead of generalization) would lead to an increase in overall organizational productivity.

Significance to leadership: Over time, *The Wealth of Nations* has been considered by some to be *the* foundational work of classical economics and one of the most influential business books ever written.

Charles Babbage

Charles Babbage (1791-1871) was a British mathematician, philosopher, inventor and mechanical engineer. Perhaps best remembered for originating the early concept of a programmable computer.

Significance to leadership: Babbage advocated that job specialization be extended to mental labor and also proposed the idea of division of labor. Division of labor is regularly practiced even today and remains one of the cornerstone concepts in leading and managing complex organizations.

Robert Owen

Robert Owen (1771-1858) was a Welsh entrepreneur and social reformer who was one of the first industrialists to improve labor-management relations by reforming factory working conditions in his push for the eight-hour work day.

Significance to leadership: Demonstrated true concern for industrial workers. Incorporated that thinking into a utopian socialism and the cooperative movement, which came to influence labor union and management cooperation.

The Behavioral Era

George Elton Mayo

George Elton Mayo (1880-1949) is credited with making numerous and noteworthy contributions to several disciplines including industrial sociology, organizational psychology, and business management. Many credit Mayo with establishing what today is referred to as organizational behavior because he combined his linking of human, social, and political issues of industrial civilization into what we know as *workplace behavior.*

Mayo's work in realizing that besides the formal organization there exists an influential informal organizational structure, as well, laid much of the foundation for what became the *human relations movement.*

During his numerous experiments and studies, Mayo is perhaps best remembered for his consulting work on a series of experiments on worker behavior at the Hawthorne Works of the Western Electric Company (1924-1927). His experiments found that employee satisfaction was a key to higher productivity and also concluded that group influences had a significant effect on behavior and worker output.

Significance to leadership: Because leadership theory is a key cognate within the larger organizational behavior theory, George Elton Mayo is certainly one of the most influential psychologists, industrial researchers, and organizational theorists in the foundation of what we know today as leadership theory.

The Classical Era

Frederick W. Taylor

Frederick W. Taylor (1856-1915) was an American-born mechanical engineer whose work focused on the improvement of industrial efficiency. Taylor's work outlined a plan for increased job specialization and mass production by scientifically selecting and training workers. His pioneering work developed into what is now referred to as industrial engineering.

Significance to leadership: In studies and experiments in improving industrial (organizational) efficiency, Taylor developed his Four Principles of Management, which continue to be a cornerstone in effective leadership thinking.

Taylor's Principles of Management

1. Develop a science for each element of a person's work. In doing so, one would analyze each movement individually in each element of a person's work.

2. Scientifically select and train workers. Today, for example, we use a position description during the hiring process and train employees in a well-thought through and written step-by-step array of actions.

3. Promote enthusiastic co-operation between workers and management.

4. Ensure that there is a division of tasks between workers and management. Therefore, ensure that we know who is both responsible for actions, goals, and outcomes and has the power to achieve them.

Karl Emil Maximilian (Max) Weber

Max Weber (1864-1920) was a German sociologist, philosopher, jurist, and political economist who published works on the theory of bureaucracy. As such, Weber's studies, experiments, and ideas heavily influenced social theory and social research. Weber is often credited along with Emile Durkheim and Karl Marx as one of the three founders of sociology.

Significance to leadership: Weber studied the importance of understanding the purpose and meaning that individuals attach to their behaviors and actions. He came to believe that individuals' actions result from multiple causes instead of any particular single cause. Over time, Weber developed his Model of an Ideal Bureaucracy.

Weber's Model of an Ideal Bureaucracy (Legal-Rational Model)

1. A rigid division of labor clearly identifying regular reporting relationships, tasks, and duties. So, carefully written job descriptions along with reporting authorities.

2. Chains of command as today would be depicted in a detailed organizational chart showing direct, indirect, and matrix reporting authorities.

3. The hiring of people with particular qualifications and certifications where appropriate as described in detailed and written job descriptions.

Weber then went on to describe the Main Principles (characteristics) of this Ideal Bureaucracy, whether in the public sector (administration) or private sector (management).

Weber's Characteristics of an Ideal Bureaucracy

- Specialized roles. Jurisdictional areas are clearly specified, activities are distributed as official duties.

- Recruitment based on merit and tested through competition.

- Uniform principles of placement, promotion, and transfer within the organization.

- Careerism (internal job opportunity) with systematic salary structure, which is often based on both position and organizational tenure (time with the organization).

- Hierarchy, responsibility, and accountability with commensurate power to achieve such responsibility and accountability.

- Formal written rules of conduct. Today, we often refer to this as an employee manual.

- Supremacy of abstract rules. Written rules and guidelines govern decisions and actions. Rules are stable, exhaustive, and can be learned. Decisions are recorded in permanent files.

- Impersonal authority. Therefore, the person holding a particular position does not bring those authorities with him or her when moved to another position. Personal property is separate and apart from office property.

- Political neutrality. Ideally, decisions are what is best for the organization and not based on political considerations.

Henri Fayol

Henri Fayol (1841-1925) was a French management pioneer who studied as a mining engineer, later becoming a mining executive, author and director of mines.

Significance to leadership: Fayol, (along with Frederick W. Taylor) is widely acknowledged as a founder of modern management methods. Fayol developed a general theory of business administration often referred to as *Fayolism*, whose theory defined Core Management Functions along with his Principles of Management.

Fayol's Core Management Functions

1. Planning. Deciding where to take the organization and planning the steps.

2. Organizing. Bringing together physical, human, and financial resources to achieve objectives.

3. Leading. Motivating employees to achieve organizational objectives and goals.

4. Controlling. Measuring and providing feedback about processes to make improvements toward goal achievement.

Originally, Fayol included a fifth Core Management Function, staffing. In recent years, researchers and authors have condensed his list to four.

Fayol's Principles of Management include the larger categories of division of labor, authority, centralization, order, equity, and discipline.

Fayol's Principles of Management

1. Division of work. The division of work is the course of tasks assigned to, and completed by, a group of workers in order to increase efficiency. Division of work, which is also known as division of labor, is the breaking down of a job so as to have a number of different tasks that make up the whole.

2. Authority and Responsibility. Authority is the right to give orders and obtain compliance, and responsibility is the corollary of authority.

3. Discipline. Employees must obey and respect the rules that govern the organization. Good discipline is the result of effective leadership.

4. Unity of command. Every employee should receive direction and orders from only one supervisor.

5. Unity of direction. Each group of organizational activities that has the same objective should have these characteristics:

   a. Be directed by one manager,

   b. Using one integrated plan,

   c. For achievement of one common goal.

6. Subordination. The interests of any one employee or group of employees should not take precedence over the interests of the organization as a whole.

7. Remuneration. All Workers must be paid a fair wage for their services.

8. Centralization. Centralization refers to the degree to which subordinates are involved or not in decision-making.

9. Scalar chain. The line of authority from top management to the lowest ranks represents the scalar chain. Communications should follow this chain. Today, this concept is typically referred to as the chain of command.

10. Order. This principle is concerned with systematic arrangement of persons, machines, materials, etc. There should be a specific place for every employee in an organization.

11. Equity. Managers should be kind and fair to their subordinates.

12. Stability of tenure of personnel. High employee turnover is inefficient. Management should provide orderly personnel planning and ensure that replacements are available to fill vacancies.

13. Initiative. Employees who are allowed to originate and carry out plans will exert high levels of effort.

14. Esprit de corps. Promoting team spirit will build harmony and unity within the organization.

While Fayol came up with his theories almost 100 years ago, many of his ideas, principles, constructs, and constructs are still represented in contemporary management theories.

Contemporary Perspectives

Systems Theory

Systems theory or Systems Science in an interdisciplinary study of different kinds of systems in determining patterns and helping explain principles that can be separated from and applied to all types of systems at different levels. For example, in business, an organizational system receives various inputs (e.g., financial, human, material, and informational) from its environment and transforms these inputs into products or services.

This type of system is still used with regularity in organizations, whether, retail, hospitality, or professional services. Picture your use of any product. There are likely both positives and negatives of the product that, presumably, you share (in the form of feedback) with the company (the system). In return, the company (the system) makes changes based on your input making their products and/or services more efficient, effective, and desirable to its customers. In this manner, the system of feedback becomes a working system for improvement.

Contingency Theory

The Contingency Theory approach to leadership embraces the concept that there is no one best way to organize an organization, lead a company, or even to make decisions. Instead, the optimal ways of doing things is contingent (dependent) upon the internal and external situation. Effective leaders carefully evaluate both the external (outside) environment with respect to issues such as competition, government regulation, and economics and the internal (inside) environment with respect to variables such as HR talent, organizational culture, leadership style, and industry, and design a customized approach to organizing and running the particular organization. We explore this concept further in view of application by theorists Fiedler, Hersey, and Blanchard in another chapter.

Interactional View

Individual behavior results from a continuous and multidirectional interaction between characteristics of the person and the situation. In this manner, the Interactional View posits that one cannot refrain from communicating (even silence is a form of communication) and that every behavior is some form of interactional communication. This is especially true since there is, categorically, no anti-behavior. Therefore, even non-communication is a form (often a strong form) of communication.

Axioms of The Interactional View

1. We are always communicating. One cannot avoid communicating. Even not communicating can become a powerful form of communication—think silence and stares.

2. Communication conveys content. Every communication has some particular content—both the words being spoken and more information relating to how the speaker expresses him or herself in terms of both verbal and non-verbal (body language) behavior.

3. Punctuation relates to cause or response. The nature of the relationship between two communicators is dependent on the ways by which the communicator expresses his or her *punctuation*. Punctuation in this sense refers to how events are labeled by sender and receiver as either the *cause* or the *response*. When one thing happens, something else always happens. For example, a supervisor is reprimanding a worker for not meeting her goals. The supervisor is upset. The worker feels guilty. One who observes may wonder, whether the supervisor is upset because of the worker's guilt or does the worker feel guilty because of the supervisor's upset-ness? One needs to be present and therefore observing the punctuation in order to properly understand the situation accurately.

4. Verbal and non-verbal communication. Communication involves both verbal and non-verbal modalities. Often, non-verbal communication, especially in the form of body language, communicates far more of the message that verbal communication. Body language may involve use of distance from someone when communicating, facial expressions, whether looking directly at or away from the person to whom you are communicating, tone and volume of voice, use of hands and arms when speaking, and others.

5. Symmetrical or complementary interchange. Communicative procedures either employ symmetrical interchange or complementary interchange. Symmetrical interchange is an interaction based on approximately equal power between communicators. Complementary interchange is an interaction

based on differences in power. These interchanges are often stratified by dominance, submissiveness, or classified as neutral. For example, if two department managers are communicating dominantly, they are engaged in symmetrical interchange. Similarly, a boss is utilizing complementary interchange over a direct report when using a complementary, dominant communicative style.

Foundations of Individual Behavior

Pavlov and Classical Conditioning

Ivan Pavlov (1849-1936), a Russian theorist developed Classical Conditioning. Pavlov posited that learning occurs when an unconditioned stimulus (e.g., layoff from a job) that elicits an unconditioned response (e.g., fear of being unemployed) is paired with a conditioned stimulus (e.g., pink slip) repeatedly, so that a conditioned response (e.g., fear) is elicited upon presentation of the conditioned stimulus (e.g., pink slip). Classical Conditioning is also widely known as *Pavlovian* or even *Respondent Conditioning*.

Pavlov's experiments were conducted using dogs. Classical conditioning involves placing a neutral signal before a naturally occurring reflex. In Pavlov's experiments, the neutral signal was the sound of a tone and the naturally occurring reflex was salivating in response to food. By associating the neutral stimulus with the environmental stimulus (presenting of food), the sound of the tone alone could produce the salivation response.

This type of Behaviorism is based on three assumptions:

- Learning occurs over time through interactions with the environment.

- The environment shapes behavior.

- Taking internal mental states such as thoughts, feelings, and emotions into consideration does not accurately explain one's behavior.

Skinner and Operant Conditioning

Pioneered by B.F. Skinner (1904-1990), an American psychologist, behaviorist, author, inventor, and social philosopher. Skinner studied observable behavior rather than internal mental events of the mind.

The work of Skinner was rooted in a view that classical conditioning was too simplistic to accurately explain the complexities of human behavior. He believed that the best way to understand behavior is to look at the causes of an action and its consequences. He called this approach operant conditioning, which means roughly changing behavior by the use of reinforcement, which is given after the desired response. Skinner identified three types of responses (*operants*) that can follow behavior.

Skinner's operants

- Neutral operants. Responses from the environment that neither increase nor decrease the probability of a behavior being repeated.

- Reinforcers. Responses from the environment that increase the probability of a behavior being repeated. Reinforcers can be either positive or negative. An example of a positive and negative reinforcer might be that progress toward monthly sales goals are posted for all to see. For those achieving high results, the reinforcer becomes positive. For low achievers, the reinforcer becomes negative and presumably encourages the salesperson to work harder and thereby avoid his or her name from appearing at the bottom of the achievement list.

- Punishers. Responses from the environment that decrease the likelihood of a behavior being repeated. Punishment weakens behavior. One example would be a statement in the employee manual that outlines a punishment policy for being late to work: 1st time a verbal warning, 2nd time a written warning, 3rd time suspension.

It is not always easy to distinguish negative reinforcers from punishers. To help clarify, think of negative reinforcement as avoidance (desired behavior is increased in the form of salespeople increasing production) and punishment as decreasing undesired behavior in view of an adverse consequence (suspension from work).

Perception

Perception is a set of processes by which a particular individual becomes aware of and interprets information about his or her environment. Perception involves signals in the nervous system, which in turn result from physical or chemical stimulation of the sense organs. For example, vision involves light striking the retina of the eye, smell is made up of various odor molecules, and hearing involves pressure waves. Perception is not passive or random. Perception is shaped over time by experience, learning, memory, expectation, and attention.

Processes of perception include individual characteristics of the person, the object, and the situation. Therefore, perception to one person may be quite different than to another.

Values

Values are beliefs that certain types of behavior are personally or socially acceptable and tend to be stable over time. Values are fundamental convictions that a certain mode of behavior or end result state is preferable to a converse mode or end result existence. Values have nested within them an element of judgment in that they are a reflection of an individual's or group's belief about what is right, desirable, or good. Values have attributes regarding content and attributes that regulate intensity. The content attribute states that some behavior or end result is desirable. The intensity attribute states the importance of such behavior or end state. By ranking values by intensity, an idea of a person's individual or work group's value system can be obtained. We will focus on values in more detail in an upcoming chapter. For now, think about some of your core values, which may be referred to as personal values.

Below is a list of core values commonly used by leadership workshops and programs. This list is not exhaustive, but it will give you an idea of some common core values. The idea over time would be to pick five to 10 core values as being *yours*. Selecting more than five to 10 suggests that the values while important, are not *core* (most important) values. These core values help individuals focus closely and specifically on what is most important to them. Think about how you might define your core values in terms that suit you.

Core Values

- Achievement
- Authority
- Balance

- Boldness
- Compassion
- Challenge
- Citizenship
- Determination
- Fairness
- Faith
- Friendships
- Growth
- Happiness
- Honesty
- Influence
- Inner Harmony
- Justice
- Kindness
- Knowledge
- Leadership
- Learning
- Love
- Loyalty
- Openness
- Optimism
- Peace
- Pleasure
- Popularity
- Recognition
- Reputation

- Respect

- Responsibility

- Security

- Self-Respect

- Service

- Stability

- Success

- Status

- Trustworthiness

- Wealth

- Wisdom

Attitude

Attitude is an evaluative judgment or statement(s)—either favorable or unfavorable—concerning objects, people, or events. *Attitude* is a settled manner of thinking or feeling about someone or something, typically one that is reflected in a person's behavior. Attitude can be formed over time from a person's past and present experiences and what he or she has been taught.

Components of Attitude

- Cognition. The cognitive component of attitude refers to the beliefs, thoughts, and attributes that we associate with a particular object. Often, a person's attitude might be based on the negative and positive attributes they associate with the object.

- Affect. The affective component of attitude refers to one's feelings or emotions linked to an attitude object. Affective responses influence attitudes in a number of ways. For example, some people are afraid of snakes—they are slippery and bite. So this negative affective response is likely to cause a negative attitude towards snakes, in general.

- Behavior. The behavioral component of attitude refers to past behaviors or experiences regarding an attitude object. The idea that people might infer their attitudes from their previous actions. For example, some would say that since the subject of math was difficult for them in high school, that they very much dislike the subject of math.

Motivation

Motivation can be defined as the forces both outside and within an individual that account for the level, direction, and persistence of expended effort. It is these internal and external factors that stimulate desire and energy in a person to be continually concerned for and committed to a job, goal, and/or objective and is used to explain behavior. Motivation results from the interaction of both conscious and unconscious factors such as intensity of desire or need incentive or reward for achievement, and the expectations of the individual or his or her supervisors and peers. These factors mix into a force and drive to achieve and are the reasons for someone behaving in a certain way. One example might be a student spending extra time studying for an exam because of that course being in his or her area of interest, major, or simply wanting a better grade. We focus more closely on the subject in another chapter devoted exclusively to motivation.

Attribution Theory

The concept of attribution theory is a theory of individual behavior and comes from the area of social psychology. Attribution theory suggests that we observe behavior of others during an event and attribute causes to it (either internal or external) depending on distinctiveness, social consensus, and consistency in order to explain it in terms that make sense to us, personally.

Fundamental Attribution Error

Fundamental attribution error is the tendency to underestimate influence of external factors and overestimate influence of internal factors of a person when judging another person's behavior in a given situation. Fundamental attribution error is also referred to as correspondence bias or attribution effect. This contrasts with interpreting one's own behavior, where situational factors are more easily recognized and can be taken into account.

Consider this example. The Slippery Path: A student named Alfred carefully walks in the rain down to lower campus using the path walkway. Alfred slips and falls. Alfred believes that this is a slippery path. Alfred continues more carefully. At the bottom of the path, Alfred pauses and sees a student named, Barney carefully walking down the path walkway. Alfred sees Barney slip on the path. Alfred believes that Barney is clumsy.

Foundations of Organizational Design

Organizational Design is a process of choosing and implementing a structural, step-by-step configuration for a particular organization. Depending upon the complexity of the organization, the design would depict relationships between and among operating and corporate entities and the alignment of structure, process, rewards, metrics and talent with the strategy of the business as a whole (grand strategy) as well as the specific business unit strategies.

Organizational design is contingent upon several factors including size of the firm, operations, environment, and growth strategy. Because organizational design is so fundamental to any complex management system, its effects on leadership are direct. Any effective leader must recognize and complement the particular organizational design.

Sociotechnical Systems Approach

The sociotechnical systems approach is an approach that views the organization as an open system that is structured to integrate two important subsystems—technology and people. The technical (inputs into outputs) and the social (interpersonal relationships between employees) subsystems form one unit. A sociotechnical system therefore is about joint optimization, with a shared emphasis on achievement of both excellence in technical performance and quality in people's work lives. This approach suggests that an organization's technical and social subsystems can be integrated largely through the use of autonomous workgroups. An autonomous workgroup is an empowered group (usually considered a team) encouraged and expected to manage its own work and working practices.

Matrix Organizational Design

A matrix organization structure is usually defined as one where there are multiple reporting lines—that is, people have more than one formal boss.

This design and structure may incorporate solid lines (direct strong reporting) and dotted lines (a weaker reporting relationship, but still indicating some formal level of 'right' to the individual's time) or it may mean multiple solid lines to more than one boss.

Matrix organizational design developed as an attempt to combine two different designs to gain the benefits of each. In this manner, lateral project (product) departmentalization is superimposed on a vertical structure. As such, each employee is a member of both a functional department and a project team and each employee has two supervisors: the department manager (from the vertical structure) and a project leader.

The move away from general knowledge managers and more toward technical and specialized work teams has spawned a dramatic increase in the use of matrix organizational structure.

The Mintzberg Framework

Henry Mintzberg (1939-present), a mechanical engineer, proposed a range of coordinating mechanisms that are found in operating organizations.

At the most basic level, Mintzberg identified five organizational frameworks.

Mintzberg's Organizational Frameworks

1. The Entrepreneurial Organization. This type of organization prides itself on being a simple, flat structure, which is a fundamental characteristic of an entrepreneurial organization. Examples might include an independent coffee shop or a mom and pop grocery store.

2. The Machine Organization. In a machine bureaucracy, work is highly standardized, work is formalized, decision-making is centralized, and tasks are grouped by functions, such as in manufacturing. Examples might include an organization that manufactures vehicle tires or computer processors.

3. The Professional Organization. In a professional bureaucracy, the environment relies on highly trained professionals who demand control over their own work, such as intellectual products. Examples might include a law or architectural firm.

4. The Divisional (Diversified) Organization. This type of organization includes many different product lines and business units. Typically a mix of manufacturing and professional, divisional organizations include a central headquarters in support of a number of autonomous divisions that make their own decisions and unique structures. One example might include a cosmetics company such as Procter & Gamble.

5. The Innovative Organization (Adhocracy). The preceding organizations describe more traditional organizations. The Innovative Organization functions and innovates on the basis of what works at the time and for the particular market, such as a refinement of products and processes organizations. Examples might include an organization like Apple or a pharmaceutical organization like Merck & Company.

According to Mintzberg, each organization can consist of a maximum of six basic parts.

Mintzberg's Organizational Parts

1. Strategic Apex, which includes top management.

2. Middle Line, which includes middle management.

3. Operating Core, which includes those working in operations and operational processes.

4. Techno-structure, which includes analysts that design systems, processes, etc.

5. Support Staff, which includes support outside of the operating workflow.

6. Ideology, which is the overall halo of beliefs, traditions, norms, values, and culture.

Organizational structure of frameworks and parts corresponds to the way tasks are divided and then coordinated. The coordinating mechanisms, which follow, correspond to stages of organizational development.

Coordinating Mechanisms

1. Mutual adjustment. Coordination by the simple process of informal communication. Examples could include two employees operating as front office agents or restaurant servers.

2. Direct supervision. One person issues instructions to others whose work interrelates. An example could include a chef telling others what is to be done, one step at a time, in processing a food order.

3. Standardization of work processes, which achieves coordination by specifying the work processes of people carrying out interrelated tasks. Those standards usually are developed in the techno-structure to be carried out in the operating core, as in the case of the work instructions that come out of time-and-motion studies. An example could include work done in this area by organizations such as McDonald's in ensuring same-ness of processes across all units.

4. Standardization of outputs, which achieves coordination by specifying the results of different work. Again, this work is usually developed in the techno-structure, as in a financial plan that specifies subunit performance targets or specifications that outline the dimensions of a product to be produced. An example could include a corporate office providing individual properties with their approved financial plans.

5. Standardization of skills (as well as knowledge). Different work is coordinated by virtue of the related training the workers have received. An example could include a control tower working closely with airline pilots during takeoffs and landings.

6. Standardization of norms, in which it is the norms infusing the work that are controlled, usually for the entire organization, so that everyone functions according to the same set of beliefs and commitments. One example could include, The Walt Disney Company.

Organizational Structure

Organizational structure is the hierarchical arrangement of lines of authority, communications, rights, and duties of an organization. Organizational structure determines how the roles, power, and responsibilities are assigned, controlled, and coordinated, and how information flows between the different levels of management.

Any structure depends on the organization's objectives and strategy. In a centralized structure, the top layer of management has most of the decision-making power and has close control over departments and divisions. In a decentralized structure, the decision-making power is distributed. The departments and divisions may have different degrees of independence.

Complex organizations may organize across geographical areas or by various products or segments. Moreover, different organizations may refer to organizational levels using different names for entities, such as division, area, branch, department, workgroup, and/or individual.

Organizational Structure affects organizational action first by providing the foundation on which standard operating procedures and routines rest. Second, organizational structure affects organizational action determines which individuals get to participate in which decision-making processes, and thus to what extent their views shape the organization's actions.

Division of Labor

The extent to which an organization's work is separated into different jobs, work groups, and individuals.

Mechanisms for coordination of tasks

- Departmentalization. Divided tasks are combined into work groups for co-ordination.

- Span of control. Span of control refers to the number of people reporting to a manager.

- Managerial hierarchy. A system of reporting relationships from the first (entry) level up to the CEO.

Vertical Structure

The vertical organization has a structure with power emanating from the top down. There's a well-defined chain of command with a vertical organization, and the person at the top of the organizational chart has the most power. Employees report to the person directly above them in the organizational structure. Each person is responsible for a specific area or set of duties.

Vertical structure is a hierarchical chain of command depicting reporting relationships. These reporting relationships are often expressed in terms of formal departmentalization, division of labor, and job specialization.

Horizontal (or Lateral) Structure

A horizontal organization has a less-defined chain of command. Employees across lines have similar input into how the organization is run. Instead of each person having clearly defined duties, employees may work in teams, with everyone on the team having input. Employees may perform many different functions and may report to several supervisors, rather than a single boss. Project managers or team leaders report to a team of supervisors, with members of each team being essentially equal in terms of power.

Chapter 07:

Management

Introduction

The purpose of this chapter on management is to call attention to the major similarities and differences between management and leadership. Leadership and management work together as if they were hand-in-glove. If we assume that the hand is leadership, management offers a structured and surrounding environment of protection. While the terms *leadership* and *management* are not synonymous, when used correctly they co-exist in a complementary fashion.

Management can be defined as the employment of human, physical, and financial resources to achieve organizational goals. *Managers* are people who conduct this process. It is important to note that management or managing differs from the work of *individual contributors* because results are achieved through coordinating the work of others. Managers are accountable for the work of their particular reports whether their areas of responsibility encompass individuals, groups and/or teams. Managers exist at different levels to form a hierarchy within the company, which is often depicted in a diagram referred to as an organizational chart (org chart). Levels and titles differ somewhat between and among entities based on organizational complexity and preferences. Characteristically, however, there typically exist three categories of management levels: first line managers, middle managers, and top managers.

Before reading further, it is essential to separate the term *management*, employing multiple resources to achieve goals from the term *manager*, a person who conducts this process and the term *leadership*, a process of social influence from the term *leader*, a person who conducts this process. Making those distinctions will assist in clarifying that an effective leader will use both leadership and management techniques. A manager will use management techniques, but may or may not use leadership techniques.

The Relationship Between Management and Leadership

Throughout this book, the terms *management* and *leadership* are often used interchangeably in broader discussion. This is a natural reference and similar to using the words *group* and *team* interchangeably. Technically, the terms *management* and *leadership* are quite different.

While management and leadership do differ significantly in their foci, they are nevertheless interdependent. Some describe leadership as the interpersonal dimension or social interaction process within management. To be a truly effective leader one also needs to be an effective manager. As covered in other areas of this book, not all leaders are effective managers. Not all managers are effective leaders. Here are some of the major points that help in clarifying the symbiotic relationship between leadership and management.

Leadership and Management Foci

1. Change and stability. The core element of leadership is using social processes in development and change. The core element of management is stability.

2. Own persons and team members. Leaders are their own persons. Managers are good soldiers.

3. Inspiration and structure. Leaders focus on leading people through inspiration. Managers focus on managing work through systems and structure.

4. Create and coordinate. Leaders create willing followers. Managers coordinate subordinates.

5. Long term and short term. Leaders have long-term horizons mostly in the form of projects and strategies. Managers have more short-term oriented horizons in the form of tasks.

6. Vision and goals. Leaders facilitate vision and mission. Managers facilitate goals and objectives.

7. Set and plan. Leaders set direction. Managers plan detail.

8. Facilitate and decide. Leaders facilitate decisions. Managers make decisions.

9. Trust and control. Leaders have passion and inspire trust. Managers rely on control.

10. Proactive and reactive. Leaders are proactive. Managers are reactive.

11. Achievement and results. Leaders focus on achievement. Managers focus on results.

12. Risk. Leaders are risk takers. Managers minimize risk.

13. Think and do. Leaders think and originate. Managers initiate and act.

14. Challenge and sameness. Leaders do the right things by challenging what exists. Managers do things right by maintaining the status quo.

15. Judgment and rules. Leaders are flexible and are not afraid to use judgment. Managers are less flexible and follow the rules and set ways of doing things.

While the direction may seem to paint managers as somehow less important than leaders, the real message is that the functions of leadership and management while different are inter-reliant and coexist in most organizations. The focus of this chapter is on the *function* of management. Effective leaders use the tools of management for guidance.

Types of Managers

It becomes confusing when thinking about the myriad of titles in a large and complex organization. Corporate office manager titles would characteristically move in ascending order from manager, to director, vice president, president, and chair. More complex organizations may recognize the additional positional titles of assistant and associate at the levels of manager, director, and vice president. Still others add additional detail such as chief operating officer (COO), chief financial officer (CFO), chief information officer (CIO), as well as senior, executive, and the like to their vice president titles. At the president and chair levels, we often see additional titles added of general manager (GM), COO, and chief executive officer (CEO).

At the property level (field level or strategic business unit [SBU]), titles are often far less complex and move in simplified ascending order from supervisor, manager, director, and GM. Larger properties may recognize the additional positional titles of assistant and associate at the levels of manager, director, and vice president. Still others add CFO, CIO, and COO to their vice president and GM levels.

Reporting authority varies widely. At times those at the property level have non-operational counterparts at the corporate level with whom they consult in their specialty areas while continuing to report to the property level hierarchy. In recent years, many multi-property organizations have instituted a matrix organizational system whereby property level management reports both to their corporate specialists and to the property level hierarchy. While well intended, such reporting cuts at the heart of the *chain of command* principle that each person should report to one and only one boss. When an employee reports to more than one boss, one can predict that conflict in priorities, goals, and objectives will occur with regularity.

Regardless of title, managers almost always fall into one or more of the following categories.

Categories of managers

1. Line managers. Line management is technically the lowest level of management in a managerial hierarchy. The line manager has direct reports that are either supervisors (quasi-managers) and/or non-managers. Line managers are responsible for the production of the main output of the company, at the level they are assigned. Non-line managers have managers as their direct reports. Examples include positions such as restaurant manager, front office manager, hotel manager, and clubhouse manager.

2. Functional managers. Functional management is where the organization is grouped into functional specialties and/or an entire department, such as operations, marketing, finance, and engineering. Functional managers have a responsibility to define how their purpose is to be carried out and how the employees will be developed to meet those functions. These responsibilities may fall on the line managers in functional organizational units. Examples include hotel manager, clubhouse manager, operations manager, accounting & finance manager, and sales and marketing manager.

3. Staff managers: Staff managers are responsible for non-operational support activities. Depending on the complexity of the organization, staff managers may fit the definition of a line or functional manager. Staff managers are those who supervise non-operations activities, such as accounting, HR, IT, and engineering.

4. General manager (GM): The general manager is responsible for all activities that make up an overall profit center, such as a property or strategic business unit (SBU).

Managerial Decision-making

Decision-making and Problem Solving

A *problem* occurs when performance is not meeting, or will not meet, objectives. This type of issue is most often a negative deviation from a standard or plan. Although the same type of situation can occur when the deviation is positive, it is not often recognized as a true problem. This is especially true when the positive deviation refers to revenues. However, when examined closely, positive deviations in revenue often relate to inaccurate forecasting or budget sandbagging. *Sandbagging* is a process whereby the person making the forecast wants to ensure that a particular forecast could be reached without too much difficulty, thereby lowering expectations.

Problem solving is the managerial process of identifying possible courses of action that will alleviate an identified problem. There are various methods involved in problem solving. However, most methods begin with careful analysis of the issue.

Problems frequently arise when *opportunities* arise. An opportunity is a possible convergence of circumstances, which, if taken advantage of, may lead to profit or gain. Opportunities often create *unintended consequences*. Therefore, adept managers ensure that steps are taken in advance of seizing opportunities in order to help eliminate unexpected problems due to unintended consequences. An example of an unintended consequence: Several years back when email users were using hotel phones to check email, hotels implemented a surcharge on each local call. Realizing this issue, users began *line camping* (make one call and then leave the line open for their entire stay instead of making multiple local calls). Hotels saw an opportunity in instituting charges for the surge in local phone calls. The unintended consequence was that line camping quickly used up all available space of outgoing lines and put additional stress on the phone lines for inbound calls.

Decision-making related to problem solving. While problem solving is identifying alternative courses of action representing viable solutions, decision-making consists of evaluating, narrowing, and selecting alternative solutions.

Decision-making environments

1. Certainty. For each alternative decision, the outcome is known. This rarely occurs in the business world.

2. Uncertainty. Not enough *reliable* information is available.

3. Risk. For each particular decision, possible outcomes have a probability attached to their occurrence. Risk may be caused by one or more of three variables:

   - Deficiency of information defining the problem.

   - Measurement uncertainty.

   - Deficiency of information about the model used.

Programmed and non-programmed decision-making

1. Programmed decisions. Programmed decisions are those made to address routine issues, such as organizational policies, procedures, rules, or computerized decision tables. An example of a programmed decision would be that when any checkout line at a grocery retailer has more than two customers waiting, another cashier automatically opens a checkout station.

2. Non-programmed decisions. Non-programmed decisions are those made for unstructured problems. Non-programmed decisions require judgment on the part of the manager. An example of a non-programmed decision would be the manager of the retailer in the preceding example, upon seeing a weather forecast for unexpected severe weather, calls in additional staff at the last moment in anticipation of an increase in business from customers preparing to be homebound during the storm.

Intuitive (sensing) vs. rational approach

1. Intuitive decision-making. Uses unknown or unproven assumptions, skips rational reasoning, and reaches a decision rapidly. Often used for complex problems where a quick decision is needed. Sensitive managers, aware of the feelings of people around them, favor such intuitive processes.

2. Rational decision-making. This is a process of inference that considers (a) the particular goals that are to be attained, (b) environmental conditions, (c) explicit representation of inferences, and (d) verifiable recommendations. Decision maker gets data from his five senses: Hearing, sight, taste, smell, and touch.

3. Heuristic approach. This approach involves trial and error, experimentation, or using a *rule of thumb*. A rule of thumb is a broadly accurate guide or principle, based on experience or practice rather than theory. Heuristic approaches employ both intuitive and rational decision-making.

Rational decision-making

Rational decision-making is a multi-step process for making choices between alternatives. The process of rational decision-making utilizes elements of logic, objectivity, and analysis over subjectivity, insight, and feelings. The word *rational* in this context does not mean saneness or clear-headedness as it does in the conversational sense.

Types of rational decision-making

1. Optimizing. When a decision maker optimizes, he or she is selecting the best alternative

2. Satisficing (non-optimizing). When a decision maker satisfices, he or she searches alternatives until some acceptability level is reached. Satisficing is often described by terms such as, the decision may not be ideal, but it is good enough.

3. Bounded Rationality. When a decision maker uses bounded rationality in decision-making, the idea is that the rationality of individuals is limited by the information they have, the cognitive limitations of their minds, and the finite amount of time they have to make a decision. Essentially, decision makers deal with inadequate

amounts of information and do not have time to investigate alternatives.

Group Decision-making

With the increased focus on collaboration, many managers think that it is a mistake to bypass the group process and make unilateral decisions. While it is true that there are distinctive benefits in utilizing groups for decision-making, there are also a number of drawbacks that managers should consider.

Benefits

- More brain power. Spreading the issues across a wider variety of people who can develop innovative solutions and, with the wider range of thought, help prevent decision-making mistakes.

- Building. *Piggybacking* off of the wider range of thought would be utilizing the combined knowledge of all group members to develop better and more thoughtful decisions.

- Risk. Increased tolerance for risk. Group input allows exploration that often goes wider than that of an individual. Consequently, decisions can be more creative because the group will normally accept more risk than an individual will allow him- or herself.

- Higher acceptance. The interplay of ideas and opinions that develop when using a group process in decision-making yield higher acceptance by all group members whether all group members agree or not with the decision. The reason for this acceptance is that those dissenting or otherwise disagreeing know that at least their positions have been considered in advance of a decision being made.

Drawbacks

While the emphasis encouraging group decision-making has been a buzzword for some time, it is not without drawbacks. Effective managers become aware of these possibilities and counsel groups before the decision-making process derails.

- Most common drawback. Domination by one particularly strong individual who foists his or her solutions in such a way as to discourage others from participating.

- Competition. When group interaction turns from collaboration to competition, it produces conflict among members. Groups whose members are particularly busy with other tasks and projects may tend to accept the first feasible solution thereby disregarding the time required to carefully consider alternatives.

- Time and effort. Because group decision-making involves individuals, the process is costly in terms of time and effort.

Summary of Decision-making Models

There exist a variety of models available from which to utilize when making decisions. This is a non-exhaustive list of the most popular models along with their major features.

1. Normative Decision Theory. Exemplified by executive writing, which yields logical solutions to problems. Normative decision theory is concerned with the best decision to take. It assumes an ideal and informed decision maker who is acting fully rational.

2. Group decision-making.

   - Brainstorming (also referred to as *brainwriting*): A group of creative and knowledgeable people is brought together to seek solutions to issues. Building on the ideas of others, the focus of brainstorming is quantity of ideas, which are later considered, ranked, and decided upon in a separate process. Therefore, brainstorming is a process instead of an outcome.

   - Nominal Group Technique aims to keep personal interactions at a minimum and is a more structured variant of brainstorming in that much of the front-end work in idea generation does not occur in collaboration. After ideas are generated and written by individuals, they are discussed and ranked by the group.

3. Bureaucratic Model. This model is used more often in larger organizations because it relies on a hierarchy of authority as depicted on an organizational chart. The model assumes departmental separation of duties and an established set of priorities and rules, defining jobs precisely, appointing experts, establishing clear rules and procedures ideally to achieve maximum efficiency. The common drawback to this type of decision-making is that it can be inflexible and inefficient (time consuming).

4. Behavioral Decision Theory. This theory describes what people really do when decisions are made. Most often decisions *satisfice* (refer back to Rational Decision-making) by accepting an available option as satisfactory instead of optimizing outcomes.

5. The Conflict-Equilibrium Model. This model is a group process whereby decisions are reached through bargaining, politicking, compromise, and persuasion to resolve conflict. While not often referred to by its formal name, the conflict-equilibrium model is a commonly used approach in decision-making.

The Changing Environments

Nested Environments

An environment is a system, which works external to some designated system. Environments are nested in the sense that each environment (system), by definition, also has its own distinctive environment. Therefore, if a particular organization is designated as the *system of interest*, its closest surrounding system (environment) is made up of its sub industry, industry, and radiates out to include other external stakeholders. *Stakeholders* are any institutions or people who affect, or are affected by, the designated organization. Think of the system of interest as, perhaps, a bull's-eye (the center) on a shooting target and the environment radiating out from the bull's-eye in concentric circles based on their relative influence on or by the system of interest.

For clarity, picture the Hilton Hotel in Long Beach, California. This particular Hilton property, the system of interest (the bull's-eye) in this case, resides inside the hotel sub-industry and the greater hospitality industry. The more obvious external stakeholders radiating outward (picture a circular target) would include its customers, competitors, The City of Long Beach, The Long Beach Convention and Visitors Bureau, The Long Beach Aquarium of the Pacific, Shoreline Village waterfront mall, the Long Beach City Council, Mayor, police and fire departments, and others up through the State of California, the United States, North America, and/or the world as a whole. Defining nested environments assists management when referring to contextual change regarding leadership, finance, economics, marketing, and strategy.

Input to an organization from its environments

Input to a business from its industry and other external stakeholders benefits any organization in developing a more comprehensive understanding of its competitive environment, task environment, as well as remote environment.

Examples of variables from the competitive environment

- Competitors and potential competitors.
- Buyers.
- Suppliers.
- Substitute-products companies.
- Other entities.

Examples of variables from the task (operational) environment

- Competitive environment.
- Government agencies.
- Activists and special interest groups.
- Trade associations.
- Financial and insurance intermediaries.
- Unions.

Examples of variables from the remote (outside) environment

- Economic.
- Social.
- Technological.
- Political including national, trading blocks, and international influence.
- Physical or natural resources including weather, climate, historical, or cultural.

Input to any organization from its environments becomes a programmed template of prompts in assisting in a comprehensive analysis of an organization's situation with regard to planning its leadership, finance, economics, marketing, and strategy functions.

Complexity and Change

In the 1960s, R.B. Duncan began researching and developing an explanation for better understanding environments. More specifically, Duncan investigated the influence of certain factors on organizational structure together with their impact on overall organizational efficiency. Among his findings, Duncan theorized that an environment is considered more complex if the following elements are present.

Complexity elements

- There are more key factors in the environment.

- There is a lack of homogeneity (similarity) of factors throughout the environment.

- Environmental change refers to both the frequency or rate of change of the environment and the extent of change.

- Complexity/change. Duncan's *environmental matrix* describes four combinations: Stable, Dynamic, Simple, and Complex.

Organization's Influence on the Environment

An organization may influence its operating environment by its behavior, size, leadership, and by negotiations with its stakeholders. Disney World, located in Orlando, Florida is a distinctive example of an organization that significantly influences its operating environment. The State of Florida, the City of Orlando, Orange County, as well as surrounding counties are all well aware of and work closely with Disney World because of its success in bringing tourism and tax dollars to the area.

Forecasting Future Environments

Forecasters within organizations use a variety of tools in predicting the future. Three techniques being used with regularity include the Delphi technique, cross-impact matrices, and scenario building.

- The Delphi technique. This is a structured communication technique originally developed as a forecasting method. A panel of experts makes predictions. The experts answer questionnaires in two or more rounds. After each round, a facilitator provides a summary of the forecasts from the previous round as well as their reasoning. After review, experts are encouraged to revise their answers in light of the replies. It is believed that during this process the range of the answers will decrease and the group will converge towards the final predictions.

- Cross-impact matrices. This method is used to evaluate the impact of various segments of the environment on each other. Cross-impact matrices are heavily reliant on statistics and were developed in the 1970s primarily by federal government intelligence agencies. First, analysts consider the number and type of events to be considered in the analysis. Typically, anywhere between 10 and 40 events are used in the analysis. It is initially assumed that every event has some effect on the others. Second, analysts calculate the initial probability of each event. Third, analysts generate conditional probabilities that events have on each other. An example would be asking statistically, *if event 'A' occurs, what is the new probability of event 'B' occurring*? This is done for every interaction between events. Fourth, analysts test their initial conditional probabilities by running simulations in a statistical program such as SPSS. Fifth, analysts can run the analysis to determine future scenarios, or determine how significant other events are to specific events.

- Scenario planning or scenario analysis. A scenario represents a possible sequence of possible visions of the future based on current and historic trends and events in which the final frame represents the most accurate vision of the future, which will be used to make decisions. Scenarios include anywhere from three to about five key factors that are forecasted from trends, patterns, and assumptions. Typically those factors would include *STEEP* trends. STEEP is an acronym defined as Social, Technical, Economic, Environmental, and Political. Scenario planning was used heavily in intelligence gathering and predicting by the federal government.

Planning For The Future

The Planning Function

While the leadership function of strategic planning is addressed in another chapter, management plays an important role in the structure. The following discussions cover a number of the key tools that build a managerial structure around what becomes and is ultimately driven at the highest level by an organization's strategy.

Planning is a combination of careful thought, input, and consideration that precede the *action* (or operations) stage. Planning is the process of establishing mutually agreed upon goals and objectives as well as the means (responsibility, power, and funding) to reach the agreed to goals and objectives. Planning may (and should) be formalized in the sense that it is written in an organized fashion. However, planning in many organizations is done informally in mental notes or brief reminders jotted on paper.

Formal planning advantages

- Formal planning sets forth goals, objectives, and actions for (ideally) everyone throughout the organization.

- Integrates the efforts of every group or department—ideally all employees—in the interests of the organization as a whole.

- Sets forth the resources required to complete the plan.

- Precedes and ties together the other management functions of organizing, leading, and controlling.

Formal planning disadvantages

- Formalized planning may result in inflexibility in the face of a rapidly changing environment.

- Erroneous assumptions may be built into the plan. Once written, assumptions may be difficult to change.

- Benefits may not be worth the cost. While this may be true at times, usually the benefits of planning far outweigh the disadvantages. Typically, the smaller the organization, the less time will be spent in a formalized planning process.

Hierarchy, Level, Time Horizons

Organizations plan in a more-or-less ordered system of planning where the preceding levels inform the next level(s) down.

The classic array echelons

- Strategic plans. At the top, strategic plans (specifically referred to as the *overall* or *grand strategy*) reside at the corporate level with time horizons going out three to five years or longer. This level plan sets the direction of the organization by answering the question as to what the business includes? By doing so, it therefore specifies the portfolio of businesses. For clarity, think about the corporate hotel entity, Marriott.

- Business plans. Moving down one level, each business would be run by a general manager with time horizons being similar to the strategic plan, normally three to five years. This level plan sets the direction of the particular business by answering the question as to how the business will compete in its particular business. Entities completing business plans are often referred to as *SBUs* or Strategic Business Units. For clarity, think about a specific hotel property within the Marriott family, such as the Ritz-Carlton, Boston.

- Functional plans. Within a business plan, there exist a number of major and minor functions led by functional managers with normal time horizons of one year. Functions in this sense are often referred to as departments or areas. Functional (and sub-functional) plans answer the questions as to who does what, in what time period, and with what resources? For clarity, think about the departments that operate within the Ritz-Carlton, Boston property. A few of the major departments and their functional managers would include the front desk run by a front desk manager, housekeeping run by an executive housekeeper, and food & beverage run by a food & beverage director. Sub-functional areas reside within functional areas, such as bell service operating within the front desk department, the laundry operating within the housekeeping department, and the coffee shop operating within food & beverage. A few of the minor operating departments or areas would include the pool department run by a pool manager and the gift shop run by a shop manager.

Objectives and Goals

Differences between objectives and goals. Much unnecessary confusion surrounds the differences in distinguishing *objectives* from *goals*. While often used interchangeably each has important differentiating attributes. They are used at different stages of the business planning process, and each serves a different purpose. Goals are statements one makes about the future of an organization or area. Goals represent aspirations and end states and represent long time frames than do objectives. A restaurant might have a goal to serve 200,000 dinner customers for the year, while a golf course may have a goal of 50,000 rounds of golf for the year. Objectives (often referred to as *interim goals*) are shorter term aspirations that would break those year-end goals down to an operational level of projecting numbers of dinner customers by the day, week, month, quarter, and so on until it reached the overall stated goals. Whether goal or objective, effective managers ensure that they meet the criteria of SMART, which is a mnemonic for remembering critical elements in creating meaningful goals and objectives: Specific, Measurable, Agreeable, Realistic, and Time bound. The strategy chapter discusses goals and objectives with additional detail.

Organizing, Staffing, And Coordinating

Organizing Work

Organization is a key management function in ensuring a smooth and cohesive workflow. Methods as to how management groups its activities to utilize its human, physical, material, and financial resources vary greatly and affect the organization's orderliness. Most organizations begin with the establishment of relationships between and among employees, functions, and tasks.

Factors affecting structure

There are several factors that should be considered in decisions regarding structure.

- Stage of growth. Referring to *stage* in terms of business growth, Porter's lifecycle classically identifies inception, growth, maturity, and decline as the stages of growth an organization experiences. Inception and growth are frequently turbulent requiring entrepreneurial thinking and temporary structures. At maturity, the organization settles into predictability. As an organization moves toward decline again becomes turbulent as structure regularly tightens as business shrinks.

- Environment. Is the outside world rapidly changing or more stable?

- Strategy and structure. Strategy and structure are work together. Careful planning of strategy guides and assists in appropriate structure.

- Technology. What level of technology is employed throughout the organization? Categories include high, medium, low or something in between any of those levels.

- Type of production. Usually this factor is related to technology.

- Type of control. Which managerial level and managerial type does what? Types to consider include line, informal, matrix of function and task, bureaucratic, delegation, and empowerment.

- Data. Consider size of the firm, geographic areas served, customary industry practice, and sources of materials and vendors.

Division of labor

A *division of labor* involves the assignment of different parts of a process or task to different people in order to improve efficiency. Division can either be horizontal or vertical.

- Vertical. Vertical division establishes a hierarchy that makes up the organizational structure by dividing large tasks into subtasks and establishing lines of authority and communication. Job depth tends to be high. An example would include a large restaurant operation requiring servers to set tables, meet and greet, interact, take beverage orders, take food orders, serve in courses, cook at the table, clear, close tickets, re-set, and complete side work associated with their stations.

- Horizontal. Horizontal division divides work into specialties that produce efficiency and boredom. Job scope is narrow. An example in a large restaurant would include pot washers or silverware sorters whose jobs would involve little interaction and repetition (versus variety).

Power, authority, responsibility, and accountability

Power is the ability to get others to act as you wish. Power may be derived from force, coercion (threat), reward, or control of resources. Authority is the legitimate right to command. Sources of authority come from the legitimacy of the organization and acceptance of authority by the people directed. Responsibility is the assignment of carrying out a task, achieving an objective, or completing a goal (for actually doing a job). Accountability is being held answerable for getting something done, whether or not responsibility is delegated. Once assigned, accountability cannot be delegated, although responsibility may be. These elements of organizing work are discussed in further detail in other chapters.

Centralization and decentralization

Whether an organization considers itself to be centralized or decentralized is a continuous sequence (a continuum) in which their particular elements are not perceptibly different from each other, although the extremes are quite distinct. *Centralization* refers to concentration of power and decisions being made near the top of the firm. *Decentralization* refers to delegating and dispersing authority and decision-making to progressively lower levels of the organization. Decentralization is sometimes referred to by the similar term, *empowerment*.

Design of Organizational Structure

Organizational structure defines how organizational activities such as tasks, projects, coordination, and supervision are directed toward achievement of an organization's goals and objectives.

Principles

When considering designing organizational structure, the following five elemental principles of structure are essential for managers to consider:

- Absolute responsibility. The *principle of absolute responsibility* states that authority can be delegated. However, ultimate responsibility cannot be delegated completely by managers to subordinates. This means that ultimate responsibility is *fixed*. The manager is always responsible to his or her superior for accomplishment of the task by delegating the powers. It does not mean that he or she can escape from ultimate responsibility for task completion. So, the commonly heard excuse that a manager delegated a task to a subordinate and therefore is no longer responsible for its completion is not valid. It is helpful to think of delegation in terms of a manager merely loaning responsibility to others.

- Parity Principle. The *parity principle* states that authority and responsibility must be matched. According to this principle, if a subordinate is delegated the responsibility to perform a task, then at the same time he should be given enough independence and power (authority) to carry out that task effectively.

- Unity of command. *Unity of command* is a classic principle of management that states that an employee should only answer to one person (direct supervisor). A worker should have one, but only one immediate manager.

- Scalar Principle. The *scalar principle* states that a series of managers link every worker directly to the top of the organization. It is an activity of the organizing function. The scalar principle is frequently referred to as the chain of command and provides a clear definition of authority throughout the organization. This authority flows down the chain of command from the top level to the lowest level in the organization. The most used device to visually depict the chain of command is the organizational chart.

- Span of Control. *Span of control* is a span of supervision, which depicts the number of employees that can be handled and controlled effectively by a single manager. According to this principle, a manager should be able to effectively supervise the work of some agreed upon number of employees. Job scope and depth, similarity of work, physical proximity of workers, and the quality of subordinates and the manager affect span of control.

Building blocks

A variety of building blocks used in managing structure.

- Division of work. *Division of work* refers to the practice of dividing a job, task, assignment, project or contract into smaller tasks. A division of work may also include a schedule or set of deadlines for the subtasks. Division of regularly takes the form of goals and objectives. Deadlines may take the form of times or counts (or both), whichever is most appropriate. Examples of time would include measuring devices that assist in supporting deadline clarity, such as seconds, minutes, hours, days, months, years, and/or dates. Counts would include almost anything that can be measured by counting in supporting deadline clarity, such as numbers, percentages, ratios, revenues, and/or expenses.

- Departmentalization. *Departmentalization* is an aspect of organizational design that includes the subdivision of an organization into units based on their function or location. Many companies, including restaurants, are likely to use two or more types of departmentalization simultaneously. Some of the standard methods of departmentalization include grouping jobs by functional activities, product types, customer groups, geography or location, processes, and chain of command. For example, McDonald's may use location where more than one store exists in a particular area. Brinker International, which owns Chili's and Romano's Macaroni Grill, and others may operate by function and separate the operations (food preparation) from the sales (serving of the customers).

- Line and staff. *Line* is a hierarchy function that relates to those involved in operations. Line managers work and contribute directly toward an organization's core business as the revenue generators. Line managers have authority over those who report to them. Examples include almost any manager who works in operations. *Staff* is a hierarchy function that relates to managers who work in support of the line employees. Staff managers almost always have advisory authority over others. Examples include those in HR, accounting, public relations, and legal.

- Committees and task forces. These groups may be permanent (on-going) or temporary (ad hoc) and therefore formed for one particular task or project.

- Hierarchical, matrix, and organic structures. *Hierarchical* is an organizational structure where every entity in the organization, except the one at the top of the hierarchy is subordinate to another entity. In a *matrix* organizational structure, the reporting relationships are set up as a grid (matrix), rather than in the traditional hierarchy. Employees have dual reporting relationships to more than one supervisor, such as both a line manager and a staff manager. This structure is regularly adopted in, for example, a hotel property where a food and beverage director might report to the property GM and also to the regional food & beverage director. An *organic* organizational structure is one that is very flexible and is able to adapt quickly and well to changes. Its structure is identified as having little job specialization, few layers of management, decentralized decision-making, and not much direct supervision. An example of an organic organizational structure would be in the early start-up days of the Internet company, Airbnb. During that period, there were very few employees, the founders made decisions largely by consensus, and anyone was free to consult with anyone else regarding problems or concerns with bringing the platform online and working through issues.

- Integration and differentiation. *Integration* (may be referred to as coordination) relates to how the different areas of the company coordinate their operations. A highly integrated company has strong connections between and among departments and product lines, with each area working under an overall set of rules and strategies. Integrated companies are highly vertical and hierarchical in nature whereby the senior levels of management dictate the structure rather than allowing the individual departments to set their own agendas. *Differentiation* often occurs in larger organizations when different properties, departments, sections, or offices create their own mini corporate cultures within the parent company's overall structure. For instance, the sales staff at a differentiated hotel company will have a different approach to their tasks than the accounting, finance, and treasury departments.

Departmentalization structures

- Functional. In a *functional* structure, the organization is divided into smaller department groups based on specialized functional areas, such as IT, finance, or marketing.

- Product. *Product* based organizations specialize by their particular product. A diversified hospitality company that organizes itself in this manner might have a private club organization, a hotel organization, a restaurant organization, and so forth.

- Geographic. In *geographic* structure, an organization organizes itself and groups its departments according to geographic location, such as city, county, state, region, country or continent.

- Customer. In *customer* departmentalization, departments are separated from each other based on the type of customers to be served. For example, customers of this type of organization, such as a travel agency, may be classified as international or domestic and in-bound or out-bound.

- Process or equipment. *Process or equipment* departmentalization separates departments based on their role in a production process. In a hospitality textile company, various processes of weaving, dyeing, printing, and others would each likely be separated from the others.

Controlling Direction And Operations

The general nature of control

- Control is bringing or maintaining performance of people, organizations, equipment, or characteristics of a variable within prescribed limits.

- Control is a requirement for an organization as a whole and for parts of the business. Control assists in evaluating whether the organization is achieving its goals and objectives.

- Control requires measurement of output compared to standards of performance. Measurement may occur in elements of time periods and/or counts, such as dollar amounts, numbers, ratios, and percentages.

- Control requires allowable limits of variation of performance. Often, variance of 10 percent either over or under target is reviewed in terms of timing issues or real change.

Control of people

- While elements of management, the social and inter-personal manner as to how these representative examples are used relate directly to leadership.

- Use of prestige and esteem, inspirational talks, opportunities for training and development, personal influence.

- *Material or utilitarian* control is achieved by granting or withholding maintenance elements. Examples of maintenance elements include salaries, working conditions, work schedules, and employment terms.

- Task or machine-paced-work in assembly lines. In the hospitality industry, we might see this type of control used in a bakery.

- Physical control, e.g., authoritarian countries.

Means of Organizational Control

There are a number of control mechanisms and techniques available to assist managers in directing the work of others.

- Leadership. As we cover in more detail elsewhere in this book, leadership is the social process of employing managerial tools and techniques.

- Culture. Establish the desired culture through organizational development. *Organizational development* is dedicated to expanding the knowledge and effectiveness of people through training and educational opportunities to accomplish more effective change and performance.

- Write and communicate policies. Communication is a fundamental element in helping people understand vision, mission, goals, and objectives.

- Establish budgets. Budgets, especially when accompanied by meaningful and carefully written assumptions are a widely used control mechanism in helping others understand expectations.

- Establish and communicate short and long-range plans. This is usually conveyed by means of the strategic plan.

- Take corrective action as needed. This element is delivered through both budget variance meetings and quarterly employee reviews.

- Centralized control where top management must approve all non-routine decisions. Centralizing control is done mostly in times of recession or otherwise hard times. Most employees resist atmospheres of centralization over long periods of time. The message here is that if or when centralization becomes necessary, it should be thought of and communicated as a short-term necessity along with an explanation as to why.

- Decentralized control whereby middle management is responsible for control of its department's actions. This is the preferred working atmosphere for most organizations.

- Empowerment whereby an employee is authorized to make all decisions necessary to get the job done. Empowerment transpires in decentralized organizations. It is essential to keep in mind that managers who empower others loan their power for others to work in their behalf. The manager does not become released from ultimate responsibility for achievement by empowering someone else.

- Employee self-control: Employee is fed back results of work and takes action without intervention of manager. This type of control is also commonly referred to as *self-evaluation and action*.

- Management By Objectives (MBO). In *Management By Objectives*, an employee sets objectives for the next three months with his or her manager. The employee and manager review progress after three months and new objectives are set. The three-month time frame is not time certain, as other time frames can be substituted.

- Management by exception. Manager receives reports only on work that falls short of or exceeds pre-established limits. Management by exception shares several of the features of a variance meeting. Assume as an example that a pre-establish limit is set of 10 percent either under or over forecast targets. The forecast target is $40,000. The manager will discuss results that are lower than $36,000 or higher than $44,000. Forecasts may take the form of times or counts (or both), whichever is most appropriate.

Quantitative operations controls

There are other operations controls that can and should be considered as part of the monthly, quarterly, and annual reports. Remember that the term, *operations*, by definition, includes all business systems viewed in the short term. In this case, short term is defined as any time period shorter that one year. A representative list includes systems for budgeting, customer service, cash flow, financial, and accounting systems, all of which are covered in other sections of this book. I also refer repeatedly to the importance of systems including quantitative measurement techniques, the times and counts. In short, we want to time anything that can be timed and count anything that can be counted. Examples of time would include measuring devices, such as seconds, minutes, hours, days, months, years, and/or dates. Counts would include almost anything that can be measured by counting, such as numbers, percentages, ratios, revenues, and/or expenses.

Other quantitative measurement system growing in popularity include Total Quality Management (TQM), Continuous Quality Improvement (CQI), and their updated heirs ISO 9000, Lean Manufacturing, and Six Sigma. Approaches vary somewhat by industry and precision of measurement. As such, a TQM program in a nuclear medicine department at a hospital would be more concerned about precision in measurement than a tire recycler. However, the fundamental idea of these types of programs is continuous improvement over time as measured by agreed upon variables. As an example, if we were to look at a simplified continuous quality improvement initiative in a bakery, it might include this scenario for blueberry muffins:

Procedure. When beginning the CQI program, first comes collecting data that becomes the baseline. A *baseline* is a minimum or starting point used for comparison. For this example, the variables are purposefully kept simple. Baseline results: Month 1, revenue $8,000, food cost $4,000 (50%), labor $4,000 (50%), and customer survey data 7.5 (with 10 being best). After referring to the baseline, a goal is set that by Month 12, revenue $16,000, food cost $6,000 (37.5%), labor $6,000 (37.5%), and survey data 8.5. The Blueberry muffin CQI program now is off and running. Everyone involved gathers to discuss both the baseline and the overall goal for the year. This group reviews pricing, purchasing, labor, equipment, and survey data and discuss ways to improve. In an ideal world, the bakery would break the year-end goal into monthly or quarterly objectives (not as good as monthly in that it does not provide enough timely updates), which would provide feedback as to progress toward achieving the goal. For each objective reporting period, everyone involved would come together to review the latest results and discuss ways to improve.

CQI programs are tremendously helpful in managing any organization. The sweet spot is finding some combination of practices that can be slowly introduced and implemented over time in improving products and/or services. In this case, the aim should be in increasing revenue and customer satisfaction while trimming food and labor expenses.

Special considerations. Lets work through and scrutinize a finding. Assume the following results Month 2, revenue $7,000, food cost $3,000

(42.8%), labor $3,000 (42.8%), and survey data 6.25. What happened? The bakery had good intentions by getting everyone together in discussing ways to meet their goal, but appears to have overacted in cutting costs and labor, which appear to have directly affected revenue and survey data. This demonstrates the importance of timely feedback and why monthly results are more helpful than quarterly results. The bakery can back off and re-consider quicker. So, what is the lesson? The lesson is simple: Continuous improvement comes in small steps. At times, an organization may find itself taking a few steps in the right direction and then making a misstep. The key is in ensuring that the steps are small enough that they can be corrected if necessary before losing customers. It is likely that the bakery's severe overreaction may have permanently cost the bakery customers. This example also helps illustrate the art and science nature of leadership. The numbers and dates (the objective measures) represent the *science* in this case. The degree of changing specs (perhaps using oleo instead of butter), competitive buying practices, and labor trimming represent the *art* (judgment-based decisions).

Chapter 08:

Strategy

Introduction

This chapter provides an overall guide to the strategic planning process. Specifically, it was written in response to the request of leaders for a comprehensive document that would explain the planning process as it relates to organizations including step-by-step guidelines, background information, helpful hints, and real-life examples.

This chapter will help executives create an integrated strategic plan that will serve both customers—whether you define customers as guests, shoppers, clients, members, dining patrons, or some other word, and paid staff. Paid staff includes managers and other employees regardless of rank and includes the overlapping constituencies of leaders, managers, assistant managers, department heads, sports professionals, supervisors, shift leaders, and hourly employees, essentially anyone who is paid by the organization.

The overarching goal of strategic planning is to help ensure that the executive management team has 1) established a vision and mission and 2) that the paid staff is achieving that vision and mission through the process of achieving the strategic plan's goals and objectives. A strategic plan is broad-based and conceptual in nature, and requires long-range, big-picture, visionary thinking. Typically, the executive management team (the leaders) has the responsibility for creating the strategic plan. Once created, a successful strategic plan leads to operations planning, which is more short-term and practical in nature (goals and objectives) and involves the managerial team, supervisors, and appropriate line staff.

Strategic planning benefits organization

1. Strategic planning offers a way to examine where the organization is presently (if it is existing) or where it should be when it opens (if it is a new). By understanding where the organization is presently in terms of operations and performance (the actual) and comparing it to where it would like to be (the benchmark), the leaders have created an opportunity for a gap analysis, which identifies what the organization needs to do in order to achieve its goals. The *needs-to-do* becomes the basis for the action plan.

2. Strategic planning allows an organization to define its future direction. Often referred to as *proactive management*, defining the organization's future direction helps managers to be intentional about managing their areas of responsibility instead of responding to ad hoc directional whims. Successful managers learn early that *whim management* is a dangerous game when trying to deliver a consistent product and treat all customers as being important.

3. A written strategic plan provides a consensus of direction that can be measured and evaluated.

Strategic planning is often a difficult challenge. Most organizations that undertake strategic planning are ongoing instead of start-ups, so the strategic plan must be formulated in the midst of operations and, in many cases, must be phased-in to allow for as little disruption to operations as possible. Therefore, strategic planning is not a clean or clear-cut process. Another difficult element of this challenge is that long-term strategies bind future leaders, an element that may be viewed as a drawback by executive level leadership teams. However, binding future direction is, from an overall perspective, a great idea, because it lends continuity to a potentially disparate series of directions.

Uniquely shaped by their tradition, size, and focus, organizations will vary widely in their approach to strategic planning. Some will want to go it alone, others will want to do some of the work themselves but will employ some outside help, and still others will want to leave it mostly in the hands of a consultant. No matter what approach, this chapter can help guide and coordinate the strategic planning process.

In gaining an understanding of the basic strategic process that filters throughout an organization, it is helpful to think of a typical organization as a single-business entity. As such, it has its own hierarchy with respect to the way the strategic plan courses through its organizational veins.

The strategic planning process flows from top to bottom

1. Strategic planning. The executive leadership team usually takes the lead in creating the strategic plan. The primary strategic-planning issues include highest-level strategies and initiatives to maintain or enhance the organization's position as a successful organization serving its customers over time. This chapter focuses on strategic management at this level.

2. Functional strategic planning. The functional department heads, typically represented by staff heading up non-operational, key support entities at the organization that function for the benefit of the entire organization, such as marketing, finance, information technology, and human resources, usually take the lead in creating functional strategic plans. The primary planning issues include creating departmental strategies and initiatives to support the organization's overall strategic plan and to create and achieve departmental performance goals and objectives.

3. Operations strategic planning. The operations managers, which are represented by department heads, managers, and supervisors of operations activities, usually take the lead in operational strategic planning. Primary planning issues include creating department-specific strategies aimed at supporting the organization's strategic plan and creating and achieving departmental performance goals and objectives.

This chapter has been written under the assumption that no formal strategic initiative exists at a particular organization. Thus, the chapter is organized chronologically: Readers can follow along, step-by-step, to see how an organized and integrated strategic plan comes together. Realistically, however, the overwhelming majority of organizations will have at least some elements of a strategic plan in place. In these cases, readers can look at the chapter more generally, to see the relationships among and the general order of the strategic planning elements. While the individual elements work best in the order and manner specified, they can also serve supplemental functions alongside a given organization's current practices. In short, this chapter works as well for existing organizations seeking to improve or adapt a strategic plan as it does for new entities attempting to create an entirely new plan.

Strategic Planning: A Step-by-Step Process

Strategic planning helps lead and guide an organization from a long-term perspective. Strategic planning always relates to the organization's self-definition of what it wants to become. Thus, strategic planning affects operational decisions and determines how the organization will practically achieve what it ideally wants to become.

Strategic planning helps ensure that an organization remains relevant and responsive to the needs of its customers and positively contributes to stability. It provides a basis for objectively monitoring progress and for assessing outcomes and impacts. It facilitates new program development. It enables an organization to look into, plan, and forecast the future in an orderly and systematic way. From a governance perspective, it enables senior-level leadership to set big-picture policies and goals to guide the organization and provides a clear focus to the managers for implementation and overall management of the programs and staff.

Undertaking the process of strategic planning can be a daunting task. There are a number of elements inherent in the creation of an integrated strategic plan that may, at first glance, confuse even the most experienced manager. However, when considered in a progressive order of importance, these elements work clearly and crucially with each other. They include the following elements that proceed in a more or less sequential order with some expectant degree of parallel and overlapping accomplishment.

Strategic planning steps

1. Agreeing on the Need.
2. Input.
3. Competitive Analysis.
4. Planning Retreat.
5. Vision.
6. Mission.
7. Goals.
8. Objectives.

9. Organizational Situation Analysis (SWOT).

10. Strategy Statement.

11. Budgets.

12. Action Plan.

13. Assessing Progress.

These elements are listed and discussed in order in this section. If any step is not already in place, the person responsible for the strategic planning process should ensure that the missing step is completed before proceeding to the next stage of the process.

01: Agreeing on the Need

The most fundamental element of the strategic planning process is an identification process in agreeing on a strategic planning process. This may be done at a board meeting with key staff present, or may require a special meeting or retreat, including the board, key staff, and some key internal stakeholders (such as successful past leaders). After the agreement on the need, the process begins and is conducted in advance of any further formalized strategic planning meetings. Typically, the GM, members of the board, and other members of the executive leadership team assign an array of duties with the goal of gathering information that will be used throughout the strategic planning process. The components include the following analyses:

Confidential Interviews

Invite both individuals and small groups in to discuss their opinions and views on the various aspects of the property including operations, physical plant, governance, attitudes—essentially anything related to the organization. Ideally, an organization would invite customers, employees, and suppliers to participate. These meetings serve as an effective way to discover general feelings and climate. One way to focus questions is to state them in terms of where the organization is currently as compared to where it should be in the future. This focus immediately creates a view of the future and when combined with discussion as to where it is presently, defines a gap, which is the change that should occur over time in moving from its present position to where the it wants to be in the future. An effective path might include these questions:

Tell me about your experience with the organization: Is it meeting your expectations presently? How would you change its direction in order to be even better in the future? Notice the broad generalities of the questions posed.

Minutes Review

A comprehensive analysis of board meetings, annual meetings, operations meetings, and other major deliberations should be conducted for the preceding five to seven years. The work product that develops from this analysis should be a listing and big-picture summary explanation of the situations, actions, and direction that could influence the future direction.

Financial Review

Similar to the minutes review, a comprehensive analysis of finances should be conducted for the preceding five to seven years. The work product that develops from this analysis should be a listing and big-picture summary explanation of each end-of-year budget to actual results (income and expenses), trend analysis on the balance sheet results, a review of budget to actual on dollars spent for annual regular capital expense for furniture, fixtures, and equipment, and a review of project capital budget to actual for significant remodeling or add-ons.

Operational Audit

The operational audit is a detailed analysis of the major and minor operating departments that would flow from past surveys, secret shopper reports, and comments from the confidential interviews. The work product should be a summary of the overall service effort with early recognition of challenges that need to be addressed.

Environmental Scan

The environmental scan, if not presently existing, is a time-consuming, yet vital document for reference. An environmental scan is a comparison of demographics, fees, charges, rules and policies, and other information within an operating area (also referred to as a *competitive set*). The work product is a worksheet with each particular member of the competitive set occupying a row and each data point occupying a column. Suggested column headings would include zip code, property type, and column headings for each competitive area that the organization would want for comparison between and among competitive set members. For example, a golf club would want to compare itself to others in categories that would include fees and charges for guests of member, carts, range program, lockers, bag storage, lessons, policies on outside play, charge for member-guest tournament, and the like. I have seen these documents become as detailed as containing more than 100 properties with more than 300 columns of detail as to dues, fees, charges, and policies (more than 30,000 cells of data). The benefit of this document in answering questions about what other organization practices is tremendously positive. Without this document, staff members spend inordinate amounts of time throughout the year researching ad hoc questions, such as this one: *What percentage of our competitive set charges a gratuity versus a service charge*? Ideally, this report should be updated annually.

Other issues to be considered in the environmental scan include forces and trends in the broader community, political, economic, social, and sometimes technological. Look at changing demographics, political trends, community values, economic trends, the implications of new or changing laws and regulations, communications, and other technological trends and consider their impact.

Identify Issues

Once these reports have been assembled, one or more appointees compiles a report identifying a master list of issues for consideration during the strategy process.

Setting Ground Rules

From the outset of the planning process, it is helpful to create an atmosphere in which contributions are welcomed. Essentially, the objective would be to help ensure that all participants can safely share ideas, without ideas being judged or ignored as being insignificant or otherwise unimportant.

Setting the tone

1. Encourage active involvement. All participants (in any meeting or planning session) should be actively involved in the process. Stating participation expectations up front can help keep impatient or more

vocal participants from controlling the process and potentially shutting down creative viewpoints and ideas.

2. Solicit different points of view. The idea during these strategic planning sessions, especially in the early stages, is to get broadness of ideas. It may be helpful to announce that the purpose is to generate a lot of ideas (quantity), and that judgment about the relevance of the ideas (quality) will come later.

3. Probe issues. Explore issues during the meetings by posing questions to the group. This probing provides encouragement to flesh-out and elaborate on ideas.

4. Manage conflict. Conflict needs to be mediated. Conflict of ideas and viewpoints is natural and should be encouraged up to a point, as healthy disagreement brings additional ideas to bear that would not otherwise be addressed. However, if personal attacks ensue or if negativity develops between certain interest groups, a respected and influential person may need to refocus the group's energy.

Before a planning meeting begins, consider what outcome is sought. Whether the GM/COO, the president, another board member, or a professional facilitator leads the meeting, the meeting's objective should be announced in advance whether the purpose is for seeking agreement or simply for insight and background. Announcing the purpose helps all participants to know where the meeting is headed and helps participants shape their comments, viewpoints, or answers accordingly.

Assuming that the meeting seeks agreement in the form of a decision, the person leading the meeting should always consider how decisions would be made. We often think that decisions are made by a majority vote. But that is not usually the case. Instead, decisions are most often made in one of the following manners.

Making decisions

- Authority. In decision by authority, the leader of the meeting typically accepts input but reserves ultimate decision-making authority; thus, meeting participants serve as advisors. If this is the case, participants should be made aware of their advisory status, so that they know what to expect of the decision-making process.

- Majority. When deciding by majority, the leader accepts input and offers his or her personal opinions before calling for a vote. (Robert's Rules of Order dictate a slightly different process with essentially the same outcome.) The decision gains approval either by a simple majority or, in some cases, by a super majority (two-thirds majority). Thus, meeting participants are both advisors and voters.

- Minority. Decision by minority suggests that the leader allows a vocal or passionate minority to mold the decision. This method is often technically decision by authority, though the authoritarian allows the vocal minority to influence the outcome to the point that the minority view is adopted. While it may not seem to be used often, we see this occur regularly. A group that is unified, vocal, and passionate no matter how small can be very influential.

- Unanimity. The perceived strength of a unanimous decision lies in the fact that all eligible voters voted on a decision whether for or against with no abstentions. Unanimity is a form of decision by majority, unique because the 100-percent vote in favor (or against) often further legitimizes the decision.

- Consensus. Decision by consensus is, by far, the bread-and-butter decision-making model most used. Consensus, like majority, is technically decision by authority. However, in consensus, the authoritarian allows participants to arrive at a decision informally and usually without a vote. The leader compromises throughout the discussion to help ensure inclusion before asking for consensus among members that is typically indicated by a simple nod of agreement or non-response. The decision is then adopted. Consensus allows a fair amount of interpretation and modification by the person in charge. Therefore, and especially in decisions involving sensitive and/or complicated issues, consensus is often preferred over a vote.

Once the strategic planning meetings are appropriately focused, including identifying a facilitator, participants are enthusiastic about the process, and everyone understands how decisions will be made at the meetings, the strategic planning process can begin by outlining vision.

02: Input

An atmosphere of inclusion in the process began in the confidential interviews section of the Needs Assessment. As the process moves forward, input should become more focused and more formalized to help create a roadmap for helping plan and create future, direction.

Conducting Focus Groups

This element of the strategy would include meeting with a wide variety of members and staff to determine their perceptions, opinions, beliefs, ideas, and attitudes toward products, services, and concepts. While there is some connection here to the confidential interviews, focus groups yield valuable insight by building upon information and comments gleaned from the confidential interviews. When participants are free to talk with and among other group members they engage in a kind of chaining, building, and/or cascading effect. The analysis that comes from the focus groups helps in the development of the survey.

Focus groups work well when kept to small sessions. While size and complexity of organizations varies greatly, I usually recommend conducting a minimum of five sessions at staggered times (maybe morning, mid-afternoon, and evening) over two consecutive days (maybe a Wednesday and Thursday). Each session would include approximately 10-12 participants (plus non-participant observers). The basis for questions in the focus groups should build on those from the confidential interviews.

The focus group sessions may either be aimed at the customers in general or one or more particular groups (such as those interested in dining, wine, golf, spa services, waterfront related areas, or tennis).

Question ideas for general sessions (ice breakers)

- What are we doing that you consider strong points (that we should continue)?

- What is not working well and needs improving (that we should change)?

- What would you like to see us do or add? What is missing (that we should start)?

- What would you like to see us stop doing (that we should stop)?

Question ideas for particular groups (using golf as an example)

- Tell me about your experience in golf: Is it meeting your expectations presently?

- What are two or three services within golf that you find particularly important?

- How would you change its direction in order to make it even better in the future?

Issues continue to surface during the focus group sessions. It is the combination of the previous analyses and the focus group sessions that become the foundation for creating the survey.

Creating and Conducting a Survey

Effective leaders all express the desire in developing and maintaining services that are meaningful and attractive to current and prospective customers. Valuable research about customers' needs, wants, and expectations will help do just that.

Conducting a survey, while a daunting and time-consuming task, produces valuable and rewarding information. Before conducting a survey, a decision must be made to decide the *purpose* of the survey. A survey is a great way to collect data that can be turned into valuable information. If not put together judiciously, however, a survey can turn into an unfocused document that will only serve to upset and frustrate customers and staff. The survey can be particularly frustrating if the survey information is wasted and nothing much happens after the survey has been conducted.

Reasons for surveys

1. To persuade. The property might collect customer views and opinions before undergoing a major renovation.

2. To create or modify a service or product. The golf department might modify its starting-time procedure based on customer input. Or, after analyzing data, the food and beverage department might modify the grill menu or change the operating hours.

3. To understand customer behavior. The property might undertake a comprehensive survey with no preconceived outcome in mind, except to simply better understand customers' wants and needs to serve customers more effectively. Of the three, to understand customer behavior is the most strategic purpose for a survey.

These three reasons: To persuade, to create or modify a service (or product), or to understand behavior often overlaps in a survey. Whatever the primary purpose, management should be realistic in their expectations about what the survey will accomplish. The primary focus of a survey for the purpose of strategy would be to understand member behavior in the form of their needs, wants, and expectations. The overlapping features in a survey would be the collection of the data that would then be used perhaps to help persuade the property owners to undertake a renovation and/or to modify service times or a product sold in the gift shop.

All of the preceding reports and analyses should have revealed material that can now be developed into a series of questions overall and each of its major and minor functional (accounting, marketing, etc.) and operating (golf, tennis, swim, dining, etc.) areas. The survey should, where specifically addressing operations, ask questions that elicit both importance ratings (such as a scale of 1-10 with 10 being most important) and performance ratings (on a report card scale from A down to D). In the past, operational surveys only surveyed on the basis of performance and erroneously assumed that the activities and products they were offering were important. A correctly written survey gauges *importance* and *performance*. Be sure to ask both questions: 1) *Is what we are doing important to you?* This is the importance question. 2) *How are we doing?* This is the *performance* question.

The more strategic questions often do not lend themselves toward *importance* and *performance* ratings because questions are being asked about future direction and offerings. As such, including an analysis axis for performance does not make logical sense.

Well-informed organizations' survey similarities

• Frequency. Survey with regularity at least every 12-16 months.

• Online. Conduct their surveys online instead of using paper-and-pencil forms.

- Cover message. Include a cover message.

- Involvement. Solicit participation by all users.

- Demographics. Contain a demographic section of 10-15 questions to obtain detail about the respondent.

- Departments. Have a separate section for and ask an average of 10-12 questions about each major department.

- Minor areas. Have one separate section to cover minor areas.

- Property grounds and buildings. Have a separate section to cover the property overall (in general).

- Open-ended questions. Each separate section includes one single, open-ended question that elicits comments on anything the respondent would like to elaborate. A survey may also include a generalized open-ended question at survey end, which serves as a catchall device.

Guidelines in creating an effective survey

1. Decide on the purpose. Whether the survey is intended to persuade, to modify a service, or to gather information about customer behavior, deciding on the purpose allows focus in questions.

2. Assemble the questions. Creating the questions is undoubtedly the most time-consuming part of the process, but should be done carefully and judiciously. Ensure that each question addresses one—and only one—specific issue or topic. Do not ask a customer what he or she might like best. Instead, ask what products or services the customer would be likely to use or buy. Keep questions brief and clear. Short questions are less likely to be interpreted incorrectly. Use normal vocabulary. Refer to the area as *The Grill* in your survey, if that's what the café is called by customers. Do not refer to the area as *the informal dining area*, which would be confusing.

3. Set a time limit. Customers are not likely to fill out an operations survey that takes any longer than about 10 minutes to complete. That time threshold decreases dramatically if surveys are distributed to customers frequently. As a rule of thumb, customers will not object to completing a ten-minute survey once each year

(or so). If you publicize the importance of a strategic and long-range planning survey, you can probably obtain an excellent response to a 20-minute survey every other year. Response rates vary considerably among different types of organizations and how customers are classified. For example, surveys targeting potential customers will respond at a far lower rate than existing customers. Those who hold an ownership position within the property, such as equity-holding club members will respond at a higher rate.

4. Beta test. After deciding on the appropriate time limit and scaling back (or adding to) the number of questions accordingly, test (*beta test*) the questionnaire for length, clarity, and interest. Get feedback on questions from a select group (of perhaps 25 respondents) and make appropriate changes before sending it out targeted customers.

5. Plan a frequency. The frequency of surveys, like the number of questions, largely determines your response rate. Some organizations survey quarterly; at the other extreme, others survey every three to five years. Those that survey quarterly are most successful when the questionnaire asks no more than ten questions and is quite easy for respondents to complete and return. Those surveying annually or less frequently can get away with longer, more comprehensive surveys, which are the best surveys for helping managers with strategic and long-range planning.

6. Decide on the target audience. This may sound obvious, but it is important to survey those who are interested in or use the facility in question.

7. Decide on a method for data collection and analysis. Will you administer the survey in-house or through an outside firm? How will the project be staged? Who will analyze the data? This is typically the point at which most organizations decide to consult with an outside source. If you take this route, remember to stay true to the purpose—the intention and motivation—for the survey.

8. Decide how the results will be disseminated. Most customers will assume that if you are asking about a product, service, or facility, you are going to develop an action plan to somehow change it—and that they will be informed about the plan.

Disseminate survey results through the website, newsletter, separate and specific mailings, e-mails, or other media, depending on the inclinations and expectations of the customers.

Informing customers about the purpose of the survey is important and related to how you will disseminate the survey results. It is acceptable to tell customers that you are unsure about what actions, if any, will be taken. However, if customers feel that the survey is waste of their time, they will respond less often and less enthusiastically to subsequent surveys.

Other Methods for Gaining Input

Soliciting input is important in helping ensure that the property is on track in its offerings of products and services. Almost any service organization can easily solicit input during the normal course of the business day.

- At point of purchase. Ask for feedback at the moment when a transaction takes place. Customers may not be as honest at this point, but ask questions related to quality, price, and service.

- Online. Add a *tell us what you think* link on every page of the website.

- Newsletter. Include a question or two at the bottom of each page.

- Comment cards. This still functions well for many. Post a comment box in one of the public areas of the property along with cards and a few golf pencils.

03: Competitive Analysis

There are many methods of collecting comparative data for analysis. In the paragraphs that follow, I will cover three of the most used methods. Often, these analyses are conducted earlier in conjunction with the external analyses. An organization's choice of whether to do the details of this competitive analysis earlier in the process or now generally lies in how the work processes and responsibilities were assigned. Either method works well.

Comprehensive Surveys. These are among the most reliable because they include data points from hundreds of similar organizations across the country. The results can be reviewed by type, size, geographic location, and other demographics of interest. The primary advantages of using comprehensive surveys are the ability to analyze and compare data between and among several geographic areas, the high numbers of respondents, and they are usually conducted by firms specializing in surveying and are therefore kept up-to-date and include multiple year comparisons, which assist in determining trends.

Regional Surveys. Regional surveys can be helpful and are essentially scaled down versions of comprehensive surveys. The primary advantages of using regional surveys are their convenience of typically focusing on one particular geographic area and that they serve as a basis for establishing competitive sets. A few of the drawbacks include that because their creation and upkeep is usually done on a voluntary basis, they may not be up-to-date, may not include multiple year comparisons, and do not provide a wider view as to what other organizations are reporting outside of the region.

Ad hoc Surveys. Ad hoc surveys are the bane of a general manager's existence because of the time involved in gathering information. Ad hoc surveying is almost always driven by a need for a few key bits of data in assisting in a decision. Ad hoc surveys are the most local form of surveying and, in this sense, focus on two or three of the closest competitors. The impetus for an ad hoc survey usually goes something like this: *Patrick, the board and I are good with most of your work on the upcoming budget. A few of us just need some re-assurance on a couple of items. Will you call around and find out what Redwood, Blue Lake, and Willow Springs charge for a Belvedere martini, their policies and charges for ocean-view rooms on weekends, and charges for a half golf cart after 3 PM?*

All three methods of surveying to help complete a competitive analysis are used with regularity. Access to this data provides the organization with information in establishing ranges, boundaries, and benchmarks for operations in defining what is customary and acceptable within a defined market. Benchmarks are service and/or product standards. For example, a resort nested in close proximity to several competitors along a beachfront strand would not be wise to charge an automatic 30 percent gratuity on food and beverage if the average charge among competitors was 18 percent.

04: Planning Retreat

The retreat is listed in and referred to as one of the integral steps in the process because it almost always serves as the venue where the foundational elements of strategy are created, discussed, amended, and decided by senior management. These foundational elements would include developing, modifying, and/or confirming an organization's basic values and guiding principles, vision, mission, and creation and prioritization of key goals and objectives. The retreat creates or reinforces a structure of continuity for governance.

In the past, the board retreat was typically an elaborate, multiple-day conference held at a location away from the organization with work sessions during the day, sports events in the afternoon, and social events that included spouses in the evenings. The extended and focused agenda allowed business and then informal time to reflect upon and discuss issues in detail among colleagues. The culminating session included deciding and agreeing to the plan.

Today, the retreat is almost always conducted in a condensed format lasting about one day and held in one of the private rooms on the property. Because of full agendas and shorter timeframes, organizations often find it beneficial to use a professional facilitator to help ensure that items are covered, discussed, and brought to conclusion.

Using A Professional Facilitator

Should the organization go it alone or use a facilitator? I get this question quite often from senior leaders. The answer: *It depends.* Here is a checklist of considerations.

- Participation. Do you want to participate? It is difficult to facilitate and participate at the same time. If you are the president or the general manager it becomes unusually complicated because participants react to you in your position as the president or the GM. As such, it is difficult to facilitate without participants already knowing your biases as to what the organization should become.

- Sensitive issues. Does the organization have internal communication and/or other sensitive issues? An outsider can diffuse prickly issues including overbearing personalities and heated exchanges and help focus the energy into work progress.

- The process. Does the organization understand the process? An experienced professional facilitator understands the process and has successfully led other organizations through the process.

I address the subject content for these agenda items in upcoming paragraphs.

Values and Beliefs

Core values and beliefs and/or operating principles are the fundamental convictions of the organization. For convenience, I will refer to them as values and beliefs.

Values and beliefs should address these prompts

- Highest level order. Some refer to this as a view of the property from 1,000 feet in the air (or the helicopter view). This view allows participants to step away from the day-to-day noise of operations and think strategically.

- Explain why the organization exists.

- List fundamental convictions.

- Strong written statements.

Careful thought and consideration spent early in the values and beliefs section help make other sections proceed more smoothly. Discussing and agreeing to what the organization *is not*, is as important as deciding what the organization *is* about. In helping explain amenities, level of service, and customer satisfaction, I will use the Jericho Golf Resort, located in the Sonoran Desert, to illustrate an example.

Examples of values and beliefs

- Amenities. The Jericho Golf Resort will focus its amenities on private, championship golf facilities, appealing to male and female players with handicaps of 10 and lower. The resort recognizes that it will limit its offerings and therefore will not appeal to a wide variety of potential resort guests.

- Guest rooms will all feature kitchenettes, golf course views, large balconies or patios with gas-fired outdoor fire pits, barbecue grills, covered golf cart parking and charging, and rooms decorated in golf themes of greens and clan plaids.

- Level of service. The Jericho Golf Resort will offer informal but high quality professional service—all oriented in support of golf. The resort will offer a modest daily menu in both the grill and lounge beginning with breakfast at 4:30 AM and serving continuously until

11 PM. Guests will have the choice of indoor or outdoor drinking and dining, all overlooking the golf course and water features.

- Guest satisfaction. The Jericho Golf Resort will be 100 percent dedicated to providing a high quality, value oriented golf experience for its chosen strategy.

- Other examples of items for consideration in any values and beliefs discussion:

- Employee satisfaction.

- Ethical business practices.

- Service to the community.

- Eco consciousness.

05. Vision

Vision is perhaps the most fundamental of the strategic planning elements. Vision is future-oriented and identifies what the organization is all about, its purpose for being, as well as where it is heading. Infusing a definite sense of purpose, the vision states both a direction and describes the destination.

At the outset of the vision, which usually begins at the executive level, it is important to assess others' concepts of vision. However, it is often difficult for board members to find a common language to describe their respective visions of the organization. One effective way to bring about an understanding of vision is to make a comparison between the particular organization and an unrelated idea or object. In making such a comparison, constructing a metaphor to describe the organization in the form of a familiar product with widespread familiarity and a high degree of stratification can be helpful in facilitating discussion. One product that I find quite helpful is to use automobiles.

It may sound unusual at first, but getting fundamental agreement on what an organization *is presently* (now) and what it *should be* (in the future) creates the opportunity for a *gap analysis*, for which an automobile-related metaphor serves as an effective tool. For example, as the strategic planning process begins, one might ask this question: *If this organization were a car, what kind of car should it be?* Notice the use of the word, *should*, as it focuses discussion on a *future* state. This question works equally well for established organizations (those that have some strategic planning elements in place) or new organizations that are seeking to define themselves. The question is straightforward, understandable, and perhaps most importantly prompts *vision*.

This discussion often goes on for some time, as participants share their definition or view of the organization in *ideal* terms. Be careful not to rush this discussion, as it is the most foundational discussion in the process. Discussing a future state sets the organization's direction. Expect a wide variety of answers. There may be less variation among answers if the meeting is attended primarily by senior executives or others not involved in day-to-day operations. Typically—and often confusingly—initial descriptors such as *Mercedes-Benz*, *BMW*, and *Lexus* top the list of responses.

A logical follow up question establishes the *current state* of the organization and highlights the disparity of customers' views and responses collected from focus groups and surveys: Continuing with our car analogy, *what kind of car is the organization presently?* This question is similar to the first, but forces participants to assess the organization's *actual* and current status, rather than an intended *ideal, future state*. Again, plan for an extended discussion as participants and respondents voice their opinions as to how the organization meets expectations and where it may fall short, all in the context of an automobile. As before, expect to get a variety of answers. In addition to the answers listed above, answers such as *Volkswagen, Bentley, Chevrolet, Ferrari*, and even *Edsel* are not uncommon.

It may seem that you have opened the proverbial *can of worms* with this question. However, the discussion and answers are important clues as to what customers actually think versus what, at least initially, executives have explained what the organization should be in the future. Celebrate the fact that you now have actual data to work with! To turn this data into useful, practical information, you must compare the ideal and actual descriptions. This becomes an effective *gap analysis* helping identify *actual versus ideal*, which hints at the *gap* between the two. The gap then becomes the *change* that needs to happen.

After comparing answers and identifying the gap, analyze the answers in terms of the participants' demographics and characteristics. For example, if most of the tennis-minded enthusiasts described the current state of your resort in terms of economy or low-end cars, then consider examining the tennis department and operation, in terms of its facilities, staff, and programs, to see why it is falling short in the collective opinion of this guest mindset.

At times it is necessary to probe for more details, in order to elicit richer information for use in decision-making. Asking the question, *what kind of car is the organization presently?* To assess customers' actual perceptions. If the discussion stalls, one can also ask more specific and probing questions, such as these:

- What model is the car?

- What is its condition?

- What is the quality of its stereo? Its tires?

- What other options does this car have?

Depending on the willingness and enthusiasm of the group, you may need to keep probing in order to get people engaged and talking. (Once you get them talking, do not forget to make sure that all of their responses are recorded. Keeping up with what was said will get more difficult as the pace of the discussion picks up.) For example, if members answer initial questions vaguely, probe for meaning: *Mr. Gordon, you stated that the present inn would be a Mercedes-Benz S-Class, with a faded paint job and broken dashboard controls. Will you please elaborate a bit, so I can get a clearer idea of what you are saying? Do the controls work occasionally? Are they missing entirely? Why is the paint faded? How does this automobile resemble this organization?* Naturally, these additional prompts will lead into more specific discussion about the organization itself, as the framework of the car metaphor generates discussion about values and qualities that apply to the organization. At the end of this process, the desired outcome is a shared vision and understanding of the property.

Earlier, I wrote about executives often initially describing the organization's future state in terms of luxurious brands and wrote that those responses are typically confused. This is all part of the process as executives come to a more realistic understanding of the organization and its intended niche. This is how vision evolves. If, for example, in the quick service burger business segment, almost no organization would *end up* describing itself in terms of becoming luxury class a la Mercedes-Benz- or BMW-like. Therefore, an adept facilitator would flesh out what executives meant if they were hearing those kinds of comparisons. In one case, the executives of a small, local burger chain becoming regional envisioned an upscale positioning along the lines of In-N-Out Burger. With work, the vision became clear to everyone involved. Menus were simplified, freezers were sold, store cleanliness and starched uniforms became paramount, wages and training increased dramatically, and the regional collection of 55 stores thrives today.

Here is an example of the vision statement for a start-up, elite level private club that used the automobile-as-metaphor process.

Example vision statement

The Country Club of Tarantula Canyon will create an exciting, innovative, differentiated, private club experience that will redefine quality in Southern California. By creating a country club experience that is second to none, continuously innovating while recognizing tradition and broadening our appeal to the members and prospective members, we will be successful in our quest for excellence. Our success in these endeavors will create greater value for our members and greater desirability for prospective members.

This is an example of a successful club that is positioned as a Rolls-Royce level club. By aligning its infrastructure, service, and facilities toward the high-end, the club has initiation fees at the upper end, expensive (and inclusive) dues, and impeccable service. Members expect to pay a premium; however, they expect exceptional value for dollars spent.

Think for a moment about this successful club. It knows what it is and who its members are. The message, that this is a Rolls-Royce level club is clearly communicated in everything that the club staff and management think, say, and do. The club does not appeal to Chevrolet-level members and does not try to do so. Instead, it focuses its marketing toward skimming the cream from the highest income earners in Southern California, such as those who routinely shop on Rodeo Drive.

However, and continuing with a private club example, do not misunderstand this concept. There is nothing wrong with being a Chevrolet-type club, and there are a number of extremely successful Chevrolet-level clubs. Those types of clubs are successful because they understand clearly that they *are* Chevrolet-level clubs. That is what they are, that is how they market themselves, and that is how they want to be defined. These clubs typically have average initiation fees, dues structures, and offer a full array of reasonably maintained (but not lavishly maintained) facilities. These clubs are dependable, but neither flashy nor extravagant. Their strength lies in their ability to know clearly *what they are* as clubs.

Problems often develop when some among a given club's population whether club managers, staff members, club members, or others do not share this clear understanding of their club's vision. Think for a moment about the member who visits another club and notices a number of the special offerings and amenities that the host club offers, only to return to his or her home club and suggest that you, the GM, immediately adopt similar offerings. The requests may be simple and easily achieved. But it may then lead to larger and more elaborate requests. Where does it stop? Without a clear understanding of what a club is about, its *vision*, club members tend to push for their Chevrolet clubs with Chevrolet prices to slowly morph into Cadillac clubs with Chevrolet prices. A clear and carefully thought through understanding of vision helps prevent this from occurring, or at least from occurring without careful examination.

For example, one private club located in North Carolina gave the impression of being a Chevrolet-level club. Modest by most standards, the club had, however, a few areas of discontinuity in operations. These inconsistencies helped explain the club's dire financial straits. All cars were parked by valets, which added to labor costs. The house scotch was Chivas Regal, a premium scotch priced at a mere $2 for a two-ounce pour (including tax and gratuity) at the bar, a cost dictated by a past club president who preferred the expensive brand to the former house scotch. Tablecloths were of an average quality, a standard polyester blend, but the china was Villeroy & Boch (premium quality) and the flatware was Reed & Barton (premium quality). Luncheon steaks were Angus beef and the sandwich bread was custom-baked at a local bakery. An interview with the general manager revealed that he had been advised by some of the club members over the years; that is, he had been pressured by governors, influential committee chairs, and powerful members to make these and other changes based on their personal wants.

In its mutated state, this club would have been more accurately described as a Frankenstein-club instead of a Chevrolet-club. Certain elements of the club were so out of line with its basic identity that the club had become a monster, featuring a bit of this and a non-related bit of that.

After beginning the strategic planning process, including identifying a clear vision, the club has become restructured into a successful and popular country club. A visionary president and GM/COO took charge of the arduous re-creation process in order to make the club a healthy and happy Chevrolet-level club once again. For example, the pouring scotch at that club is now the more suitable Grants. Who would have thought that Grants could be the better choice than Chivas Regal? At this club, it clearly is, because it fits in with the club's image and perception more effectively and appropriately.

Secrets of Creating a Strategic Vision and Mission

If the organization does not have a clear vision and mission, make the process more manageable by considering these guidelines:

- Encourage Flexibility and Inclusion. Many organizations that go about the business of creating a vision and/or mission do so with one person, such as the senior-most executive, acting as the visionary. This is expedient, but not usually effective. The expedient method for creating a vision and/or mission, and the one often observed, is for a strong senior executive to step forward and push a predetermined outcome. While the job gets accomplished, the product is compromised, because it is not fully accepted by customers and staff who have been excluded from its creation. Ideally, all stakeholders should have an opportunity to help mold and shape the organization's vision and mission. This takes flexibility and an attitude of inclusion on the part of the executives.

- Avoid Perfectionism. Organizations are not well served by attempts to create the perfect vision and mission, because the perfect one of either vision or mission does not exist. Instead, organizations are better off setting the goal that is focused and clear enough to infuse the staff and the customers with a definite sense of the organization's purpose and direction. One world-famous real estate development located along coastal Florida, which became Sawgrass, began with a unique—but not necessarily perfect—visionary element. Built by an owner-developer who was also an avid outdoorsman, the development was located in an area known for a number of dressy, stuffy, old-line and blue-blooded formal developments. He envisioned a development that would do things differently—a development that would be first class without *acting* first class. He described this vision as, *barefoot elegance*. Buyers, guests, prospective and current owners, and staff all understood what he meant. The development became a casual and laid-back and gated resort development known for exceptional service and high-end amenities. Your organization's vision and mission likely cannot—and perhaps should not—be fully expressed in such a simple way. (If it is, it should not be expressed in that manner alone.) Nevertheless, this development's president had the creativity and focus to paint a picture of its purpose with just two words, and *barefoot elegance* became the reference point for everything that the development would think, say, and do over the years.

- Challenge what holds you back. The vision and mission stage of the strategic planning process is more concerned with ideals than with present states in elucidating purpose. During this step of strategic planning, someone might say of an idea, *that's a great idea, but we can't possibly be that*. These types of challenges to your ideal will develop. In many instances, they should be seen not as stopping points but as starting points for determining, Why not? One small neighborhood country club in inland southern California was trying to establish its reason for being. As the story goes, the club's vision and mission grew from the interests of one young member who had the potential to become a world-class swimmer. Among the major problems he faced in fulfilling his potential were the lack of an infrastructure for coaching and training, which were seemingly insurmountable drawbacks, both for his interests as a young swimmer and for the club itself. However, vision and mission drove the club in everything that it would think, say, and do for the next 25 years to become a powerhouse swimming club with one of the top amateur programs in the nation. In hindsight, it is clear that a specific vision nurtured a strong commitment. With that strong commitment, potential members flocked to the club so their kids could be a part of this new, unprecedented swimming program. Over the years, the club produced scores of world-class swimmers, including several Olympic medalists. At the club's peak, there was a three-year waiting list of people wanting to join.

- Realize that consultants are not magicians. Nobody understands the organization better than its managers, staff, and customers.

Given this reality, why do scores of organizations pay thousands of dollars each year for consultants to come in and tell them what to do in terms of strategic planning? While consultants can be very helpful, they are not magicians. Consultants can lay out the elements of the strategic planning process and they have the additional experience of having seen and analyzed a wide variety of solutions to fairly common issues. Their external expertise, however, cannot substitute for internal knowledge of an organization's own personality. In the end, what works successfully is based on that particular organization's personality or culture.

Generic Business-Level Strategies

Ultimately, all this talk about cars is intended to bring us closer to a full understanding of where the organization is currently and where it should be going in terms of planning and operations. Professor Michael Porter devised a solid method, which has been used successfully for many years to examine strategic planning in terms of four different leadership strategies:

- Low cost. The focus of low-cost leadership is high sales at low cost, the high sales being achieved by coming up with a product that will appeal to a broad target market. Typically, organizations offering a *no-frills* approach would adopt this sort of strategy, which allows them to be competitive by undercutting others in costs and therefore providing low prices to the customer. Theoretically, a larger pool of potential customers would join or be able to buy this organization's products and/or services because of those low costs. Henry Ford's Model T epitomized this strategy: cheap, simple, reliable, and only black as the color choice. When it first entered the US market, Volkswagen used low cost strategy with its original Beetle. It was low cost, uncomplicated, and popular with car buyers across a wide range of social and economic backgrounds. An example of an economy lodging property following this strategy would be Motel-6. An example of a retail store chain would be Wal-Mart.

- Differentiation. With differentiation, the strategic focus is on uniqueness and price. Real estate developers might adopt this strategy, entering a market at several economic levels with a variety of residential communities. They would create communities of different types at a range of price points, from low to high, thereby capturing a large number of total real estate sales. This strategy could be compared to that of General Motors, which offers brands Chevrolet, GMC, Buick, and Cadillac; essentially, it offers something for every car-buyer, from entry-level to high end. Toyota uses the same strategy under its unified brand in Yaris, Corolla, Camry, Prius, Venza, and Avalon, and the separate Lexus brand that contains its own stratification of offerings.

- Focused low cost. Focused low-cost leadership emphasizes high sales at low cost to a narrow target market. Private clubs offering a no-frills approach in a particular area, such as tennis, use this strategy. Undercutting other tennis clubs in initiation fees, dues, and other charges allows this type of club to attract a larger pool of potential tennis members. Years ago, sports car manufacturer MG, used this strategy to develop its Midget brand and sold a relatively large volume of cars to a very narrow market of people who sought a low-priced sports car. Popeyes Louisiana Kitchen used this strategy to when they first opened because all of their fried chicken was highly spiced. Jeep, while very different in recent years, used the same strategy when it brought its original automobile to market. It was inexpensive, appealed to a narrow segment of car buyers, and dominated its niche. With a focused low-cost strategy, private clubs understand that they are not for everybody. Members have access to great tennis services and facilities, but little else. However, they offer great value to tennis enthusiasts.

- Focused differentiation. Focused differentiation emphasizes uniqueness and price, but for a narrow market. For example, some high-end, independent, destination resorts offer an all-inclusive and high price, marketing themselves as elite and thereby appealing to a narrow, affluent audience. Gray Goose vodka became hugely successful in finding its niche in the gigantic vodka category of distilled spirits by adopting this strategy. Certain boutique collection cruise lines have found success utilizing this strategy. Their intangible array of desirable relationships and excellent facilities helps them capture a low number of total sales, but at high price. Rolls-Royce and Ferrari successfully market themselves employing this strategy.

The desirability of each strategy depends on the unique goals of the organization. During the vision stage of strategic planning, it is essential to clarify the generic strategy. Are we going to choose low-cost, differentiation, focused low-cost, or focused differentiation? The important thing is to not allow the organization to get stuck somewhere between these positions. When an organization is neither fish nor fowl, it gets into trouble. Often, competing forces within a customer base demand both high quality and low price, which can lead to an untenable middle ground if it tries to satisfy both demands. The conversation may proceed like this:

At a restaurant: Look, I know that the regular price for a banquet is $39 per person. However, this is an important function for a great cause. We need for you to do it for $30, including tax and tip, and it has to be the best event of the year because the senator will be attending. There are scores of other restaurants that will gladly do this function if you insist on your price.

Or:

At a high-end private country club: Okay, here's the plan, we really need to get a ton of new members in here. So, for the next 50 members who join at the regular $100,000 initiation fee, let's give them free dues for ten years.

To begin such a fire sale on a Rolls-Royce club should be unthinkable, because to do so would betray the vision, cheapen the product, and upset current members. Clubs and other organizations that consistently stick to their chosen strategy in every decision they make, whether it is about pricing for a banquet or ways to recruit new members, are, over time, the most successful organizations.

Figure 04: Four Leadership Strategies

		Competitive advantage source	
		Cost	Unique
Breadth of competitive scope	Broad target market	Low-cost (quantity)	Differentiation (price)
	Narrow target market	Focused low-cost (quantity)	Focused differentiation (price)

Connecting Vision with Operations

For vision to become reality there should be a strong connection between the vision and the day-to-day operation of the property.

MBA students often speak of operations as *a burning platform*. Envision an ongoing business operation as an offshore oilrig that has caught fire. The oilrig's engineers and laborers are trained to expect fires as part of daily operations, and are so well trained that the operation continues even in the midst of such catastrophes. The idea behind this illustration is simple: a vision should be so well integrated into operations that, even under stressful conditions, everyone executes his or her duties in a manner consistent with that vision.

To connect the vision with operations, make sure that discussions about the vision address these issues:

1. Define the organization. This may seem an obvious task, but it should not be underestimated. Such discussion is essential, especially if the organization has never established a definite purpose and reason for being. Comparing the organization to automobile brands, as suggested previously, is one way to help define. An organization can also be defined by answering three questions:

- Who are the customers?

- What are the customers' wants and needs?

- How will the organization satisfy the customers' wants and needs?

2. Decide the long-term strategy. The long-term strategy should consider a timeframe reaching five to ten years or more into the future. Generally, the more established the organization, the farther out into the future the timeframe.

3. Communicate the vision. The vision should be stated clearly and in a way that inspires staff and customers alike. Communicating the vision in everything that an organization thinks, says, or does is as important as the creation of the vision itself. Share the vision! Construct a concise, well-worded vision statement to empower employees with a higher sense of purpose. For example, a painter in the engineering department who is in tune with the property's vision might consider it his job to maintain a treasured showplace, not simply to paint the white trim.

4. Recognize the difference between strategy and operations. Strategy is aimed across the organization and across time. Operations (often referred to generically as tactics) is aimed across the various departments and occurs in day-to-day, week-by-week, and month-by-month increments.

06. Mission

Mission is a broad description of an organization's fundamental purpose. A correctly crafted mission should include the broadest and highest level of goals and objectives. A written mission statement includes not only the vision and purpose, but also the basic services the organization provides. The mission statement states why the organization exists and how it contributes to its overall goals. Generally, the mission statement is one that, if realized, helps ensure successful operations.

To make the distinction between vision and mission, vision is a broader conceptual approach, while mission includes the vision and then adds the basic products and services provided. More organizations are merging the discussion of values and beliefs and vision along with mission and achieving excellent results. Discussing these items together is time efficient and results in the desired product, which is a well-developed mission statement.

More than any other element of the strategic planning process, the mission statement picks up where the vision leaves off and spells out the first-order reasons for the organization's existence in more detail. The mission statement flows directly from the values and beliefs and vision and helps crystallize desired outcomes.

The mission statement should be used everywhere to communicate and reinforce the vision. The mission statement reminds the community, its customers, staff, guests, vendors, and others, as to *why* the organization exists and the *basic products* and services it provides.

To achieve this end, the mission statement should be reproduced and featured in all publications including newsletters, websites, stationery, brochures, advertisements, public relations articles, employee handbooks, orientation manuals, and even the backs of business cards. In short, any time one is creating any communications piece, consider including the mission statement as a complementary element. Some print the mission statement on signs above employee bulletin boards, in break rooms, locker rooms, and service delivery areas.

Questions answered in a properly constructed mission statement

- What do we do?
- How do we do it?
- For whom do we do it?

Questions to test the value of a mission statement

- Does it foster common goals?
- Can anyone outside the organization understand what we do?
- Can we use the statement to evaluate what we do?

An example mission statement for a start-up guest ranch

The Tarantula Canyon Resort was created as a haven for its guests. We are second to none in our purpose to offer an extraordinary array of outdoor recreation and dining experiences, in our commitment to the highest level of guest service, and in our willingness to recognize our employees as our most valuable asset. Our allegiance to these basic elements will ensure long-term success for our guests and staff.

Mission statement elements for consideration

1. Common features. What are the fundamental products and services? What markets or potential customers does the property pursue? What are the core values? What are a few of the broadest goals? What is the competitive position? What is the image that the property wants to portray to the public?

2. Internal scans. What are the unique strengths that the organization should be known for and build upon? What weaknesses should be improved upon internally? If considering reinvention, what did not exist in the present model that should included in the future? If considering reengineering, what would the organization look like in a complete redesign? Is the organization focusing major attention toward continuous quality improvement and total quality management?

3. External scans. What demographic shifts should be anticipated? What changes in products and services may come about over the next five-to-10 years? What changes in the economy are forecast? What is the available source of labor? What laws and regulations could change the ways that the organization does business? What are the strengths and weaknesses of the competition? What technological factors are available or developing? What ecological factors should be considered?

07. Goals

I have covered goals in detail in other sections and chapters of this book. In this discussion, we cover goals as they specifically relate to creating strategy. Goals focus on desired and planned future states of existence. Goals help ensure fulfillment of the mission. How well an organization achieves those goals dictates its effectiveness.

The strategic vision transitions to performance targets through goal-creation. Goals are evidence of the commitment by leaders to achieve specific outcomes in keeping with the vision. Leaders who insist on achieving only mutually agreed-upon and focused goals are far more effective in reaching those goals than are managers who have only a vague idea of what they should be doing. Goals are the *meat and potatoes* of strategic planning. When a goal is written correctly, the goal achiever should feel some degree of both apprehension and exhilaration. Apprehension would be in knowing the goal requires greater-than-normal effort, creativity, and tenacity (and not just business as usual) and exhilaration from the positive excitement in anticipation of the improvements that will come from such goal achievement.

At this point in the process, the pure planning of strategy is beginning to mix with the implementation of the strategy, which most of us know by the name of *operations*. To ensure that the strategic planning process does not become corrupted with actual operations (a phenomenon referred to as *micromanagement*), I will make a few important distinctions between and among concepts:

Strategy can be referred to in terms of two broad categories: strategic planning and strategic implementation. Strategic planning is the part of the process that occurs before creating major goals and objectives. Strategic implementation picks up at the creation of major goals and objectives and continues through the creation of the multiple-year economic model along with agreed upon methods for reviewing, measuring, and evaluating goal achievement. The planning portion of strategy is fairly distinctive in that it is a broader and more creative process. Strategic implementation focuses on creation of goals and objectives. During this process, it can become difficult for executives to resist the temptation of assuming the responsibility for goal achievement. The achievement function is clearly a function of the paid staff working under the direction of a management staff as depicted on the organization chart. When goals move from the implementation stage (while still part of the strategy) to the operational stage, they are turned over to management levels working closer to the day-to-day operations staff.

Goal timelines

1. Short-term operational goal (range 0-6 months): In general terms, an operational goal that can be accomplished within approximately six months (or less) is a short-term goal. Just because a goal is short term does not mean it is not vital to success. For example,

a golf department may decide in January to eliminate errors in sign-up process for tee times before the end of February—a very important goal.

2. Mid-term operational goal (range 6-12 months): An operational goal that can be accomplished within six to 12 months is a mid-term goal. For example, a golf course maintenance department might decide in January to rebuild the bunker drainage system before the end of August.

3. Long-term operational goal (range 1 year or longer): A goal that requires 12 months or more to be accomplished is a long-term goal. The aquatics department may be rebuilding the summer swim team program and, in May, might set a goal of winning the league championships held in August of the following summer.

Note that a long-term operational goal can become as long or even longer term than some strategic goals. At first this may seem confusing. However, when considering the *originator*, a long-term operational goal instituted at the *department* level (an operations level and not an executive level) is technically considered operations and therefore operational.

Unlike operational goals, strategic goals are usually larger in scope, typically have longer timeframes, and originate from the highest levels of the organization. Strategic goals are, by definition, those that focus on timeframes one year or farther out.

Examples of goal timelines

1. Short-term strategic goal (range 1-2 years): In September 20X0 a restaurant's corporate executives set a goal to increase its daily average covers across all units from 425 to 550 before the end of December 20X1.

2. Mid-term strategic goal (range 2-5 years): A private country club board of directors decides in January of 20X1 that it wants to re-build all of its greens with Bent grass before the end of December 20X3.

3. Long-term strategic goal (range 5 years or longer): A hotel development company creates the strategy in January 20X0 of

doubling its number of properties from 100 to 225 before the end of December 20X9.

08. Objectives

Objectives are often described as the specific *whats* of an organization. Objectives include short-term, departmental aspirations and aims. Objectives should be quantifiable, measurable by counting and/or timing, and should serve as steps toward goal-achievement.

As with operational and strategic goals, the distinction between operational and strategic objectives is sometimes difficult. For example, one could argue that the short- and mid-term strategic goals used in the examples above are actually interim objectives of the long-term goal to increase the club's net total membership by 50 members within five years.

As one proceeds through these initial stages of strategic planning, do not be overly concerned about distinguishing an objective from a goal. Instead, be concerned with aligning everything that the organization thinks, says, does, and plans with the vision, mission, and its highest, broadest goals. Arguing about whether a given proposal is a goal or an objective wastes time on unproductive word games.

The executive management team plays a critical role in reviewing progress and assuring that strategies are changed as appropriate. Staff working under the direction of a general manager should execute the objectives as well as carry out monthly monitoring in the form of budget variance meetings. Typically a quarterly budget variance meeting is attended by department level managers and higher. If supporting staff members are included, typically they are invited in during their particular segment and then excused. If the organization has a planning and evaluation unit (such as treasury, strategy, and/or long-range planning), it should play an ongoing role in monitoring progress towards goals and objectives, and analyzing reasons for shortfalls in accomplishments. The main report cards for measuring accomplishment of goals and objectives are the budget, the management performance review using a dashboard (described later in this chapter), and the recurring operations survey data.

09. Organizational Situation Analysis (SWOT)

Situation analysis is a concept that has existed for many years. Situation analysis helps establish a sense of identity and direction as to where it is currently and where it might go in the future. Such analysis helps evaluate strengths, weaknesses, opportunities, and threats (SWOT). SWOT analysis is a valuable tool for planning strategic direction.

The SWOT analysis is both an internal and external appraisal. The internal appraisal identifies strengths and weaknesses. The external appraisal identifies the threats and opportunities that exist in the outside environment (such as competitors and government). These strengths and weaknesses along with opportunities and threats help managers establish a set of *key factors for success* (KFS).

Strengths and Weaknesses

Strengths and weaknesses are internal. A *strength* is something positive about the organization or what the organization is good at doing. Conversely, a *weakness* is where the organization falls short or has a limitation. Curiously, in conducting a SWOT analysis, an identified strength may also help identify a corresponding weakness, and vice versa. For example, that a resort facility is a grand-style, 150-year-old architectural treasure may be a strength, in that the age adds value to the guests' perception of their overall experience. On the other hand, the facility's age would undoubtedly be a factor in several internal problems, such as high maintenance costs, faulty wiring, and outdated plumbing, which are all weaknesses.

Do not become overly concerned that a strength in one sense could also be considered a weakness in another. Use good judgment to determine if the strengths of a particular attribute outweigh its weaknesses, so that the attribute should be placed in the strength column rather than the weakness column (or vice versa). Many managers have heard the cautionary tale of a hotel company president who convinced the board that the operational difficulties associated with maintaining an antebellum mansion as a hotel facility were insurmountable. The building was razed and a modern and efficient facility was constructed in its place, but the new building's sterile atmosphere lacked character. The new hotel was little more than a sterile and uninteresting box, and the company suffered greatly from this misjudgment.

Lists of strengths and weakness are developed during brainstorming sessions, formal surveys, or informal conversations with and interviews of customers, staff members, and suppliers. Following this collection of data, a session (or several sessions) should be held to help ensure agreement and consensus. During this process of *consideration and assessment*, perceived strengths and weaknesses should be considered individually in terms of relativity and duplicity.

For example, some guests might report that the restaurant is too expensive. Managers and the executive team must use honesty and sound judgment to determine whether this is a valid statement of weakness or simply a relative weakness—that is, a general statement that could be attributed to all white tablecloth restaurants.

Eliminating or allowing duplication (listing an element as both a strength and a weakness) requires judgment in sorting through strengths and weaknesses. For example, suppose that a golf course has the highest USGA slope rating of any area course. A golf club could perceive this as a strength as it may be a prestigious award that earns bragging rights; or, the difficulty lures the finest golfers to the club; or, the undulating terrain is spectacular in its beauty and elevation change. But the fact that the club's golf course has the highest USGA slope rating may also be a weakness, if the course's difficulty frustrates golfers with average to high handicaps, thereby severely limiting the market for the club's course as an *everyday home course*, or if the difficulty creates an average round time of five hours, which is a full hour longer than the typical average round target of four hours. In this case, the managers and others must collectively determine whether overall the club's golf course is a strength or a weakness. Alternately, the listing could appear in both places (as both a strength and a weakness), as long as the particular context was explained. Do not be concerned if strengths also end up being listed as weaknesses. Just ensure that the context is explained.

Once complete, the internal assessment of strengths and weaknesses helps establish a bundle of distinctive competencies and qualities that the property is adept at either doing or being, along with a set of issues that the property is not good at either doing or being.

In conducting this analysis, remember that strengths and weaknesses are, by definition, *internal* to the organization.

Opportunities and Threats

Opportunities and threats are *external* to the organization. An *opportunity* is something that the organization could explore capitalizing upon. A *threat* can come from a competitor, or from government regulations, or from any other external situation that presents a challenge.

As with the determination of strengths and weaknesses, success in determining opportunities and threats lies in careful analysis and judgment. Often, some are quick to dismiss a finding as insignificant. However, few findings are insignificant. In fact, those who are particularly successful in identifying opportunities and threats are those who can identify emerging trends that go unnoticed by others.

A growing trend among seasoned strategy experts is to work through opportunities and threats before identifying strengths and weaknesses. These experts believe that opportunities and threats from the outside drive the relativity of the internal strengths and weaknesses, rather than the other way around. Consequently, this group might refer to this analysis as OTSW (pronounced *ott-swa*), which is undoubtedly less catchy than SWOT.

An opportunity based on competition may be that a neighboring property burned to the ground, and present zoning only allows it to build back 50 percent of its pre-fire square footage. This creates an opportunity for a neighboring property's growth, because the rebuilt property may no longer have the capacity to handle its former house count.

A situational opportunity for a remote location property may be that the state transportation department has approved the construction of a new bridge, which will put the property within 20 miles of the major population center of the area, as opposed to the 40-mile journey that people in the populated area must currently take to reach the property. Because of the new bridge, the property will become more geographically accessible and thus potentially more desirable to a larger number of people creating a clear opportunity for growth.

Threats can be classified similarly. A threat from the competition may include plans for a major new national restaurant to be built within three blocks of an existing restaurant. A governmental threat may be a lowered blood-alcohol level tolerance for DUI or DWI offenses. Such a mandate might then threaten the restaurant's beverage sales, and might also put the property at greater risk for alcohol liability and liquor-related lawsuits.

SWOT Analysis Examples

Aligning strength with opportunity

If the external analysis uncovers an opportunity and the internal analysis reveals corresponding internal strengths, then the organization has a tremendous chance to capitalize on the opportunity.

Continuing with one of the previous examples, if the property that has a new bridge being built nearby, thereby bringing the property closer to the population center (external opportunity) has excess capacity (an internal strength due to availability to take on new business), then that property has a tremendous opportunity to capitalize on the coming availability of new and increased potential customers.

Aligning weakness with opportunity

Assuming that a property's external analysis identifies an opportunity but its internal analysis reveals weaknesses that make it difficult or impossible to take advantage of the growth opportunity (slack capacity), the property has a limited ability to capitalize. For example, if the property is currently maxed out on capacity issues, it has a relative weakness due to availability, and thus has only a limited opportunity to capitalize on increased business. This situation can be represented as follows.

Aligning strength with threat

If a property's external analysis reveals a threat, but its internal analysis reveals a strength that can help the property offset or cope with the threat, then the property has the ability to respond to the threat successfully. For example, if the state lowers the BAC threshold for DUIs, but the property has an outstanding alcohol awareness program in place, the property has the ability to minimize the impact of this threat. This example could be illustrated as follows.

Aligning weakness with threat

If a property's external analysis determines a high degree of threat and its internal analysis reveals weaknesses in its ability to respond to the threat, the property faces its worst operating position. For example, if a new, popular restaurant concept known for excellent service and food will open next year within two blocks of a restaurant that has not provided acceptable levels service or quality food to its dining patrons, the existing restaurant faces a severe threat to which it likely cannot respond effectively.

In any SWOT analysis, whether organization-wide or by department, a key to extracting meaningful information is to compare the strengths and weaknesses along with the opportunities and threats. SWOT *analysis* (the comparing) is the payoff to the SWOT *exercise* (the creating). The outcomes from the analysis flow into the action plan.

10. Strategy Statement

The object of effective strategy is to capitalize on strengths in a way that helps it develop sustainable advantages in its marketplace. After all, organizations want their particular property to be *the* property of choice in their particular market. To develop and highlight their strengths, organizations can choose one or more of the strategic methods listed in the following paragraphs.

Enhancing Differentiation

With the *enhancing differentiation* strategy, the property concentrates on becoming more appealing in one particular area that the competition may not share. The internal SWOT analysis identifies the internal strengths (and weaknesses). To enhance its differentiation from others, the property simply focuses on improving its strength in particular areas.

For example, one golf resort located in a competitive area with high demand for golf times might add lights, thereby allowing play long past sundown. In fact, one resort in Arizona worked through this exercise and added lights to its five finishing holes, effectively accommodating an increase of almost 50 players per day.

Another example of a property improving on a strength. A resort with a Golf Digest-rated top-100 golf course spent an extra $200,000 on grooming and conditioning its course. This spending of capital dollars to enrich an already superior aspect of the course is strategic. The executive leaders made this decision in order to attract new and more guests, further satisfy existing guests, and perhaps move up in the Golf Digest ratings.

Enhancing Superiority

Using the *enhancing superiority* strategy endeavors to exploit a competitor's weaknesses or to emphasize its own noncompetitive strength.

Exploiting weakness: To exploit another's weakness, a Nevada golf resort rebuilt all of its greens with pure, Bent grass greens, thus highlighting the course condition of a competitor, which had bumpy, 25-year-old Poa Annua infested greens and not an ideal course, by comparison.

Enhancing Noncompetitive Strength

Enhancing noncompetitive strength fits technically under Enhancing Superiority, but with a twist: A West Virginia resort emphasized its noncompeting strengths by publicizing the indoor bowling center, equestrian center, *dive-in* movies at the pool during summer, and indoor shooting range. Exploiting noncompetitive strengths, especially when perceived as having real desirability, can add tremendously to the property's value equation in terms of attracting potential members and/ or retaining and satisfying existing members.

Innovating

Properties interested in *innovating* would develop new products or services that do not presently exist at the property or at competing properties. The list of potential new products and services is endless. The key is to innovate into areas that will be appreciated and used by customers or at least be perceived as providing new, different, and desirable products and services. One example of innovating would include a well-known hotel in Texas that, over time, added a dry-cleaners, tailor shop, stylist, casual-use office space, retail-type convenience store, business center, and a hotel-sponsored American Express card.

Revolution

Revolution can be an effective strategy, especially when drastic measures are required to improve the facilities or performance. A *revolution* strategy changes the fundamental and accepted way the organization conducts business. For example, a private golf club located in Louisiana adopted a policy of nondiscriminatory tee times among male and female members. At the time, this was seen as a revolutionary initiative by surrounding communities. Revolution is an extremely effective strategy for an organization hoping to gain new customers and distinguish itself in a market dominated by old-line, established, and traditional competitors.

Statement

Once an organization has identified and chosen a strategy, the strategy is then written as a statement. This becomes the *strategy statement*. A strategy statement explains how external opportunities will be exploited by internal strengths. Threats and weaknesses, in the strategy statement, are either avoided or mitigated with suggested counter-measures.

Specific Strategies

Major departments and constituencies often refer to themselves as being the *drivers* of their organizations. The golf department at a luxury resort may not value another sport or activity highly, forgetting that an integrated resort must offer a wide variety of interests to keep guests involved, engaged, and welcome. The following list of strategies helps properties allocate resources to a wide variety of constituencies.

Allocation of resources

Allocation of budgeted resources follows a step-by-step approach in choosing the most appropriate method. Methods to consider are provided below.

- Surplus maximization. A family-owned hotel chain in Southern California operates in a manner that retains and stockpiles surplus dollars at the end of each year with the idea of undertaking a major renovation and/or expansion when enough money is retained to do the project without borrowing or diluting stock. Example: Retaining surplus dollars each year for five years and then has enough money set aside to fund the building and equipping of a health spa.

- Usage or targeted maximization. A fried chicken restaurant sets a goal of serving the highest number of customers of their services by offering a limited menu at low cost and high value. This is a common goal in the casual, limited menu restaurant business.

- Full or partial cost recovery. A private spa resort in Utah manages its programs and services so that they break even, providing only as much as finances allow. Typically, full cost would be defined as covering labor and cost of goods, so it is not actually full cost recovery. Perhaps this property agrees to do a Napa wine tour if it can get 10 advance sign-ups. If not, the trip is cancelled.

- Budget maximization. An old-line, formal restaurant in New York City maximizes the size of its staff, services, and operating expenses regardless of revenue. This is an older operating concept. A specific example may be that this restaurant offers a dinner dance with elaborate buffet and three-piece combo every Friday night (because it is thought of as tradition) but on certain nights serves as few as 8-12 customers. The tradition is maintained by allocating what many would consider a disproportionate amount of subsidy.

- Customer satisfaction maximization. A cruise line offers extreme value on selected events and services as a recurring *thank you* to its existing customer base. This thank you becomes a customer reward and thereby an effective customer retention tool. An example may be that a cruise line offers a deeply discounted, all-inclusive, special cruise to existing cruisers only (not available to those who do not already cruise with this company). Typically, the offering will occur during a shoulder season and/or when ships are being repositioned. The price will be set covering variable, but not fixed costs.

11. Budgets

There are three types of budgets that hospitality organizations must create and manage. The processes are referred to as *normal capital budgeting*, *project capital budgeting*, and *operations budgeting*.

Normal Capital Budgeting

Most organizations do not have unlimited capital reserves. In fact, most properties do not fund depreciation. Instead of funding depreciation, they traditionally spend a range of two to nine percent of *gross annual revenues* on normal capital items such as furniture, fixtures, and equipment (often referred to as *FF&E*). Restaurants would fall into the lower percentages averaging around two percent, private country clubs about three-four percent, with hotels and resorts trending up to about nine percent or higher if considered world-class properties.

A rule of thumb for classification of a *capitalized item* versus an *expensed item* is an accounting term regulated by the Financial Accounting Standards Board (FASB). FASB is a private, non-profit organization market regulator whose primary purpose is to establish and improve generally accepted accounting principles (GAAP) within the United States in the public's interest.

A capitalized item is a new item (asset) that has a material useful life of longer than 12 months. Examples would include a new sofa for the reception area or floor mixer for a restaurant kitchen. However, a capitalized item may also be a procedure or repair that materially extends the useful life of an existing item longer than 12 months. An example would include rebuilding the engine on an existing catering truck. Capitalized assets are depreciated over time (over their useful lives).

Expensed items appear in operations budgeting and are considered paid for and used up within 12 months. Examples of expensed items would include cleaning supplies used to shampoo the new sofa; flour used in the floor mixer; and fuel, such as gas, oil, and lubricants used on the catering truck.

Project Capital Budgeting

Properties refer to funding for major rebuilding, remodeling, and adding-on as *project capital*. While technically classified in essentially the same manner as normal capital, the distinction, project capital relates to the methods frequently used for funding. Funding for project capital may come from a variety of sources: Capital reserves (reserved and earmarked monetary commitments from normal capital over time), borrowing (debt) from commercial banks or insurance companies, assessments imposed on owners (in the case of private clubs), stock sales, and others.

Operations Budgeting

The process of operations budgeting by department is a tremendously time-consuming part of effective business management. Operations budgets consider how and when revenues will flow in and how and when expenses will flow out of the organization. Operations budgets should be created in painstaking detail and should be broken down into expected monthly increments. When completed, operations budgets should answer the questions, *Who? What?* Where? When? Why? and *How many?* or *How much?* (as the case may be).

For example, if the membership department of a fitness club were to be budgeting revenues, *budgetary assumptions* would be supported by answers to the following questions:

- *What?* The goal at The Punch and Judo Fitness Club is 20 *net new members* (the difference between member joins and member resignations) for the year. (Also answers *How many?*)

- *Why?* The club is a *growth club* and, consistent with its strategic plan, *we desire a growth of 20 net new members per year.* A growth club is one that has not reached its maximum number of members.

- *When?* This would be a statement that projects when during the year the new members will join.

For example, managers might project the following forecast:

Consistent with the resignation and join patterns over the past five years, the following monthly and quarterly seasonality forecast is depicted across the coming year in the chart shown below: (Note that assumptions are usually written in third person and passive voice.)

Figure 05: Member Forecast Example

Month and Quarter	Number of members at month start	Resignations during month	New member joins
Quarter 01			
January	360	0	0
February	360	0	2
March	362	1	3
Quarter 02			
April	364	0	2
May	366	2	6
June	370	0	3
Quarter 03			
July	373	0	2
August	375	0	2
September	377	1	3
Quarter 04			
October	379	0	1
November	380	0	0
December	380	0	0
Total	380	4	24

The written assumptions will help explain any subsequent variance. Assumptions help managers determine whether budget variances are permanent or the results of timing issues that can be made up in subsequent months. The chart also provides a basis for forecasting membership revenues by month. Many leaders use quarter changes as intervals in adjusting thinking for timing issues occurring over the preceding months. In this manner, a seasoned leader may accept one or up to two months of explanations for budget variances due to timing, for example, unexpected weather. However, using the quarter change as a reminder, experienced leaders would likely consider the third month to indicate a trend instead of a blip and adjust accordingly.

Departmental operations budgets should flow from the organization's grand (overall) strategy and reflect the supporting departmental (SBU) strategies.

Creating an Economic Model

The culminating effort of the budgeting process includes normal capital budgeting, project capital budgeting, and operations budgeting. The effort is to forecast these budgeting elements for the next five to seven years and create a package that is often referred to as the *economic model*. The economic model is also commonly referred to as the *cash flow forecast*. The creation of an economic model aids any organization in that it shows revenue sources and expenses, as well as functioning to prioritize and forecast major and minor regular and project capital expenditures.

An economic model helps in smoothing the annual budgeting process. As years progress each year moves one place to the left toward becoming the operating year (referred to as year 1). As this moving occurs, years two and three are typically refined to the point where they are a natural progression in the budgeting process instead of the stressful and demanding October push to come up with an operating budget and package that goes into effect in January (assuming that a fiscal year begins in January). The creation of an economic model has the added advantage of helping with continuity in that it assists in binding decision makers into continuing with the established strategy.

12. Action Plan

The action plan comes together after planning and budgeting are completed. Often referred to as *operations* or *implementation*, the action plan is the realization or practical application of the strategic planning effort. Strategy and operations come together during the action planning. The strategy is what the organization will do. The term, *operations*, otherwise known as the *action plan*, is how the organization will do it.

There are four scenarios in which strategy meets operations. Knowing these scenarios provides an understanding as to how implementation is likely to occur. In the best case, the organization has clear strategy and effective operations; the likely result is that the organization has enjoyed success in the past and will also do so in the future. If the organization has a clear strategy but ineffective operations, it has likely enjoyed some success in the past; however, future success is in doubt. Similarly, if the organization has an unclear strategy but effective operations, it has probably enjoyed success in the past, yet future success is doubtful. In the worst scenario, the organization has an unclear strategy and ineffective operations. Most likely, it has failed in the past and will likely fail in the future unless major changes are implemented.

Figure 06: Implementing Action Plans

		Strategy (What)	
		Clear Strategy (+)	Unclear Strategy (-)
Operations (How)	Effective Operations (+)	Success in past and future. (+/+)	Success in past; doubtful future. (+/-)
	Ineffective Operations (-)	Some success in past; doubtful future. (-/+)	Failure in past and future. (-/-)

13. Assessing Progress

In whatever form the action plan takes, being able to measure whether the organization is accomplishing its goals, objectives, and strategic initiatives is vital. The foundational element for controlling and monitoring progress is a connection to the *counts* and *times* (the objective measures) created in the budgeting process. For example, a renovation of a café within a resort, which was approved in the capital budget, would have developed from a strategic initiative and would include assumptions of what, why, when, and how much. The objective measures for evaluating its success—timing and dollars spent—are the answers to when, and how much and help an organization to make the decision regarding whether funding comes from normal or project capital. Monitoring and assessing progress should be continuous, occurring during the renovation as well as after completion of the project. Monitoring serves two purposes: (1) it keeps all departments and functional areas on track, and (2) it ensures that accomplishments move the organization toward achievement of its long-range goals (those outlined in the strategic plan).

Strategic Implementation Analysis

Strategic implementation analysis is the process of examining an organization's efforts to ensure that operations efforts are driven by strategic initiatives. Often, properties spend tremendous effort, time, and money to create a strategic plan, and then fail to integrate it successfully into operations. The flurry of day-to-day operations creates confusion between what the organization would like to become (its ideal, as defined by its strategic plan) and what it is (its current state, as defined by operations and implementation). The strategic implementation analysis form allows a manager to rate how well the organization aligns and coordinates its strategic plan with implementation, and helps the manager bring these two aspects more into alignment, if necessary. Ideally, operations flow naturally from the organization's overall strategic efforts.

The headings of the following sections provide a checklist of issues that leaders and managers should concern themselves with in managing the effective implementation of the strategy.

Creation of the Grand Strategy

Has the executive management team determined what it wants the overall organization to be in both nature and direction over the next several years? An overarching approach and agreement to organization-wide direction from the executive management team is referred to as the *overall* or *grand strategy*. This effort is perhaps the most fundamental of the strategic planning elements. Much like a road map, the grand strategy provides a direction for the organization and should be the foundation and reference point for everything the organization thinks, says, and does. This grand strategy should take the form of a highly organized and tabbed written document, readily available, and referred to often.

Agreement

Is there agreement as to the grand strategy? As the foundation for everything the organization thinks, says, and does, the grand strategy should be agreed to by all: Board members, officers, senior leadership, staff members, and managers alike. Do not be surprised if agreement does not come easily; agreement usually develops over time. However difficult a process, agreement about the grand strategy is a valuable outcome. Efforts made to bring all organizational constituencies into agreement and alignment create a strong identity.

The Leader as an Integral Part of Grand Strategy

Though unlikely, it is conceivable that the organization does have an agreed-upon master plan in the form of the grand strategy, but management has been left out of the loop. The senior leadership team should, to the extent possible, ensure that they are made an integral part of the planning and development process when grand strategy is a new initiative. In organizations that already have a grand strategy, the senior leadership team should reinforce the importance of the agreed-upon outcomes as guiding principles.

Successful senior leaders position themselves not only as chief operating officers, but also as chief administrative officers for board proceedings. As such, they become chief advocates for continuity of the grand strategy across all constituencies. Senior most leaders are responsible for authorizing the implementation of the elements of the strategic plan to the operational level. They can be much more effectively implemented if all levels of management and departments become familiar with the grand strategy. Doing so helps ensure that departments understand their roles in complementing the grand strategy.

Current Management Standard

Business management continues to evolve. Many organizations have adopted a *current management standard* that values managers who can encourage and influence others positively without using coercion or intimidation. Along the same attitude of thinking, organizations are realizing the importance of professional delegation by the senior leaders in utilizing *open book management* with their staff members. In open book management, department heads, sports professionals, supervisors, and essentially anyone who has both the power and responsibility for achieving goals and objectives also has access to the financials for his or her area of responsibility. Doing so helps eliminate feelings of secrecy, suspicion, and distrust.

Communicating the Strategy

Assume that as the organization's senior leader you are familiar with the organization's grand strategy. Are you sharing that plan with direct reports as well as other employees? Are you reinforcing the importance of the plan and using it as a central theme in everything that you think, do, and say, whether with subordinates, committees, consultants, or suppliers? Do key managers understand and share the same vision of the grand strategy and use it as a guide for their departmental strategies? All managers who work directly with the senior leadership team should refer to and reinforce the importance of the strategic plan when discussing any issues.

Clarity and Conciseness

There is an exercise referred to as the elevator test that works well in illustrating the need for clarity and conciseness when expressing the organization's overall strategy. Imagine for a moment that you are riding down from the 20th floor to the 1st floor in an elevator with a someone who knows that you work at a particular organization, and he or she asks you to explain what your organization is all about. Could you do it before the doors opened on the 1st floor? Where would you begin? What would you say?

The *elevator test* suggests that the senior leadership team and down—VPs, directors, department managers, and sports professionals—should visualize the organization's strategic plan (including its vision, mission, and major goals and objectives) as a daisy chain of connectedness. As such, you should be able to organize your thoughts and answer the questions simply, clearly, and in less than 30 seconds. Impossible? If the answer is *no*, then you need to better organize your thoughts and/or simplify or clarify the strategy. Practice the 30-second version of the strategic plan until the answer becomes second nature. If you cannot explain the strategy clearly and concisely before the elevator doors open, you or the organization's written documents are stating the strategy in terms that are disorganized, too broad, or too complicated. Organize. Simplify. Clarify. Refine. Reflect. Repeat. Practice.

Use Strategy to Create New Services

A clear grand strategy allows departments to align their daily operations with the strategy and guide the creation of new services, products, and markets. Additionally, a clear strategy suggests services, products, and markets that the organization will not pursue. This *here-and-now* application of the strategic planning process is an important key to the success of the overall effort and has within it a tremendously important focusing quality.

Consider the scenario of a private club: Members visit another club and return with operations procedures and offerings that they want the club to adopt. A clear strategy can be an effective filter for these types of suggestions. Do the members' suggestions fit in with the club's strategy? If not, they should not be implemented.

A clear strategic plan, like the vision and mission that help define it, is a foundational element of the club. Refer to the strategy to ensure that your Chevrolet club, Mercedes club, or Ferrari club—whatever its type stays true to its roots, maintains its distinctive identity, and does not become a Frankenstein club, as I wrote about earlier.

Strategy Should Complement Long-Range Planning

The operational foci of strategy and long range planning lie mainly in formulating big picture overall goals vis a vis capital improvement projects, land utilization, and the development and maintenance of an integrated, multiple-year plan consistent with the vision and mission. Ideally, this plan is continuously updated.

While both strategic and long range planning are often spoken of as being synonymous, there are a few key fundamental differences in the functions that each perform. Essentially, long range planning focuses on what an organization wants to look like over time and strategic planning focuses on how an organization will get there.

Long-range planning forecasts both internal and external conditions and realities and plans how an organization can function effectively within them. Since it involves planning and predicting over multiple year periods, it cannot be as specific as short-term or operational planning, which generates a work plan with detailed annual objectives, tasks, methods, timelines, and responsibilities.

Strategic planning is process by which leaders pick up on the long range planning of what an organization intends to become in the future and develops a plan as to how it will get there by creating and assigning priorities, procedures, and operating strategies to achieve that vision. Included are measurable goals, which are realistic and attainable, but also challenging; emphasis is on long-term goals and strategies, rather than short-term (such as annual) objectives, which almost always appear in the present-year operations budget.

Just as the strategic and long range plans should complement each other, so too should the hierarchy charged with those planning efforts work fluidly and consistently. There is much variation among organizational strategic and long range planning efforts, but typically one of the following three scenarios occurs

Disconnects between strategy and long range planning

1. No strategic or long range planning. The least desirable scenario for an organization is that it has neither a strategic planning nor a long range planning committee. Organizations without either committee are at a distinct operational disadvantage; their product offerings, markets, and services tend to develop as reactions to customer comments, without cohesion or structure. If the formation of strategic and long range planning committees is currently impractical for the organization, an ad hoc committee that occasionally reviews strategic and long range planning efforts is better than nothing at all.

2. Merging strategic and long range planning. The second configuration merges strategic planning with long range planning into one standing committee. While this is often a very effective model, the demands on the committee members are numerous. The success of the

single committee depends on the organization of work: What is the committee charged with accomplishing? If duties are not carefully decided, assigned, and prioritized, the committee members can become overwhelmed with work. This is especially the case in an existing organization that establishes a combination long-range planning and strategy committee for the first time.

3. Separate strategic and long range planning. The third governance model separates long range planning and strategic planning into two discrete standing committees. The functional advantage of having two committees is the potential division of work among the committees. There is not an unreasonable time commitment required of either committee. The main disadvantage is the separation of planning issues and coordination of the committees' efforts. Simply stated, long range planning efforts should not be separated from strategic considerations.

Given these three scenarios, the one most common and perhaps most practical for the average organization is the single-committee model. Though the demands on committee members are larger, coordination of effort is streamlined, which is often the most important consideration in planning efforts. Organizations without a long term planning and/or strategic planning committee should create one.

If we assume that an organization merges the functions of its strategic planning and long range planning committees into one effort, it is that committee whose function helps ensure the future success of the chosen strategy. It becomes one of their most important functions to serve as the gatekeeper for proposed programs and major changes. It is also incumbent on this committee to serve as a consistent and reliable committee for making sure that the agreed upon strategic plan is followed closely and achieved. I go into the importance of gatekeeping in the next section.

The Strategic Plan as a Living Element

Is strategy treated as if it were the blood, which courses throughout the body of the organization? If not, it should be treated as such. A strategic plan should be the *nourishment* for everything that an organization plans, projects, and budgets, as it is the lifeblood of all discussion within the organization.

At times some may feel frustrated and confused as to why it seems as if all planning and operations are funneled through the strategic planning committee. Take heart; that is the very purpose of the committee. When a long range planning committee and/or strategic planning committee is established, the committee becomes its gatekeeper for two important reasons:

1. New products, changes, or improvements. The strategic plan flows from the vision and mission, while operations flow from the strategic plan. Because strategy flows from vision and mission, all ideas for new products or changes or improvements must be filtered through the strategic planning committee to ensure that they are consistent with the vision and mission. With this system in place, ideally the executive team, departments, and staff members at all levels of operations will soon begin to ask themselves the question: *Is this idea consistent with the strategy*? If yes, the conversation should continue and perhaps the idea will move toward implementation. If no, the idea should be either discarded or filed away for future discussion and possible implementation, should the strategy change.

2. Current practices. The strategic planning committee is also important because all current practices should be filtered through the strategic plan; the committee becomes an evaluation tool not only for new ideas, but also for what's currently going on in operations. Sometimes older products, services, or operational procedures pre-date the current strategic plan. These unfiltered elements should pass through the strategic planning committee to ensure that all elements are aligned with the strategic plan. Otherwise, filtered or committee-approved operations are mixed in with unfiltered operations, to the detriment of the strategic vision. This type of organization is a conglomeration of misaligned functions and is in danger of becoming a Frankenstein entity.

Understanding the Internal and External Environment

Strategic planning includes an internal analysis of what an organization is adept at doing and where it falls short, as well as an outward look at the external environment and its challenges and opportunities.

As discussed previously, the SWOT analysis, which identifies strengths, weaknesses, opportunities, and threats, indicates current position. As such, a SWOT analysis is often referred to as a *situation analysis*. A SWOT analysis may be used on a macro level to evaluate an overall entity or on a micro level to get a snapshot of a particular aspect, such as the golf course, food and beverage department, rooms division, or any other department or area. SWOT could be taken as micro as a particular meal service in a particular restaurant or some special function.

During a SWOT analysis, the organization serves as its own critic. Besides providing perspective and understanding of position, a SWOT analysis supports and helps create a clear strategic plan, either for the entity (grand strategy) or by department (business strategy), which should align with and complement the grand strategy.

A SWOT analysis should be performed the organization for as a whole (grand strategy) and for each department (business strategy) at least one time each year. It can be a valuable exercise if it is carried out in a frank and honest manner. On the other hand, if it is handled in a political manner, the exercise can become a useless waste of time.

Using the Strategic Plan to Allocate Capital

Throughout the budgeting process, the strategic plan should play a major part as a reference tool for prioritizing needs and distributing capital. Capital requests should be made with the strategic plan in mind.

For example, suppose that the Golf Department supported a proposal by the GM, the golf course superintendent, and the director of golf to begin hand-mowing greens instead of tri-plexing greens, to begin tri-plexing fairways instead of gang mowing fairways, and to begin gang mowing the rough instead of flail mowing the rough. In the proposal, the economic impact of the mowing changes has been stated in terms of operations (increased labor) and capital expense (purchasing hand-mowers and gas carts with trailer combinations for transport).

Since this is a comparatively expensive proposition, it is likely that the proposal would be turned down unless it dovetailed with the overall strategy. In this case, the resort had a strategic initiative to improve the condition of the golf course by 25 percent within two years. Therefore, the executive leadership team approved the proposal as consistent with the strategic plan. In this case, everyone involved—the GM, golf course superintendent, director of golf, and the executive leadership team—kept the strategic goal for the golf course in mind, and so time was not wasted on a proposal that had nothing to do with the strategic vision, and the proposal was approved without difficulty. Organizations that use the strategic plan to allocate capital do not waste money on projects that have nothing to do with advancing the strategic vision.

Envisioning and Initiating Change

Strategic management recognizes that organizations change over time. Normally, change is instituted and occurs from the executive levels of management and leadership. Change can involve physical structures or equipment, but change almost always involves staff including attitudes, behaviors, processes, and ways of doing things. The following discussion helps define and identify the people, positions, and steps involved in visualizing and implementing change.

Change sponsors. *Change sponsors* can be defined as individuals who are convinced of the need for change and have the power and influence to both initiate and implement change. Change sponsors usually include members of the executive leadership team and key department heads or sports professionals.

Change agents. *Change agents* can be defined as persons who are convinced of the need for change and are responsible for assigning initiatives, projects, tasks, and day-to-day efforts that make change happen. Change agents include the general manager, department heads or sports professionals, and supervisors.

Change targets. *Change targets* can be defined in terms of physical structures or equipment, but change almost always involves staff including attitudes, behaviors, processes, and ways of doing things that must change in a way that meets or exceeds new expectations.

Change process example. The GM (change sponsor) recognizes that the café needs to be remodeled and prioritizes the project as one of his or her initiatives for the year. The Food & Beverage Director (change agent) agrees with the GM and takes on the responsibility for getting the project accomplished. The café (the physical remodeling) and the staff who will work in the newly remodeled grill are the change targets.

Model for Organizational Change

The steps in the model for change include planning, doing (implementing), checking and monitoring results, and conducting business in a manner that ensures continuous improvement.

- Planning. In the planning stage, change sponsors recognize the need for change, establish a vision, assess the current status as to the way things presently exist, and develop a plan.

- Doing. In the doing phase, change agents become involved by completing the planning, communicate the vision, use their power to ensure the change is accomplished, use times and/or counts to establish a method by which to measure accomplishment, and celebrate the success of the completion of the change.

- Checking and monitoring. In the checking phase, change sponsors and change agents become involved in re-evaluating the accuracy of the vision for the change, re-assess the plan for the change, and evaluate the direction of the change using times and/or counts to help ensure that the actual change is in alignment with the intended change.

- Acting. In the acting phase, the focus becomes one of looking for additional opportunities to improve the change. The terms, total quality management and continuous quality improvement become methodologies used by change agents and change targets to help ensure steady improvement in operations over time. On a regular and planned basis, change agents consult with change sponsors (repeating the cycle) to confirm that operations are meeting or slightly exceeding the intentions of the original plan.

Operations Strategies

As the process trickles down from grand strategy to department (business) strategy to operating in a strategic manner, this list of guidelines will help ensure that goals, objectives, projects, and tasks align with those created at higher levels.

Where are we going? Supervisors and department managers should reinforce the communication and plans for the department making it clear exactly where the department is heading, including its goals and objectives for the year.

How do we want to get there? In addition to communicating and clarifying where the organization and department are headed, it is vital for supervisors and department managers to communicate in detail how the department will achieve its goals and objectives. It is helpful to break goals and objectives into weekly, monthly, quarterly, semi-annual, and year-end segments. Creating this level of detail helps focus attention as to how overall goals and objectives funnel down into daily operations.

Establish goals and objectives for individuals and teams. In an ideal situation and over time, all employees, departments, and teams should be involved in the establishment of goals and objectives that they can be given the power and accept responsibility for achieving.

Prioritize. Employees at all levels are often bombarded by so many tasks, projects, objectives, and goals that they can become overwhelmed, lose track of a clear focus, and actually become less productive as a result of the ensuing confusion. Effective supervisors and leaders anticipate these scenarios and solicit questions about priorities on a regular and recurring basis.

Monitoring Goal Achievement

If, over time, we have succeeded in getting departments, groups, teams, and individuals utilizing systems of mutually agreed upon and acceptable goals and objectives, one must now create a system whereby achievement can be monitored easily. The foundational elements in an effective monitoring system ensure that goals and objectives can be tracked easily, that the supervisor and the person responsible for the outcome can access progress and results, and the progress and results are reported using objective terms instead of subjective terms.

Reporting in Objective Terms

Objective terms include times, counts, dates, and other details that refer back to an agreement (such as budget or goal) that are written in such a way that they become self explanatory to almost anyone who sees them. Many results are expressed in subjective terms, which is an imprecise method suggesting that the reporter has not done his or her homework in knowing the precise answers.

Examples of subjective terms:

- *We were really busy and did a lot of covers.*
- *We will probably finish up that project by about summer.*
- *Food cost at the snack bar was relatively low.*
- *Labor at the Front Desk is quite expensive.*

Examples of objective terms:

- Last week we did *463 covers on a budget forecast of 450.*
- *We are on track to complete the project as planned by June 30, 20XX.*
- *Food cost at the snack bar was 27% for July on a budget forecast of 30%.*
- *Labor at the Front Desk for February was 51% on a budget forecast of 51%.*

It is obvious to see the benefit of getting everyone using a common business language. Common business language suggests using objective terms (counts and times) when referring to progress on achieving goals and objectives. Common language also suggests referring to budget line-item assumptions (explanations and justifications) when delivering financial reports. The preciseness of using common business language improves efficiency and communication and reduces time spent discussing drama and noise. Using objective terms and assumptions helps add quantification and richness to statements, thereby reducing chances of misunderstandings.

Building a Scorecard

Effective leaders create scorecards (also referred to as flash reports and dashboards) to help them monitor goal achievement of their direct reports. While this may appear to be a daunting task, time spent in organizing a scorecard on the front end saves tremendous amounts of time into the future and pays huge benefits in organization. Follow these steps and examples to help get started:

- Agree on the right measures. When created, goals and objectives should all have associated objective measures (timeframes and numbers) associated with them. Ensure these times and counts are meaningful. If not, change them.

- Seasonalize forecasts instead of flat lining. Make certain that time is taken to spread the times and numbers across timeframes that make sense. From an earlier example, if the Membership Director assumes a goal of 24 member joins for the year, spreading the joins over the year at two per month (flat lining) makes little sense. Take time to plug the actual forecasting into the months where joins will occur (seasonalizing).

- Assign responsibility. State who has the responsibility for goal achievement (and make sure that person has been given both the power and responsibility for achieving it). Identify where the number is coming from and who is responsible for reporting it. The data source will almost always be the budget and/or the survey. These two data sources are the two major scorecards within any organization.

- See the big picture. The primary purpose of the scorecard is to provide an overall view of the entity with a relatively small amount of information. If the big picture is not coming through, change the measures. Creating a visual depiction (a dashboard) is an effective way to see the information quickly. I refer to the concept of a view from 1,000 feet in the air in the values discussion. More specifically, the concept of a dashboard would be continuing to see the entity from 1,000 feet (as if looking down at a map), but having five to seven map tacks pointing out important details for each area or department.

- Monitor and Act. Taking action means doing so in a timely fashion. Many managers rely on the venue of budget variance meetings for this step. If that method functions well, do not change. If we back up a few steps and remember that everyone who is involved in goals and objectives has done so using quantified (objective) budget line-item assumptions (explanations and justifications) that are properly seasonalized (and not straight lined) and those assumptions have been used in the creation of an operating budget (and perhaps a multiple year economic model over time), one is able to center-in on actual results when compared to the budget forecast (plan).

- Timing. When does a timing issue become a real change? There is no hard and fast answer. However, from experience I generally rely on quarterly updates as a major indicator of real change as suggested earlier. If direct reports have been given both *responsibility* and a commensurate amount of *power* for goal achievement, then they should also be leading the discussion in terms of objective reporting, analysis, along with a plan and recommendations and as to how to get the underperforming outlier results back in line with plan. Unfortunately, the analysis, plan, and recommendations for correction are often left to the executive leaders and their analysts. Not having operations staff involved in this process is not an indication of effective management.

- Construct a dashboard. The easiest way to build a dashboard is to use either *Excel* or *Tables* inside of a Word document. The advantage of using Excel is the ability to use formulas and update. Use icons such as smile, blank, and frown icons to quickly indicate position. Here is an example of a simplified dashboard for Golf Course Maintenance for January and February (created in Tables). Enter the words, *dashboard scorecard* into Google to see examples of dashboards. Tip: Ensure that the dashboard is kept simple enough to maintain and that it provides adequate detail (stay 1,000 feet above the property with map tacks). Over time, have a dashboard for each department manager and sports professional.

Figure 07: Golf Course Maintenance Dashboard

	Goal	Actual Jan	Plan Jan	Icon	Actual Feb	Plan Feb	Icon
1	Greens avg Stimp	8	7	:)	8	8	:|
2	Payroll	$71K	$72K	:)	$78K	$75K	:(
3	Sand, seeds, fert	$6K	$7K	:(	$5K	$8K	:)
4	Rolling stock ready for use	100%	100%	:|	75%	100%	:(
5	FTEs	13	15	:)	16	16	:|

Working With Dashboards

Using the dashboard should complement the budget variance meetings. In referring to the example dashboard for Golf Course Maintenance, it is apparent that the dashboard provides (by design) an incomplete picture of that department in that it does not report all line item expenses (remember that there is no income attributed to Golf Course Maintenance), no actual versus budget variance numbers with percentages, and no year-to-date (cumulative) actual versus budget variance numbers and percentages.

However, the dashboard does its work: It functions as a snapshot of how the department functioned in its designated five key items. Moreover, it contains information relative to major non-financial goals (speed of greens, availability of rolling stock, and headcount) that would not be included in the financials. In that manner, it provides a quick look and complements the monthly financial package in a manner that would be reflected in customer survey data.

The responsibility of maintaining the dashboards should lie with the department heads and sports professionals. After a format is agreed to as to how the dashboard will be reviewed (assume during the monthly budget variance meeting) each department head and sports professional should be prompted as to the order of review and expectations for analysis to be completed prior to the meeting.

Reporting example for reviews and variance meetings

- Revenues (assuming the area has income). Review any line item with a variance (either positive or negative) of 10% to plan when comparing actual results to budget. Identify the cause of the variance and form an opinion as to whether the variance is due to a timing issue (and will therefore correct over the coming months) or if the variance will continue and therefore become permanent. Explain the cause along with a proposed action plan if the variance becomes permanent.

- Expenses. Review the trial balance with the Controller for any line item with a variance (either positive or negative) of 10% to plan. Identify the cause of the variance and form an opinion as to whether the variance is due to a timing issue (and will therefore correct over the coming months) or if the variance will continue and therefore become permanent. Explain the cause along with a proposed action plan if the variance becomes permanent.

- Non-financial goals. Review each goal's actual performance for the period compared to forecasted performance. Formulate an opinion and action plan for dealing with underperformance on any goal (negative variance). Analyze and explain over performance on any goal (positive variance).

- Timing (blip) issues, as a rule of thumb, should correct within one to three months. Issues considered due to timing, but trending longer than three consecutive months, are good candidates for re-classifying as permanent change.

A note about variances. Many organizations dwell on negative variances and celebrate positive (revenue) variances. While understandable for the short term, positive variances should receive as much scrutiny as negative variances. Both positive and negative variances suggest errors in forecast budgeting. Errors in forecast budgeting may come from sandbagging, failure to conduct due diligence, failure to put for the required effort, lack of access to information, and/ or lack of reporting history (in newer operations). Conducting analyses on variances will aid in the preciseness of the budgeting process in the future.

Ensuring the Strategic Plan is used

Organizations often go through a strategic planning process only to allow day-to-day operations to edge out the strategy in terms of importance. As the strategy ages without updates, it begins to feel like a dusty and tired burden instead of the exciting and powerful lead-sled-dog status it deserves.

- Get a wide variety of people involved. Ask questions. Solicit opinions. Make everyone feel like they are part of the process. Let them know that what they have to say is important to the future of the organization.

- Keep the strategy simple. The work that goes into creating the strategy is time consuming and detailed. However, the product that filters down from all of the questions, analyses, and work should be simple. A strategic plan is a guide that serves like a roadmap in getting the entity or department from where it is presently to where it wants to be in the future. This is not a business plan that explains the business to the customers. It is an action piece.

- Communicate with the staff. Summarize portions of the strategic plan. Let everyone know (in summary format) what was said, what was decided, and when people might begin to notice changes. Use big picture language to describe what the property is presently and what it will become in the future. Do not be afraid to report what the organization is not going to become in the future.

- Refer to and publicize the strategic plan. The strategic plan should become *the* foundational element. The strategy should be the primary driver for everything the organization thinks, says, and does. The executive leadership team, department heads, and all contributors to publicity should reference and draw subject material from the strategic plan. Make the strategy important. The strategic plan should be the first document referred to before the annual budget process begins and before adding, changing, or discontinuing any product or service.

- Charge the long range planning committee. The long range planning committee, in the absence of a strategic planning committee should assume the role of *strategy gatekeeper*. If we assume that an organization merges the functions of its strategic planning and long range planning committees into one effort, it is that committee whose function helps ensure the future success of the chosen strategy. It becomes one of their most important functions to serve as the gatekeepers for proposed programs and major changes. It is also incumbent on this committee to serve as a consistent and reliable committee for making sure that the agreed upon strategic plan is followed closely and achieved.

Article 01:

The Effect of Leader Values on Behavior

Article authors: Edward A. Merritt and Dennis Reynolds

Abstract

The purpose of this study was to examine the interpersonal work values of leaders in work settings and to determine the influence of such variables on their consequential behavior. A total of 301 participant managers were drawn from private industry. A survey questionnaire, personal interviews, and unobtrusive observation methods were utilized. Checks were used to verify that the data were free from regional and/organizational bias, test for response stability, and guard against response bias. Support was found for the hypothesis that manager values and certain demographic variables of interest will lead to manager behavior. Applications, limitations, and research implications are discussed.

Introduction

Values are attitudes about what is correct and incorrect, fair and unfair, honorable and dishonorable (Yukl, 1998). Examples include fairness, integrity, trustworthiness, courtesy, and support. Values are salient because they influence manager choices, awareness, and behavior, which, in turn influence and shape the work place. Manager values and their consequential behavior play an important part in shaping organizations. In this research, work values held by leaders were investigated.

A second concept that is addressed is that of managerial behavior. The concept of managerial behavior suggests that managers may use certain behavior in order to contend with the varying demands of their positions.

There is a gap in the research that addresses work values and behavior of managers, the subject of this study.

Background

Values are fundamental convictions that a certain mode of behavior or end result state is preferable to a converse mode or end result existence (Rokeach, 1973). Values have nested within them an element of judgment in that they are a reflection of an individual's or group's belief about what is right, desirable, or good. Values have attributes regarding content and attributes that regulate intensity. The content attribute states that some behavior or end result is desirable. The intensity attribute states the importance of such behavior or end state. By ranking values by intensity, an idea of a person's individual or work group's value system can be obtained (Bales, 1999; Bales & Cohen, 1979).

Values are important to the study of management and organizational culture because they help establish a foundation for the understanding of attitudes and motivation and because they influence perceptions, attitudes, and behavior (Connor & Becker, 1994). Individuals enter organizations with interpretations and ideas of what should and should not be. Furthermore, such interpretations imply that some behavior or end states are preferable to others. As a result, individuals' value systems may be incongruent with those of the organization. With an increasing demand by consumers for a higher level and quality of service (Cline, 1996; Coyle & Dale, 1993; Zeithaml, Parasuraman, & Berry, 1990), the effect of values on employee organizational culture becomes a key issue to help ensure that individual value systems are aligned with those of the employing organization's staff, in order to meet such demand.

Individual values as a person's established, enduring beliefs and preferences about what is worthwhile and desirable will differ to some degree across managers (Rokeach, 1973). Behavior is the manner of acting in a given circumstance—what a person says and how he or she says it—as observed by that person and others. Behavior is influenced by a person's values and his or her particular circumstances (Bales, 1970). Understanding that values tend to reflect important events and influences can be helpful in gaining insight into and predicting behavior.

This study, then, is designed to determine the work values of leaders and to study the relationship of this variable to the outcome variable of manager behavior.

Literature Review

In 1956, Bronowski stated that values are deep interpersonal illuminations of justice and injustice, good and bad, and means and ends. Expanding this, Rokeach (1973) defined values as abiding ideology that one mode of conduct or end state is preferable to another mode of conduct or end state. Hofstede (1991) interpreted this definition more holistically and suggested that values are manifestations of one's basic approach toward life—broad tendencies to favor specific states over others—to which Schwartz (1996) added that values equate to trans-situational goals that vary in importance, and serve as guiding principles. Yukl (1998) expanded this further and defined values as attitudes about what is right and wrong, ethical and unethical, moral and immoral; examples include fairness, honesty, loyalty, courtesy, and cooperation. Coalescing the preceding definitions,

Bales (1999) defined values as enduring, trait-like, and high-order abstractions in the mind of a person, which correlate fantasies, images, perceptions, and concepts. Central to the study reported here, then, this definition suggests that values are an individual's lens through which he or she interprets experiences and their meanings. Moreover, this understanding of values underscores the construct's centrality to the self concept and suggests values influence predominately behavior whether or not the individual thinks about values (Bales, 1999; Feather, 1992).

The literature review substantiates Bales' work in integrating interpersonal behavior and values. Many researchers treat behavior as phenomena characteristic of developing lists of traits. Others, such as McDougall (1918), and Lewin (1951), theorized that behavior is part of a higher-order system. In this higher-order system, values are considered to be more complex than behavior and the product of multiple filters. For example, McClelland (1980) attested that values guide interpersonal behavior, and stated that they are best obtained from questionnaires and non-obtrusive observational methods. Triandis (1989) posited that values are a critical determinant of social behavior while Elizur et al. (1991) asserted that values motivate goal-directed behavior. More pointedly, Hofstede (1980, 1991) suggested that values determine the meanings of people's behavior.

Kluckhohn and Strodtbeck (1961) offer, from an anthropological perspective, their definition of value orientations as being complex, rank-ordered principles developing from cognitive, affective, and directive elements. And, such influences provide order and direction for the ever-changing situations. Feather (1992) contends that individual values, as they relate to behavior and social interaction, were largely ignored by psychologists in favor of behaviorism, personality theories, and group dynamics.

Bales (1999) suggested that behavior is observed. And, that once observed, certain evaluations are placed on such behavior. The evaluations inform a behavioral response to the original initiated act. These evaluations can be treated as sets of values held by both the observer and the person being observed. This builds on Bales' (1985) earlier contentions that values' primary focus is the evaluation tool for the behavior of the self and others in interaction. Thus, values and behavior are closely intertwined. Empirical evidence as to what moderates such a relationship, however, is lacking.

Methodology

This study utilized an integrated field theory of social psychology developed by Bales (Bales & Cohen, 1979) as a theoretical foundation and as a measurement system to investigate managerial work values and behavior. Field theory can be defined as a broad set of theories that focus on the total psychological environment and attempt to explain behavior because of interactions between people (Reber, 1995). The isomorphic properties of Bales' model make it possible to assess values and behavior using the same three-dimensional, factor-analytic framework (Bales, 1985, 1988; Bales & Cohen, 1979).

Using the values and behavior scale forms, participant managers' direct reports (such as department heads) considered the actual values and behavior of their managing supervisor when answering statements. The results of respondent statements were then examined in order to understand how these values related to the outcome variable of behavior.

The three bipolar dimensions for both the values and behavior scales are classified by using names that relate to their location in the model that resembles a three-dimensional schema:

- The Upward-Downward (U-D) dimension.

- The Positive-Negative (P-N) dimension.

- The Forward-Backward (F-B) dimension.

The three dimensions are measured independently of each other. For example, the U-D dimension is not affected by ratings on P-N or F-B. On the other hand, each of the dimensions is bipolar. For example, if a value or behavior measures as more of a dimension, such as *up* on the U-D dimension, that score, because of its bipolar nature, indicates a lack of *down* (Bachman, 1988; Hogan, 1988; Koenigs & Cowen, 1988). Therefore, the model measures the two ends of each of the three bipolar dimensions as well as the intermediate points between the ends.

First, the direct reports rated current work values. Second, the direct reports rated on-the-job behavior. The two questionnaires elicit responses about perceptions of the current interpersonal work values and behavior of their supervising managers.

Importance of the Study

This study has theoretical importance in that it will help provide a better understanding of managerial work-related values and behavior in the club industry. In this context, we contend that values help mold and direct the workplace behavior. Offering practical importance, this study explores whether the identification of groups of meanings expressed through values produce elements that may help in understanding an organization's behavior.

These groups of meanings are the foundations of behavior expressed as values and principles reflected in customs, traditions, and symbols. The central meanings are not discrete points. Instead, they represent ranges, which are recognized within an organization. In other words, values and behavior reflect a unique organization-wide variation in culture, which is as defined and as basic as is the variation in biological phenomena (Kluckhohn & Strodtbeck, 1961).

Previous research suggests that a blending of the positive components from the three dimensions of values and behavior in the workplace typically correlate with effective managerial outcomes (Bales & Isenberg, 1980; Hogan, 1988; Koenigs & Cowen, 1988). The question of interest involved investigating whether managerial values may predict behavior.

Findings

The research question: Do manager values and certain demographic variables of interest predict U-D, P-N, and F-B manager behavior?

Support was found for the hypothesis that manager values and certain demographic variables of interest will predict manager behavior.

Behavior U-D

The U-D (Up-Down) dimension of behavior scores can be predicted by the U-D dimension of values. This suggests that manager scores on the U dimensional element defined as *values on dominance* values or the D dimensional element defined as *values on submissiveness* values will reflect a positive relationship with the U dimensional element defined as *dominant* behavior or the D dimensional element defined as *submissive* behavior. Moreover, managers who have value sets that are more dominant—demonstrating value sets focusing on individual financial success, personal prominence, and power—will likely display more dominant behavior. Managers who have value sets that are more submissive—demonstrating value sets focusing on giving up personal needs and desires, passivity—will likely display more submissive behavior.

The U-D dimension of behavior scores can be predicted by the interaction of the U-D dimension of values and the P-N (Positive-Negative) dimension of values. This suggests that at any particular values U-D level, there is an inverse relationship between the interaction with values P-N in predicting the U-D dimension of behavior. Moreover, in the interaction, as the U dimensional element defined as *values on dominance* values element increases in values U-D, the P dimensional element defined as *values on friendly behavior* values in values P-N decreases. An inverse relationship is indicated between the interaction term and the U-D dimension of behaviors. This suggests that the interaction of managers who have more dominant values and who are also less friendly will exhibit more submissive behaviors.

The implications for application suggest that senior managers and boards of governors should carefully examine their hiring practices. If, for example, a more dominant manager is identified who is also less friendly, the corresponding behavior will likely be more submissive. On the other hand, if a more submissive manager is identified who is also friendlier, the finding suggests that the manager's behavior will be more dominant.

The U-D (Up-Down) dimension of behavior scores can be predicted by annualized bonus pay average. This suggests that managers who make more in bonus (the scale was an ordinal, continuous scale, which was used to rank-order level of bonus from less to more, including, 1. *no bonus* to 7. *30 percent or more of base*) are also more dominant. Moreover, managers who make less in bonus are also more submissive.

The implications for application suggest that senior managers and boards of governors should carefully examine their bonus programs. If a more dominant manager is desirable for the club, consider increasing the bonus plan to the upper end of the scale toward 30 percent or more of base. If a less dominant (more submissive) manager is desirable, consider decreasing the bonus plan to the lower end of the scale toward zero.

Behavior P-N

The P-N (Positive-Negative) dimension of behavior scores can be predicted by the P-N dimension of values. This suggests that manager scores on the P dimensional element defined as *values on friendly behavior* or the N dimensional element defined as *values on unfriendly behavior* will reflect a positive relationship with the P dimensional element defined as *friendly* behavior or the N dimensional element defined as *unfriendly* behavior. Moreover, managers who are more friendly—demonstrating value sets focusing on equality and democratic participation in decision making—will likely display more friendly behavior. Managers who are more unfriendly—demonstrating value sets focusing on self-protection, self-interest first, and self-sufficiency—will likely display more unfriendly behavior.

The P-N (Positive-Negative) dimension of behavior scores can be predicted by the F-B (Forward-Backward) dimension of values. This suggests that manager scores on the F dimensional element defined as *values on accepting task orientation of established authority* or the B dimensional element defined as *values on opposing task orientation of established authority* will reflect a positive relationship with the P dimensional element defined as *friendly* behavior or the N dimensional element defined as *unfriendly* behavior. Moreover, managers who are more oriented toward accepting the task orientation of established authority—demonstrating value sets focusing on conservative, established, correct ways of doing things—will likely display more friendly behavior. Managers who have value sets that are more oriented toward opposing task orientation of established authority—demonstrating value sets focusing on change to new procedures, different values, and creativity—will likely display more unfriendly behavior.

The P-N (Positive-Negative) dimension of behavior scores can be predicted by Marital status. This suggests that married managers are friendlier than single managers. Moreover, single managers are more unfriendly.

The implications for application suggest that senior managers and boards of governors should consider their hiring criteria. If a friendlier manager is desirable for the club, consider hiring a manager who is married. If a less friendly manager is desirable, consider hiring a single manager.

Behavior F-B

The F-B (Forward-Backward) dimension of behavior scores can be predicted by the U-D (Up-Down) dimension of values. This suggests that manager scores on the U dimensional element defined as *values on dominance* or the D dimensional element defined as *values on submissiveness* will reflect a positive relationship with the F dimensional element defined as *instrumentally controlled* behavior or the B dimensional element defined as *emotionally expressive* behavior. Moreover, managers who have value sets, which are more dominant, will be more instrumentally controlled. Managers who have value sets, which are more submissive, will be more emotionally expressive.

The F-B (Forward-Backward) dimension of behavior scores can be predicted by the P-N (Positive-Negative) dimension of values. This suggests that manager scores on the P dimensional element defined as *values on friendly behavior* or the N dimensional element defined as *values on unfriendly behavior* will reflect an inverse relationship with the F dimensional element defined as *instrumentally controlled* behavior or the B dimensional element defined as *emotionally expressive* behavior. Moreover, managers who have value sets, which are more positive—oriented toward values on friendly behavior, equality, and democratic participation in decision making—will be more emotionally expressive. Managers who are more negative—oriented toward values on unfriendly behavior, self-protection, self-interest first, and self-sufficiency—will be more instrumentally controlled.

The F-B (Forward-Backward) dimension of behavior scores can be predicted by the F-B dimension of values. This suggests that manager scores on the F dimensional element defined as *values on accepting task orientation of established authority* or the B dimensional element defined as *values on opposing task orientation of established authority* will reflect a positive relationship with scores on the F dimensional element defined as *instrumentally controlled* behavior or the B dimensional element defined as *emotionally expressive* behavior. Moreover, managers who have value sets oriented toward accepting task orientation of established authority—conservative, established, and correct ways of doing things—will be more instrumentally controlled. Managers who have value sets, which are more oriented toward opposing task orientation of established authority—change to new procedures, different values, and creativity—will be more emotionally expressive.

The F-B (Forward-Backward) dimension of behavior scores can be predicted by the interaction term V_U-D*V_F-B. This suggests that at any particular values U-D level, there is a positive relationship between the interaction with values F-B in predicting the F-B dimension of behavior. This suggests that the interaction of managers who have more dominant values and who demonstrate values on accepting task orientation of established authority would also likely exhibit behavior that is more emotionally expressive.

The implications for application suggest that senior managers and boards of governors should carefully examine their hiring practices. If, for example, a more dominant manager is identified who also demonstrates more values on accepting task orientation of established authority, the corresponding behavior will be more emotionally expressive. On the other hand, if a more submissive manager is identified, who also demonstrates more values on opposing task orientation of established authority, the finding suggests that the manager's behavior will be more instrumentally controlled.

The F-B (Forward-Backward) dimension of behavior scores can be predicted by type of ownership. This suggests that managers whose clubs are owned by the members are more instrumentally controlled. Moreover, managers whose clubs are owned by corporations, developers, individuals, or others are more emotionally expressive.

The implications for application suggest that senior managers and boards of governors should carefully examine the perceived fit when hiring a manager who is crossing over from a member-owned club to a corporate-owned club or vice versa. Managers from member-owned clubs are likely to keep their emotional arousal more closely in check, while managers from corporate-owned clubs feel freer to express their feelings. It is reasonable to suggest that due to these attributes, the move by a manager from a corporate-owned to member-owned club may be a more difficult transition than from member-owned to corporate-owned club.

The F-B (Forward-Backward) dimension of behavior scores can be predicted by number of members. This suggests that managers at clubs that have fewer members are more emotionally expressive. Moreover, managers at clubs that have more members are more instrumentally controlled.

Again, the implications for application suggest that senior managers and boards of governors should carefully examine the perceived fit when hiring a manager who is crossing over from a club with fewer members to a club with more members or vice versa. Managers from clubs with fewer members feel freer to express their feelings. Managers from clubs with more members are likely to keep their emotional arousal more closely in check. Due to these attributes, it is reasonable to suggest that the move by a manager from club with fewer members may be a more difficult transition than from a club with more members.

Limitations

The goal of this study was to detect relationships that might exist among the independent and dependent variables. Therefore, the nature of the study was classified as correlational instead of causal (Tuckman, 1998) and the type of study suggested a one-shot or one-time investigation correlational survey design instead of an experimental design (Campbell & Stanley, 1963). The study design therefore, can only suggest bases for correlational relationships that may exist.

This was the first time that leader values and behavior had been studied in this fashion. Therefore, conducting this study opens a research stream for organizational behavior. Additional studies in this area of organizational behavior would have helped suggest hypothesized relationships more precisely. Furthermore, this study included 301 managers from across the six geographic regions. Additional participants may have added to the validity of the findings.

The nature of this study as being cross-sectional rather than longitudinal may also be viewed as a limitation. However, the job at hand was examining leader values and behavior at one point—the situation—as described by Bales (1999). Moreover, as suggested by Merritt (1995), almost one half (44 percent) of leaders planned on leaving their present jobs within three years. (Note: This study found that almost one third [32.9 percent] of leaders surveyed planned on leaving their present jobs within three years.) Therefore, concern arose about erosion of sample size due to turnover. Concern also existed about managers' willingness to participate in multiple versions of the study over time, as was suggested during the club visits.

Significant differences between how the direct reports rated their managing supervisors and how the managing supervisors rated themselves were found. Future research could investigate this gap from the perspective of management development. This could be of benefit to senior managers who counsel managers in the employee review process.

This study included managers from six geographic areas included in the CMAA regions. However, expansion of CMAA's boundaries to include an international chapter of clubs and interest in international expansion by corporate-owned clubs suggests a possibility for future study. It might also prove interesting to study the relationships of values to behavior from a cultural perspective. For example, managers from the present study could be compared to international managers—expatriots from the U.S. and home-country managers outside the U.S. Furthermore, these findings suggested in the present study beg the question: Will these findings hold across other sectors of the hospitality industry such as hotels and resorts, restaurants, and contract management? A next logical step could be to replicate the present study to the hotel industry and compare findings between industries.

Concluding Remarks

This study achieved two significant purposes: First, it enabled us to gain insight into leader values and how these values relate to behavior. In doing so, to the findings contribute to the stream of literature and further gusset the foundation of Bales' theory. Second, the findings fulfill many formative steps toward developing a model that integrates values, behavior, and—as moderators—demographic variables. Ultimately, these findings represent yet another small step at understanding human behavior in the workplace.

References

Bachman, W. (1988). Nice guys finish first: A SYMLOG analysis of U.S. naval commands. In R.B. Polley, A.P. Hare, & P.J. Stone (Eds.), *The SYMLOG practitioner: Applications of small group research* (pp.133-153). New York: Praeger.

Bales, R. (1970). *Personality and Interpersonal Behavior.* New York City: Holt, Rinehart, and Winston, Inc.

Bales, R. (1985). The new field theory in social psychology. *International Journal of Small Group Research*, 1, 1-18.

Bales, R. (1988). A new overview of the SYMLOG system. In R.B. Polley, A.P. Hare, & P.J. Stone (Eds.), *The SYMLOG practitioner: Applications of small group research* (pp. 319-344). New York: Praeger.

Bales, R. (1999). *Social interaction systems, theory and measurement.* New Brunswick, NJ: Transaction Press.

Bales, R., & Cohen, S. (1979). *SYMLOG: A system for the multiple level observation of groups.* New York: The Free Press.

Bales, R, & Isenberg, D. (1980). SYMLOG and leadership theory. In J.G. Hunt, U. Sekaran, & C.A. Schriesheim (Eds.), *Leadership: Beyond establishment views* (pp. 165-195). Carbondale, IL: Southern Illinois University Press.

Bronowski, J. (1956). *Science and human values.* New York: Harper & Row.

Campbell, D, & Stanley, J. (1963). *Experimental and quasi-experimental designs for research.* Chicago: Rand McNally College Publishing.

Cline, R. (1996). Hospitality 2000: A view to the millennium. *Lodging Hospitality* (August), 20-26.

Connor, P. & Becker, B. (1994). Personal values and management: What do we need to know and why don't we know more? *Journal of Management Inquiry*, March, 68.

Coyle, M., & Dale, B. (1993). Quality in the hospitality industry: A study. *International Journal of Hospitality Management*, 12, 141-153.

Elizur, D., Borg, I., Hunt, R., & Beck, L. (1991). The structure of work values: A cross cultural comparison. *Journal of Organizational Behavior*, 12, 21-38.

Feather, N. (1992). Values, valences, expectations, and actions. *Journal of Social Issues*, 48 (2), 109-124.

Hofstede, G. (1980). *Culture's consequences: International differences in work-related values*. Beverly Hills, CA: Sage.

Hofstede, G. (1991). *Cultures and organizations: Software of the mind*. London, UK: McGraw-Hill.

Hogan, D. (1988). The SYMLOG leadership profile as a predictor of managerial performance. In R.B. Polley, A.P. Hare, & P.J. Stone (Eds.), *The SYMLOG practitioner* (pp. 191-210). New York: Praeger.

Kluckhohn F., & Strodtbeck, F. (1961). *Variations in value orientations*. Evanston, IL: Row Peterson.

Koenigs, R., & Cowen, M. (1988). SYMLOG as action research. In R.B. Polley, A.P. Hare, & P.J. Stone (Eds.), *The SYMLOG practitioner: applications of small group research* (pp. 61-87). New York: Praeger.

Lewin, K. (1951). *Field theory in social science*. New York: Harper and Row.

McClelland, D. (1980). Motive dispositions: The merits of operant and respondent measures. In L. Wheeler (Ed.), *Review of Personality and Social Psychology*, 1, 10-41.

McDougall, W. (1918). *Social psychology*. Boston: John W. Luce.

Merritt, E. (1995). *Hospitality management: A study of burnout in private club management*. Master's thesis: Pepperdine University, Malibu, CA.

Reber, A. (1995). *The penguin dictionary of psychology* (2nd ed.). New York: Penguin Books.

Schwartz, S. (1996). Value priorities and behavior: Applying a theory of integrated value systems. In C. Seligman, J. M. Olson, & M. P. Zanna (Eds.), *The psychology of values: The Ontario symposium* (Vol. 8, pp. 1-24). Mahwah, NJ: Lawrence Erlbaum.

Triandis, H. (1989). The self and social behavior in differing cultural contexts. *Psychological Review*, 96, 506-520.

Tuckman, B. (1998). *Conducting Educational Research*. New York: Harcourt Brace Jovanovich.

Yukl, G. (1998). *Leadership in organizations* (4th ed.). Englewood Cliffs, NJ: Prentice-Hall.

Article 02:

Burnout in Private Club Management

Article author: Edward A. Merritt

Summary

Club management is a difficult segment of the hospitality industry because of the emotional energy it consumes. The continuous amount of social effort required by managers represents extensive amounts of emotional labor. There is a high degree of mental and psychological work involved in treating every person and situation as individually important.

When managers reach the point of being used up and burned-out from too much emotional labor, their hearts are no longer in their work. Quality begins to slip. The staff and members react negatively to such a downturn, which further exacerbates a difficult situation.

As demonstrated by the results of this study, many managers suffer high levels of burnout working their way to the top. However, successfully reaching the top—becoming a general manager—does not always create a significant drop in burnout.

Different types of responsibilities seem to function differently as stressors. One way to categorize this variable is responsibility for people versus responsibility for things. The effects of long-term stress can lead to burnout and turnover.

According to Maslach, burnout is a multidimensional construct of emotional exhaustion, depersonalization, and reduced personal accomplishment that can occur among individuals who work extensively with others under considerable time pressures. Furthermore, burnout is particularly relevant to individuals when working with people in emotionally charged situations. From that reference, it seems likely that club managers are prime candidates for burnout.

Turnover is a major topic throughout this study for these reasons: Turnover is a major contributor to burnout for managers because of the constant need for recruiting and training of new workers. Moreover, turnover is often the result of what happens to managers after they become burned-out. Therefore, turnover is both a cause, and an effect of burnout. Hospitality turnover averages well over 100 percent annually as an industry. This means that employees stay on the job, on the average, about one year.

Turnover has become a more serious challenge recently as the supply of available workers has dwindled. As a result, the industry now finds itself filling jobs with almost anyone willing to work. Sometimes, jobs cannot be filled at all, further compounding the stress levels of managers.

This study includes the feelings of management staff of private clubs throughout the United States. Its purpose was to determine the demographics and other information that, when compared to the results a burnout inventory (The Maslach Burnout Inventory), identified a manager profile more susceptible to burnout than that of other managers.

The Maslach Burnout Inventory (MBI) is used to assess the three aspects of the burnout syndrome: Emotional Exhaustion, Depersonalization, and lack of Personal Accomplishment. Maslach contends that burnout exists in each of us by degrees. From that viewpoint, it seems that stress and burnout are more closely related than separate.

By Maslach's measures, high burnout is reflected in high scores in Emotional Exhaustion and Depersonalization and in low scores in Personal Accomplishment. Average burnout is reflected in average scores on the three subscales. Low burnout is reflected in low scores in Emotional Exhaustion and Depersonalization and in high scores in Personal Accomplishment.

Overall Sample

The Emotional Exhaustion question group for this study totaled 20.09—Average when compared to the Overall Categorization.

Depersonalization scored 8.81 for the study, also Average. Personal Accomplishment also ranked Average range with 37.03.

Cross tabulating results of the Burnout Inventory by demographic selectors, the study identified both expected and unexpected findings. A summary of some of those findings follows:

- Clubhouse Managers are the single-most burned-out group.

- Golf Club Managers experience highest burnout; Athletic Club Managers, the least.

- Managers with less than 5 years in the club profession are the most burned-out. Managers with the most years in the industry are the least burned-out.

- Managers with the least amount of time at their clubs are most burned-out in each subscale.

- Managers that work the least amount of hours per week are the most burned-out. Those that work the most are the least burned-out.

- The youngest Managers rate far above anyone else in burnout. The oldest Managers show the least burnout.

- Men are considerably more burned-out than women.

- Managers from the North experience more burnout than anyone else. Managers from the West experience the least.

- Single, Previously Married Managers exhibit the lowest burnout; Married Managers exhibit the most.

- Managers planning to stay at their clubs less than 1 year are the most burned-out.

- Managers with the fewest members are the most burned-out; Managers with the most members are the least.

- Managers at clubs not performing well are the most burned-out. Managers reporting club performance as better than in past show the lowest amount.

- Managers predicting the industry as doing worse than in past are the most burned-out. Managers expecting it to do better are the least.

- Managers predicting their clubs will do better than in past show the least amount of burnout. Managers predicting worse, show the most.

The growth in numbers of private clubs creates an increase in need for more and effective managers. Boards of governors and senior managers that supervise private club managers should understand burnout's causes and effects. However, identifying and documenting problems alone does not lead to solutions—it serves instead as an important first step. From there, boards and senior managers must examine data to isolate factors that contribute to burnout, and develop a plan to reduce or eliminate such factors.

Introduction

Dealing with members and employees is different from solitary work where you are developing ideas, working with numbers, or operating equipment. To manage a club effectively, you must be visible and engaged. You work with expectations and misunderstandings. You deal with personalities—you must cope with their frustrations. It can be difficult, and therefore, stressful.

Physical Versus Mental Labor

Some jobs are difficult because of the physical labor involved. People must move things or perpetually be on the go. Some of this activity is involved in managing clubs. But that is not the answer to why managing is difficult. Club management is challenging because of the emotional energy it consumes. The intangible quality of communicating with and working well with people—the social effort—consumes an extensive amount of emotional labor.

Managers must greet people constantly and enthusiastically; and they must serve and please. Managers must treat people as special. There is a great deal of mental and psychological work involved in treating every person and every situation as being individually important.

Working with people can be gratifying when it all goes well. However, a manager still must invest great amounts of energy into such a process. The emotional expenditure is much greater when people become uncooperative. Dealing with these situations requires physical stamina; in addition, such situations test a manager's psychological stamina. Eventually, it can lead to emotional fatigue.

When managers reach the point of being burned-out from too much emotional labor, it shows in their work. Quality begins to slip. The staff and members react negatively to such a downturn, which creates an even more difficult situation. It can become a vicious cycle where everyone loses—the manager, the club, and the member or employee. To a large degree, members measure the quality of a club by the quality of service. In their eyes, the managers and staff are the organization. A manager helps shape that reputation every day. That amount of responsibility can be exhilarating in the sense that a manager has great flexibility to orchestrate a successful operation. On the other hand, it can also become a negative reflection upon that same manager when the club fails to meet member expectations.

Changing population demographics are causing hospitality organizations to place more emphasis on employee retention and productivity than ever before. As the availability of labor dwindles, the focus is on organizational climate. Clubs need to know that there is a direct relationship between employee withdrawal (including turnover, absenteeism, and burnout) and job satisfaction.[1] As demonstrated by the results of this study, many managers suffer high levels of burnout on their way to the top. Achievement of a general manager's position does not translate to a significant overall drop in feelings of burnout.

Stress and Burnout

Interest in burnout in the hospitality industry has become widespread in recent years. The demand for quick financial fixes, a nagging club president, low job security, and the constancy of working closely with people in difficult situations are some of the causes of such interest. Over time many managers leave clubs because they feel burned-out by the hectic pace.

During the past two decades, the term burnout has become commonplace. Burnout might be defined as psychological distress that may develop into physical illness when no relief appears to be forthcoming. Personal definitions of stress differ widely. The club manager may view stress as frustration; a pilot sees it as a problem of concentration; a biochemist thinks of it as a chemical event. Nelson and Quick define stress as the unconscious preparation to fight or flee a person experiences when faced with any demand.[2] A variety of dissimilar situations—work effort, fatigue, uncertainty, fear, or emotional

---

1 Gary K. Vallen, "Organizational Climate and Burnout," Cornell Hotel and Restaurant Administration Quarterly February 1993: 54.
2 Nelson, Debra L. and Quick, James C., Organizational Behavior (St. Paul, MN: West Publishing Company, 1994) 188.

arousal—are capable of producing stress. Therefore, to isolate a single factor as the sole cause of stress is extremely difficult.

Past Studies

Burnout is perhaps easier to observe than to define. In an effort to define burnout, one author offered these insightful comments:

> *Billions of dollars are lost each year . . . because of workers who can no longer function in, or cope successfully with, their jobs. More than just the monetary loss . . . is the loss suffered by the people in the process. In recent years the signs and symptoms of these problems, i.e., turnover, absenteeism, lowered productivity, psychological problems, etc., have become increasingly predominant in our society. . . . To attempt to define the condition itself is difficult. . . . This condition . . . can be defined as all of those . . . problems on the job that result in a negative interface between individuals and environments as people attempt to adapt within the organization.*[3]

Freudenberger was the first to use the term burnout to denote a state of physical and emotional depletion that results from conditions of work.[4] Maslach used the term to describe an over-extension of self that evolves into a severe loss of energy and deterioration in performance.[5]

According to Maslach, burnout is a multidimensional construct of emotional exhaustion, depersonalization, and reduced personal accomplishment that can occur among individuals who work extensively with others under considerable time pressures.[6] From that reference, it seems club managers are prime candidates for burnout.

> *A key aspect of the burnout syndrome is increased feelings of emotional exhaustion; as emotional resources are depleted, workers feel they are no longer able to give of themselves at a psychological level. Another*

---

3 Vallen "Organizational Climate and Burnout." 55.

4 H. J. Freudenberger, "Staff Burnout," Journal of Environmental Issues Number 30 1974: 159-65.

5 Christine Maslach, "Burned-out," Human Behavior Number 5 1976: 17-22.

6 Christine Maslach and Susan E. Jackson, Maslach Burnout Inventory Manual, 2nd edition (Palo Alto, California: Consulting Psychologists Press, 1986) 1.

aspect of the burnout syndrome is the development of depersonalization—i.e., negative, cynical attitudes and feelings about one's clients. . . . The development of depersonalization appears to be related to the experience of emotional exhaustion, and so these two aspects should be corrected. A third aspect of the burnout syndrome, a feeling of reduced personal accomplishments, refers to the tendency to evaluate oneself negatively, particularly with regard to one's work with clients. Workers may feel unhappy about themselves and dissatisfied with their accomplishments on the job.[7]

Burnout, as studied by those early researchers, was assumed to be particularly relevant to individuals whose work focused on working with people in emotionally charged situations. Later, studies involving a psychological profile frequently represented in managerial occupations found that burnout was also associated with increased mental demands.[8] It seems the dimensions of the burnout described in these two types of job situations are different.

Statement of The Problem

Burnout leads to substantial direct and indirect business operating costs.[9] The consequences of burnout are potentially dangerous for the staff, the members, and the clubs in which they work.[10] Research of Lang; Reynolds and Tabacchi; and Krone, Tabacchi, and Farber reveals that other hospitality-industry managers experience destructive feelings that should be addressed. It was clear the subject of burnout warranted further investigation.

About the Study

The Research Question

What is the sample profile of the most, down to the least burned out club manager?

Purpose

The purpose of the burnout study is to rank the variables identified in focus groups to compare to the burnout instrument, and thereby create

---

7 Maslach and Jackson 1.

8 Maslach and Jackson 1.

9 Krone, Tabacchi, and Farber 58-63.

10 Maslach and Jackson 1.

a sample profile to determine the most, down to the least burned-out manager. This study reveals the results of the survey and documents what managers had to say about the effects of burnout. Additionally, the survey, through cross tabulation, is interpreted as to its possible meanings and ramifications. Finally, insight gained during personal interviews, comments, and conversations is shared with the reader, as are recommendations that can be implemented to reduce burnout in private clubs.

Participants

This study was conducted among management-level staff working at private clubs. Typical position titles include General Manager, Manager, Clubhouse Manager, and Assistant Manager. One hundred fifty-two managers (n=152) of private clubs throughout the United States participated in the study. The survey was conducted by mail with a three-part instrument including demographic and descriptive information, the Maslach Burnout Inventory, and one optional, open-ended question soliciting comments about successes or challenges of club management.

Demographics

The demographic and descriptive information component of the survey contains 14 variables:

1. Job title.
1. Type of club.
1. Years in club management.
1. Years at their present club.
1. Hours worked.
1. Age.
1. Gender.
1. In which of five areas of the country they were located.
1. Marital Status.
1. Length of time they plan to stay at their club.

1. Number of members.

1. Club performance over the past year.

1. Expectation for industry performance over the coming year.

1. Expectation for club performance over the coming year.

The demographic and descriptive information statements were developed from small focus-group studies and telephone conversations conducted during spring 1995. The focus groups included a total of 25 participants composed of managers, hospitality educators, and association executives. During the sessions, participants were asked open-ended questions to loosely-guide the subject matter. However, the focus-group sessions were allowed to develop on their own to uncover areas of importance. For example, the following question began each session: *How do you feel when you hear the subject of burnout mentioned?* Following the focus-group sessions, educators and association executives responded to direct questions. For example: *After reading the list of questions proposed from focus-group studies, please make suggestions for additional questions or modifications.* The idea was to use the educators and association executives as editors in finalizing and smoothing questions, and to clarify answers.

Burnout Inventory Instrumentation

Along with the completion of demographic and descriptive information, respondent managers were asked to comment on 22 statements regarding their feelings and attitudes about burnout—The Maslach Burnout Inventory (MBI). The survey instrument instructed them to mark the selection that most-closely indicated their feelings on a Likert-type scale answer grid (0 = Never, 6 = Every day).

> *Burnout can lead to deterioration in the quality of service provided by the staff. It appears to be a factor in job turnover, absenteeism, and low morale. Furthermore, burnout seems to be correlated with various self-reported indices of personal dysfunction, including physical exhaustion, insomnia, increased use of alcohol and drugs, and marital and family problems. The generally consistent pattern of findings that emerged from this research led . . . to an instrument to assess it. This measure, the Maslach Burnout Inventory (MBI),*

contains three subscales that assess the different aspects of experienced burnout. It has been found to be reliable, valid, and easy to administer.[11]

The MBI has been validated as a reliable tool for measuring burnout, and has been used many times within the hospitality industry.[12] Maslach views burnout as a combination of three factors or dimensions: depersonalization, emotional exhaustion, and the lack of personal accomplishment. Accordingly, the Maslach Burnout Inventory (MBI) rates people on these three subscales (dimensions) by determining how people respond to each of 22 statements. Respondents state the frequency of such feelings, ranging from never to every day. The higher the respondents score on depersonalization and emotional exhaustion, the higher their levels of burnout. The lack of personal accomplishment scale measures in the opposite direction. That is, the lower the scale, the higher the burnout level. A list of the questions from the MBI is provided below:

1. I feel emotionally drained from my work.

1. I feel used up at the end of the work day.

1. I feel fatigued when I get up in the morning and have to face another day on the job.

1. I can easily understand how people I work with feel about things.

1. I feel I treat some people in an impersonal manner.

1. Working with people all day is a strain for me.

1. I deal very effectively with problems people bring me at work.

1. I feel burned-out from my work.

1. I feel I am making a difference in other people's lives through my work.

1. I've become more callous toward people since I took this job.

1. I worry that this job is hardening me emotionally.

1. I feel very energetic.

1. I feel frustrated by my job.

11 Maslach and Jackson 2.
12 Maslach and Jackson 2.

1. I feel I'm working too hard on my job.

1. I don't really care what happens to some people I encounter at work.

1. Working with people directly puts too much stress on me.

1. I can easily create a relaxed atmosphere with people at work.

1. I feel exhilarated after working with people closely on my job.

1. I have accomplished many worthwhile things in this job.

1. I feel like I'm at the end of my rope.

1. In my work, I deal with emotional problems very calmly.

1. I feel others at work blame me for some of their problems.

Open-Ended Question

The final component of the survey instrument included one open-ended question that encouraged managers to write about successes or challenges in their work. The statement at the end of the survey states, *Please attach an additional sheet if you would like to share any challenges or successes of working in the private club industry.*

Measuring Tools

The authors used Microsoft Excel and Minitab to analyze answers, counts, and averages, and cross-tabulation to draw relationships among demographic components and burnout.

About the Study Participants

Sample Selection, Strategy, and Procedures

Addresses for survey participants were obtained from the Club Managers Association of America Yearbook. An equal number of survey recipients was selected from 50 of the 51 CMAA Chapter Cross References. Due to distance, unreliable mail delivery, and high postage costs, the Far East Chapter was excluded. The study included the 48 contiguous States, plus Alaska and Hawaii. A total of 316 individually addressed envelopes were posted with first-class stamps and mailed. Managers were asked to complete and return the survey within 30 days.

In addition to the primary survey, a second survey was enclosed in each envelope requesting that managers ask one of their senior assistants to fill-out and return a survey to help broaden the sample of the industry.

Respondents

Of the respondent base of 152 managers, the job title profile includes General Managers (61 percent), Managers (13 percent), Clubhouse Managers (10 percent), Assistant Managers (9 percent), and Other management-level staff members (7 percent).

A variety of types of private clubs are represented in the survey. Country Clubs represent the majority in the club-type affiliation category at 70.9 percent, followed by City Clubs (12.6 percent), and Golf (8.6 percent). Minor club categories round out the profile with Yacht Clubs (2.6 percent), Athletic Clubs (1.3 percent), and Other types of clubs (4 percent).

The majority of the respondents have worked many years in the club profession. The profile of managers in the survey on the number of years worked in the industry includes 10-15 years (29 percent), 5-10 years (26 percent), 15-20 years (17 percent), more than 20 years (16 percent), and less than 5 years (12 percent).

The largest percentage of managers in the survey have worked at their present club more than 7 years (33.1 percent). The remainder of the profile in order from most to least, includes 1-3 years (27.2 percent), a tie in the categories of 3-5 years and 5-7 years (16.6 percent), and less than 1 year (6.6 percent).

Manager respondents help corroborate the industry reputation for long work hours. Almost half work 50-60 hours per week. An astounding 80.7 percent of the sample work between 50-70 hours each week or more. The manager profile for the survey includes 50-60 hours (47.3 percent), 60-70 hours (28.7 percent), 40-50 hours (19.3 percent), and more than 70 hours (4.7 percent). Although listed as a possible answer, no manager selected less than 40 hours per week.

As expected, the majority of managers (approximately 70 percent) in the survey range from 30-50 years of age. The manager profile includes 30-40 years old (35.8 percent), 40-50 (33.8 percent), more than 50 (18.5 percent), 25-30 (7.9 percent), and less than 25 (4 percent).

Male respondents outnumber female respondents by a wide margin, but in keeping with the demographics of the mailing list itself. The gender profile includes male (86 percent) and female (14 percent).

The geographic location tabulation divides the country into five regions: North (27 percent), South (26 percent), Central (23 percent), West (17 percent), and drops off sharply with Mountain representing just 7 percent of the sample.

The overwhelming percentage of respondents in the survey sample is married. The marital status profile includes Married (76.8 percent), Never Married (11.9 percent), and Single, Previously Married (11.3 percent). For clarification, the category Married includes those managers that are presently married, although they may have been previously divorced.

Managers vary in their answers on how much longer they plan to stay at their present club. The most frequently chosen option is a disappointing 1-3 years (30.6 percent), followed by more than 7 years (25.2 percent), 3-5 years (21.8 percent), less than 1 year (13.6 percent), and 5-7 years (8.8 percent). When combining the 1-3 year group with the less than 1 year group, it is significant to note that more than 44 percent of managers plan to leave their present job within 3 years.

Over half the clubs in the sample have memberships of more than 600 members (57 percent), followed by 500-599 (20 percent), 400-499 (12 percent), 300-399 (7 percent), and finally the classically envisioned club of less than 300 members representing a mere 4 percent of the survey.

Club performance over the past year is improved for 65.5 percent of the respondents, followed by same as in past (20.5 percent), and worse than in past (13.9 percent).

Managers are optimistic in their expectations for the industry over the next 12 months. 43.7 percent expect the industry to perform better than in the past, followed by same as in past (40.4 percent), and worse than in past selected by just 15.9 percent.

Similar to past club performance and feelings about future industry performance, managers believe their clubs will improve in the coming 12 months. 69.5 percent predict better than in past, 20.5 percent say it will be the same as in past, and a low 9.9 percent predict worse than in past.

Aspects

In this study, the Maslach Burnout Inventory (MBI)[13] is used to assess the three aspects of the burnout syndrome identified by Maslach: Emotional Exhaustion, Depersonalization, and lack of Personal Accomplishment. Each aspect is then measured by a separate subscale. The Emotional Exhaustion subscale measures feelings of emotional over-extension and work exhaustion. The Depersonalization subscale measures an unfeeling and impersonal response toward club members, employees, or others. The Personal Accomplishment subscale measures feelings of competence and successful achievement in a manager's work with people.[14] Respondent managers selected one answer out of a possible six for each of 22 statements.

Burnout: A Continuous Variable

Maslach considers burnout a continuous variable, ranging from low to average (moderate) to high degrees of experienced feeling. In her opinion, burnout is not viewed as a variable that is either present or absent. From that viewpoint, it seems the words stress and burnout become more related than with the more popular lay reference to a condition of burnout developing at some imprecise point after experiencing periods of long-term stress.

Scores are considered high if they are in the upper third of the normative distribution, average if they are in the middle third, and low if they are in the lower third. Furthermore, according to Maslach, given limited knowledge about the relationship between the three aspects of burnout, the scores for each subscale are considered separately and are not combined into a single, total score. Thus, three scores are computed for each respondent.[15]

Aspect Measuring

Emotional Exhaustion

The range of experienced burnout for this survey overall in Emotional Exhaustion is 20.09—Average when compared to the Overall Categorization of MBI Scores.

---

13 Maslach and Jackson Maslach Burnout Inventory Manual.
14 Maslach and Jackson 2.
15 Maslach and Jackson 2.

Depersonalization

The range of experienced burnout for this survey overall in Depersonalization is 8.81—Average when compared to the Overall Categorization of MBI Scores.

Personal Accomplishment

The range of experienced burnout for this survey overall in Personal Accomplishment is 37.03—Average when compared to the Overall Categorization of MBI Scores.

Findings and Implications

This study identified a number of both expected and unexpected findings regarding burnout in the private club segment of the hospitality industry. What follows is a summary of some of those findings:

- Clubhouse Managers are highest in burnout by each measure: Emotional Exhaustion, Depersonalization, and Personal Accomplishment.

- Golf Club Managers experience highest levels of burnout—by far— than others; Athletic Club Managers, the least.

- Managers with less than 5 years in the club profession are more burned-out than any other group. Managers with the most years in the business are the least burned-out.

- Managers with the least amount of time at their clubs are most burned-out in each subscale.

- Managers that work the least amount of hours per week are the most burned-out. Those that work the most are the least burned-out.

- The youngest Managers rate far above anyone else in burnout. The oldest Managers show the least burnout.

- Men are considerably more burned-out than women.

- Managers from the North experience more burnout than anyone else. Managers from the West experience the least.

- Single, Previously Married Managers exhibit the lowest burnout; Married Managers the most.

- Managers planning to stay at their clubs less than 1 year are the most burned-out.

- Managers with the fewest members are the most burned-out; Managers with the most members are the least.

- Managers at clubs not performing well are also the most burned-out. Managers reporting club performance as better show the lowest amount.

- Managers predicting the industry as doing worse than in past are the most burned-out. Managers expecting it to do better are the least.

- Managers predicting their clubs will do better than in past show the least amount of burnout. Managers predicting worse show the most.

Recommendations

The growth in numbers of private clubs creates an increase in need for more and effective managers. Boards of governors and senior managers that supervise private club managers should understand burnout's causes and effects. However, identifying and documenting problems alone does not lead to solutions—it serves instead as an important first step. From there, boards and senior managers must examine data to isolate factors that contribute to burnout, and develop a plan to reduce or eliminate such factors.

From the findings of this study, examining other research findings, and interviewing other managers, the authors propose the following recommendations to reduce factors that contribute to burnout:

- Examine the club culture. Vallen found that 20-30 percent of absenteeism and turnover is related to job dissatisfaction, involving either personal factors, the work environment, or job conflict. Burnout is often associated with the same factors.[16] It therefore makes good sense to examine your corporate culture and make changes if necessary.

- Ensure job descriptions are honest and clear. Reduce misunderstandings about duties and expectations.

- Work to help motivate the staff.

16 Vallen "Organizational Climate and Burnout." 55.

- Encourage networking. Association and peer group networking opportunities help provide an outside support group atmosphere so that managers do not feel isolated and uninformed.

- Allow an informal, relaxed atmosphere. Encourage everyone to laugh and have fun at work.

- Weigh the extent of club policies and attitudes that encourage burnout. Change policies where appropriate.

- Create Employee Assistance Plans (EAPs). Club managers and staff work long and unusual schedules and do not always take time to strengthen personal and family relationships. Furthermore, the festive atmosphere and constant presence of alcohol can prove to be a difficult environment for those dealing with weaknesses, habits, and addictions. Programs such as those listed below, provide opportunities for employee retention.

- Understand the lifestyle of a private club manager does not encourage socializing outside of work. Single managers often stay single or marry someone in the industry. Married managers can become pressured at home, especially when the spouse has a 'normal' job. Encourage creative work policies to help address these issues.

- Reduce role conflict.

- Ensure overall goals are mutually agreed upon—and that they are achievable.

- Emphasize overall results. Allow managers to do their jobs.

- Educate young managers about the challenges and realities of the industry. Ensure they do not develop unreasonable expectations. *The learning curve flattens significantly after a year or two. That is when management turnover problem really starts. The first year it is fun to beat the numbers; the second year, you beat your own; the third year is a real pain.*[17]

- Reduce burnout and turnover substantially by keeping managers involved.[18]

- Empower others to do their best. People want to work in an atmosphere where they are given the tools, responsibility, and support to get the job accomplished.[19]

17 Lang 138.
18 Lang 138.
19 Lang 138.

Article 03:

Establishing and Managing Goals and Objectives

Article authors: Edward A. Merritt and Florence Berger

In Brief

Managers are expected to perform a multitude of functions including executing their responsibilities through others. They cannot expect to manage others if they cannot manage themselves. Establishing a system of goals is a valuable tool that will enable managers to manage themselves and others. Effective goal setting can provide managers with many benefits including: directing attention, encouraging high-level performance, developing innovation and persistence, and diminishing stress. The goal-setting process includes six steps: specify the goal and how to accomplish it, create a SMART goal, identify resources and risk involved, and obtain feedback. Two effective ways to approach goal achievement are through visualization and setting objectives. Once managers have established their goals and have moved toward achieving them, they can begin to coach their employees on goal setting. Effective methods of coaching include: staying in contact, praising, communicating the importance of the process, ensuring capability, allowing employees to reward and critique themselves, choosing the right time and method, publicizing goals, considering using negative feedback in a non-evaluative way, and mitigating conflict. For this paper, I interviewed 22 hospitality industry leaders (my expert panel) regarding their use of goal setting. Of these participants, only one said that he did not use principles of goal setting on a daily basis.

Statement of The Problem: Why Goal Setting?

When managers do not care where they are going, goals are not important. In Lewis Carroll's, Alice's Adventures in Wonderland, Alice and the Cheshire Cat had the following conversation:

Alice: *Would you tell me, please, which way I ought to go from here?*

Cheshire Cat: *That depends a good deal on where you want to get to.*

Alice: *I don't much care.*

Cheshire Cat: *Then it doesn't matter which way you go.*[20]

Goal setting is vital when managers want to know where they are going. The key to success for many senior-level managers is their ability not only to manage others but to discipline and manage themselves. Through this skill one is able to set realistic goals and objectives and determine the most efficient and effective way to achieve them. Continual goal setting and achievement helps assure continued success.

Managers are expected to perform a multitude of functions including planning, organizing, leading, and controlling, and perhaps most important, executing their responsibilities in a way that produces desired goals. Successful managers must be able to make efficient use of time, delegate responsibility to others, and be aware of both the long and short-term effects of their decisions. Managers cannot expect to manage other people if they cannot use time wisely, complete tasks as scheduled, and provide leadership and direction to the employees they supervise. Establishing a system of goals is a valuable tool that will enable managers to do both—manage themselves and others.

The successes of Steve Wynn, then chairman and president of Mirage Resorts (named by Forbes Magazine as one of America's 10 Most Admired Companies) and Rich Melman who has built his Lettuce Entertain You Enterprises into a $140-million empire in 25 years are probably familiar to you. Each enjoys success because of diligently pursued goals.

First, I will discuss some of the details of the study—including its purpose, methodology, findings, implications and lessons, and

20 Gardner, M., The Annotated Alice: Alice's Adventures in Wonderland & Through the Looking Glass (New York: Clarkson N. Potter, Inc., 1960), p. 88.

discuss an idea for a future study. Second, I introduce the subject of goal setting by discussing some of its many benefits identified by the study participants. The third section is devoted to the step process in establishing a goal: Problem identification, strategy mapping, setting a performance goal, identifying necessary resources, recognizing risk, and obtaining constructive feedback. The fourth section is a discussion of a variety of methods for goal achievement once the goal is established. The fifth and final section lists techniques managers can use in managing others through goal setting. If managers need an incentive to read further, remember that organizations that implement goal setting reap greater profits than organizations that do not.[21] An astounding 100 percent of study participants state that goal setting increases their organizations' bottom lines by at least 10 percent.

About the Study

Purpose

The purpose of this study is to determine if the time and effort necessary to develop and implement a system of goal setting are beneficial to a hospitality organization's success. The expert panel overwhelmingly agrees that the time and effort are, indeed, beneficial and worth the trouble. In addition to asking if managers use goal setting, I asked those that answered *yes*, to quantify the impact of such programs on their bottom lines. Given the strong findings in favor of a goal-setting program, I then utilized respondent comments in developing a tool kit for managers to use in creating such a system.

Methodology

I contacted a stratified sample of 30 senior-level hospitality throughout the country to ask if they would participate in a qualitative study on goal setting. Of the 30 managers contacted, 22 (n=22) agreed to individual, in-depth interviews to help us probe further into the subject.

My assumption was that the positive results that could be derived from an effective system of goal setting and implementation are worth the effort in terms of increased bottom-line profit to the hospitality organizations. However, I wanted to find out from the panel if the benefits are worth the time and effort involved in developing and implementing

21 Terpstra, David E. and Elizabeth J. Rozell. "The Relationship of Goal Setting to Organizational Profitability." Group and Organization Management. Vol. 19, No. 3, (September 1994), pp. 285-294.

such a program. Furthermore, assuming managers answered in the affirmative—that the benefits are worth the time and effort—I would use such information as the basis to help answer another question: How can hospitality managers develop and institute effective goal setting and implementation programs in their organizations?

Study Participants

This study was conducted among 22 (n=22) senior management staff working at hotels, resorts, private clubs, and restaurants across the United States. Typical position titles include Owner, Corporate Executive, District or Regional Manager, General Manager, and Manager. The interviews were conducted by telephone and mail.

Demographic Information

First, I asked the expert panel to tell us about themselves. The demographic and descriptive information component of the study contains six statements to determine answers to such variables as these:

- Job title.
- Length of time in the hospitality management profession.
- Length of time in present position.
- Age.
- Gender.
- In which of five areas of the country they live.

Study Questions

Next, I asked the panel to tell us about their work. Participants were asked eight major questions to help guide the subject matter. However, interview sessions were allowed to develop on their own to uncover areas of importance. From those answers, extemporaneous focus questions were asked where appropriate to help clarify information provided:

- Amount of management functions performed. Note: The idea of this question is to determine a broad spectrum of general management responsibilities in the areas of planning, organizing, coordinating, and controlling, as opposed to the narrow focus of technical segment specialists.

- Number of direct reports.
- If they use goal setting.
- If yes, its effect on the organization's bottom-line.
- Observed benefits of goal setting.
- Steps used to create goals—the process.
- Once goals are set, methods used for goal achievement.
- Techniques used in managing others through goal setting.

Findings

Job title:

- 45% (10 individuals) of study participants hold the job title of general manager.
- 41% (9) of study participants hold a job title such as area manager or regional manager, corporate executive, or owner.
- 14% (3) of study participants hold the job title of manager.
- Years in hospitality profession:
- 41% (9) of study participants have been in the hospitality profession for 15 to 20 years.
- 36% (8) of study participants have been in the hospitality profession for up to 15 years.
- 23% (5) of study participants have been in the hospitality profession for more than 20 years.

Years in present position:

- 36% (8) of study participants have been in their present position up to 3 years.
- 32% (7) of study participants have been in their present position 3 to 5 years.

- 32% (7) of study participants have been in their present position 5 years or more.

  Age:

- 54% (12) of study participants are 30 to 50 years old.
- 23% (5) of study participants are more than 50 years old.
- 23% (5) of study participants are up to 30 years old.
- Gender:
- 68% (15) of study participants are male.
- 32% (7) of study participants are female.
- Area of the country where working:
- 32% (7) of study participants work in the North.
- 23% (5) of study participants work in the West.
- 23% (5) of study participants work in the South.
- 14% (3) of study participants work in the Mountain region of the country.
- 9% (2) of study participants work in the Central region of the country.

  Number of management functions performed:

- 55% (12) of study participants state that they perform many (> 7).
- 36% (8) of study participants state that they perform a moderate amount (4-6).
- 9% (2) of study participants state they perform few (1-3).

  Number of direct reports:

- 55% (12) of study participants supervise seven or more direct reports.
- 36%(8) of study participants supervise 4 to 6 direct reports.
- 9% (2) of study participants supervise 1 to 3 direct reports.

Those using goal setting daily:

- 95% (21) of study participants use principles of goal setting daily.
- 5% (1) of study participants do not use principles of goal setting daily.

Does goal setting increase your organization's bottom line?

- 76% (16) of study participants say goal setting increases their bottom line by 15% or more.
- 24% (5) of study participants say goal setting increases their bottom line 10 up to 15%.
- 0% (0) of study participants say goal setting increases their bottom line less than 10%.

Benefits of goal setting:

Interview participants mentioned a variety of benefits that are derived from goal setting. Through focus questions, I was able to categorize their answers into four major categories:

- Directing attention.
- Encouraging high-level performance.
- Developing innovation and persistence.
- Reducing stress.

Steps of goal setting:

Interview participants mentioned a variety of steps they use in the goal setting process. Through focus questions, I was able to categorize their answers into six major steps including:

- Specifying the goal and how to accomplish it.
- Creating a SMART goal—specific, measurable, acceptable, realistic, and timely.
- Identifying resource sources and evaluating risk involved.
- Obtaining feedback.

Approaches to goal achieving:

Interview participants mentioned two approaches that they utilize for achieving goals:

- Visualization.

- Setting objectives.

Coaching methods:

Interview participants mentioned a variety of methods they utilize in effectively coaching their employees toward goal achievement. Through focus questions, I was able to categorize their answers into 10 categories including:

- Staying in contact.

- Praising employees.

- Communicating the importance of the process.

- Ensuring employee capability.

- Allowing employees to reward and review themselves.

- Choosing the right time.

- Choosing the right motivational methods.

- Publicizing goals.

- Using negative feedback.

- Avoiding goal conflict.

Implications and Lessons

Findings help support my hunches. However, with the small sample (n=22), I cannot generalize findings to the larger population of hospitality managers.

The panel of participants indicates an increase in the business pace due to competition, smaller staffs due to reorganization, and higher expectations by their ownership. The majority of respondents (68 percent) have been in their present jobs five years or less—a shorter time than I expected. While some of the job turnover can be accounted for by advancement, much of the turnover is due to turmoil. Fortunately, managers' skills are portable; as 87 percent of study participants have been in the hospitality industry at least 10 years.

Findings indicate that it is still a *man's world* in the higher ranks of the hospitality industry within the sample population. Men outnumber women by more than two to one as managers.

Participants describe their management functions as *many* (7 or more) indicating that these truly are managers in the sense that they exercise a broad spectrum of general management responsibilities in the areas of planning, organizing, coordinating, and controlling, as opposed to the narrow focus of technical segment specialists. This may help explain the seemingly large number of direct reports managers supervise.

It is in the coordinating function where I am a bit surprised—specifically span of control (the number of people who report to one manager). The majority of manager participants (55 percent) supervise at least seven employees. While I classified the highest category as seven or more; the average within this category is 10. One manager supervises 15. Managers indicate their having a wider span of control necessitates a system such as goal setting to help organize the interaction and communication among their employees.

The fact that 95 percent of the study participants utilize the principles of goal setting on a daily basis is as I expected. I am puzzled to find that one manager—considered by most measures as quite successful—does not use goal setting. This finding may provide the basis for an interesting future study.

The finding that 76 percent of participants believe that goal setting has a positive effect on their organizations' bottom lines by at least 15 percent is particularly noteworthy. When I set out to undertake this study I thought that managers would say that the outcome is worth the time and effort. However, I did not anticipate such dramatic results. An unexpectedly large 19 percent of study participants say that goal setting improves their bottom lines by over 20 percent.

Finally, I was interested to hear managers' thoughts concerning the goal-setting process as a whole. Relating back to their comments about their work being more demanding than in the past, manager participants believe that they must first be able to manage themselves before they can manage others. In other words, managers must implement an effective system of goal setting and achieving for themselves before they can embark upon an organization-wide goal setting program for others.

Future Ideas

Seizing Opportunity

I was intrigued to find one successful manager, a chief operating officer that does not use goal-setting methods per se. His techniques include focusing on opportunities that arise. Here are some excerpts from the write up: *I believe that when my chance happens I must focus on that opportunity or it will come and go without positive results. I wanted to do well in my career...but I never got too specific.*

While the majority (21 of 22 participants) of the managers in this study clearly utilize goal-setting methods on a regular basis, it may be interesting to examine the balance between focusing on goals and seizing unexpected opportunities as they arise.

Benefits

Study participants believe goals help managers translate general intentions into specific actions. Debra Mesch defines a goal as a plan for a desired outcome.[22] And goal-setting theory posits that people who set goals perform more effectively than those who do not set goals.[23] David Chag, GM of the Country Club of Brookline, Massachusetts, states, *Goals establish an end result, a direction of pursuit, a method of measurement, and foster teamwork and achievement. Goals help us perform beyond our capabilities and keep us focused when the going gets tough.*

There are many benefits of goal setting. Some of the more notable advantages identified by study participants include:

- Directing attention and actions because they give managers a target.[24] People can become confused if they do not have a specific

22 Mesch, Debra J., Jiing-Lih Farh, and Philip M. Podsakoff. "Effects of Feedback Signs on Group Goal Setting, Strategies, and Performance." Group and Organization Management, Vol.19, No.3, (September 1994), pp. 309-333.
23 Locke, E. A. and Latham, G. P. A Theory of Goal Setting and Task Performance (Englewood Cliffs, NJ: Prentice Hall, 1990).
24 O'Hair, D. and Friedrich, G. W. (1992). Strategic Communication in Business and the Professions (Boston: Houghton Mifflin Company, 1992).

goal toward which to direct their efforts. Goals nurture an atmosphere that produces specific results within specific time periods.

- Performing at peak levels. Setting goals makes managers aware of the mental, emotional, and physical energy they will need for the task and encourages them to conserve and mobilize energy carefully.

- Bolstering persistence. The absence of strong goals can distract from one's mission and foster a temptation to quit when facing a challenge.

- Developing innovative strategies. Managers that set important goals will be surprised at how ingenious they can be in devising their strategies to reach their goals.

- Providing a short and long-term game plan. If set properly and realistically, managers can map out their futures with their companies, or effect plans to achieve other aspirations.

- Preventing stress. A comprehensive goals program can help avoid burnout and produce positive feelings.[25]

Steps in Establishing a Goal

Step One: Identify the Problem

As a first step toward goal setting, specify exactly what is to be accomplished: the job, assignment, or responsibility. Managers can use brainstorming methods to assist in identifying problems and then rank the ideas that emerge.

Brainstorming

Create a list of wants or desires as they relate to the job, assignment, or responsibility. Try to put aside inhibitions and be creative—in a dreamlike state. This is the time to catalog all options. Resist the temptation to evaluate whether or not these dreams are practical, logical, or even possible. Jerry McCoy, a certified club manager and consultant living in Columbus, Georgia, shared these thoughts about the brainstorming process: *Our most successful and creative ideas come from brainstorming. We brainstorm for special projects and in general sessions to help improve overall operations.*

---

25 Stallworth, H. (1990, June). "Realistic goals help avoid burnout." HR Magazine, Vol. 35, 6, (June 1990), p. 171.

Ranking

Next, prioritize to determine which of these desires is most important. Select the most important option as the goal.

Step Two: Map Strategy

Create a plan for how to accomplish the goal. Brainstorm to develop a list of possible alternatives—regardless of how impractical they appear. After recording possibilities, begin the culling process by considering the limitations of each alternative. Discard those that are unreasonable.

Step Three: Set a SMART Performance Goal

A SMART goal is a goal that is: Specific, measurable, acceptable, realistic, and timely. The following points discuss the importance of incorporating these five components into the goal-setting process.

Specific

Goals should be both explicit and unclouded—something to aim toward without misinterpretation. It is not enough simply to set positive-sounding goals (*I want to become more fit*). O'Hair found managers are more likely to succeed if their goals are specific and clear.[26] Harry Waddington, GM of the Piedmont Driving Club in Atlanta believes, *Focus is the key to my success. If I focus specifically on something long enough, I know that I probably can achieve it. If we properly plan a function and carefully focus on the details as it unfolds, we are likely to produce a huge success.*

Goal-setting theory asserts that specific goals improve performance by producing higher levels of effort and planning than unclear or general goals. People strive for a higher standard of success by increasing effort.[27] When people pursue vague goals, they may obtain satisfaction from even low levels of performance.[28]

26 O'Hair 1992.
27 Shalley, Christina E. "Effects of Productivity Goals, Creativity Goals, and Personal Discretion on Individual Creativity." Journal of Applied Psychology, Vol. 76, No.2, (1991), pp. 179-185.
28 Latham, Gary P. and Edwin A. Locke. "Self-Regulation Through Goal Setting." Organizational Behavior and Human Decision Processes, 50, (1991), pp. 212-247.

Managers can channel some of this extra effort into the development of appropriate plans. Studies show that people with specific goals tend to plan and organize more than those with general goals that, in turn, create a motivational effect to follow through with the plan.[29] Using the example about desiring to become more physically fit begins to transform from a general wish to a distinct possibility by amending the statement to the more specific statement, *I will become more physically fit by beginning a jogging program*. This idea becomes more salient and develops into a goal as the process evolves.

Measurable

It is very important that goals are measurable because measurement permits objectivity that helps define goals in terms of actions that one can readily see. Measurement can be as simple as an informal checklist, or it may be a complex and sophisticated evaluation form that measures performance in a variety of categories. For example, at the beginning of your jogging program, you could establish a baseline by timing yourself over a one-mile course. If your time is 14 minutes, you have established that as your baseline. It is reasonable to infer that with proper training, your time can improve—an indication of enhanced fitness. You may decide that you will jog 45 minutes, five days a week, for four weeks. And at the beginning of each week, you will time your first mile to see how you are progressing.

Acceptable

Goals should not be imposed, but rather self-desired and thereby acceptable—whether assigned or self conceived. When managers accept their goals and make a commitment to achieving them, goals have a much better chance of being realized. However, if the goal is more imposed than desired, the goal may be perceived as more difficult to attain, thereby resulting in frustration instead of accomplishment. Is achieving an improved fitness level an acceptable, self-desired goal to you—one that you are committed to achieving?

Acceptance and commitment create determination for reaching a goal—regardless of the goal's origin. Locke summarized the

29 Earley, Christopher P, William Prest, and Pauline Wojnaroski. "Task Planning and Energy Expended: Exploration of How Goals Influence Performance." Journal of Applied Psychology, Vol.72, No.1, (1987), pp. 107-114.

determinants of goal acceptance and commitment into three categories: external influences, interactive factors, and internal factors.[30]

External influences—legitimate authority. Managers have both personal and work related goals. Companies have goals that are often times pushed down on managers from higher levels such as from corporate, to division, to region, and to the property level. In order for managers to be as effective as possible in goal achievement, they must deal with this dilemma of sorting out which goals are most important. In effect, managers must try to reconcile conflicting goals and attempt to make them congruent for themselves as well as for those they supervise. This merging of individual and organizational needs is seen as the biggest challenge in goal attainment.[31]

Managers should take responsibility for and assume ownership of their goals—all goals. Those that are sent down from the corporate or divisional offices should be carefully incorporated as guiding principles into property-level goals where they become more salient. It may not be easy. The culture of the organization will regulate the amount of influence managers have on top-down goals. Michael Mooney, manager at the Annapolis Yacht Club in Maryland offered insight regarding his past experience in a restaurant company: *Corporate set the goals, the general managers were the enforcers. Department heads had very little say. Now that I am a manager, I try to involve everyone in the process, so our goals become more meaningful.*

Ideally, managers should go about the process of developing and implementing work-related goals with the same structure and zeal they would utilize with their personal goals, instead of accepting them as habitual responses, respect for authority, or due to the power of the person assigning the goal.[32] With long workweeks the norm for hospitality managers, the process of buying off on and personalizing organizational goals is a key issue with which to make peace.

Assigned goals do the following:[33]

30 Locke, Edwin A. "The Determinants of Goal Commitment." Academy of Management Review, Vol.13, No.1, (1988), pp. 23-39.

31 Gatewood, R. D., Taylor, R. R., and Ferrell, O. C., Management Comprehension, Ana lysis, and Application. (Burr Ridge, IL: Richard D. Irwin, Inc., 1995).

32 Earley, 1987.

33 Earley, 1987.

- Afford a feeling of purpose, guidance, and explicitness concerning expectations.

- Broaden individuals' convictions of what they think they can realize.

- Direct individuals toward developing high quality plans to realize their goals.

- Interactive factors—participation and competition. Although assigned goals increase commitment, studies suggest that participatory goal setting produces even greater commitment. Participation was a subject of primary concern to management during the 1960s.[34] Maier's research asserts that employees tend to set higher goals for themselves in a participatory setting than supervisors alone would dare to impose, since employees seem to be more acutely aware of the factors within their control.[35]

Studies have not yet definitively proven how competition affects commitment. However, Locke found that employees set significantly higher goals and performed significantly better in competitive situations than those who were not competing.[36]

Internal factors—personal goals, self-efficacy and internal rewards. Personal goals and self-efficacy judgments have direct effects on performance. Zander suggested that individuals are equally committed to self-set and participatively-set goals.[37]

Individuals will set more difficult personal goals for themselves than for others because they see themselves as more able to perform. In other words, individuals have lower expectations for others than for themselves. *We see evidence of this all the time. Our corporate targets are quite aggressive, but our managers set even higher goals for themselves. Essentially, they become entrepreneurs within a billion dollar organization*, states Ed Evans, vice president of human resources for the Business Services Group of ARAMARK.

---

34 Mathis, R. L. and Jackson, J. H. (1997). Human Resource Management. (St. Paul, MN: West Publishing Co., 1997).
35 Maier, Norman R. F. "Assets and Liabilities in Group Problem Solving: The Need for an Integrative Function." Psychological Review, Vol.74(4), (1967), pp.233-249.
36 Locke, 1988.
37 Zander, Alvin, The Purposes of Groups and Organizations. (San Francisco: Jossey-Bass, Publishers, 1985).

During the goal-setting process, individuals experience a normative shift that shapes their self-efficacy—the belief in their capabilities.[38] When an individual believes that they can accomplish a task, they will push themselves. By contrast, not even incentives will motivate an individual with low self-efficacy. In other words, self-efficacy is more a more fundamental internal value than reward. People will not strive for rewards they believe are unattainable, but they will commit to goals they believe they can reach.

Realistic

Not only should goals be specific, they should also be challenging—but within an individual's capabilities and limitations. Goals should not represent whatever levels of achievement a manager decides would be *nice*. Dreaming has no place in effective goal setting. For goals to serve as a tool for stretching an individual to reach their full potential, they must be challenging but achievable. Therefore, before beginning goal setting, managers should consider their stretch capabilities and honestly examine whether they have the knowledge, skills, resources, and abilities needed in successfully accomplishing their goals. Satisfying this criterion means setting goals in light of several important considerations:[39]

- What performance levels will conditions realistically allow?

- What results will it take to be a successful performer?

- What is an individual capable of accomplishing when pushed?

Managers should emphasize that their goals extend their abilities. Though it may take extra determination and hard work to achieve difficult goals, it will be far more rewarding than those goals that can be achieved with little effort. Research has found that when challenging goals are set instead of easy goals, performance is usually better. This is true because achieving only easy goals may keep one from realizing their full potential.[40] Bill Kendall of Woodmont Country Club in Rockville, Maryland stated, *the process of lofty goal setting keeps everyone*

38 Gellatly, Ian R. and John P. Meyer. "The Effects of Goal Difficulty on Physiological Arousal, Cognition, and Task Performance." Journal of Applied Psychology, Vol.77, No.5, (1992), pp. 694-704.
39 Thompson, Jr., A. A. and Strickland III, A. J., Strategic Management Concepts and Cases. (Burr-Ridge, IL: Richard D. Irwin, Inc., 1995).
40 O'Hair, 1992.

striving for improvement, rather than allowing the easier alternative. We want our managers continually stretching their limits. On the other hand, managers should not set goals that will be impossible to achieve, thereby setting themselves up for failure. Experiencing failure makes people less apt to set goals in the future.

For example, you may never be able to run a four-minute mile, so stating that as a goal for your fitness program is not productive. But it is a good idea to push yourself beyond what you honestly feel would be your best performance. You know from your baseline measurement that you can jog a 14-minute mile in your present fitness condition. Furthermore, you may remember three years ago, after one month of easy-to-moderate training, you were able to run a 12-minute mile. To set that as a goal would not allow you to reach your full potential. On the other hand, you may feel that if you really train hard, you may be able to jog a 10-minute mile—two minutes faster than ever before. The 10-minute mile goal—one that broadens your previous capability—will be a far more rewarding goal.

Timely (or Time Bound)

Managers should not constrain themselves with procedures and deadlines. While goals should be specific, they must be allowed to change over time. *As the world evolves, circumstances change*, says Mohammad Memar'Sadeghi, manager at the Carousel Hotel, Resort, and Athletic Club in Ocean City, Maryland, *We can't just set and achieve goals in a vacuum—there are too many external variables such as weather, regulations, or economics affecting our business. We must be able to change too—even if it means abandoning a goal altogether and creating a new one.* Setting highly specific, inflexible goals may give a manager an unfavorable reputation as being too rigid, or unresponsive to the real world. For example, if you have set achievement of your 10-minute mile goal over a four-week timeline and sprain your ankle at the end of the third week, you will likely need to adjust your deadline.

Step Four: Identify Necessary Resources

Time, equipment, money, favors, encouragement, and moral support are just a few of the resources managers may need to achieve their goals. Anticipating resource needs will strengthen plans and actions, and planning how to utilize resources can make goals more real and concrete. Using the 10-minute mile example, you should consider issues such as how you will work your run into your daily schedule, where you will keep your workout clothes (and your new $135 Nikes), how you will freshen-up afterward, and if your staff will support your quest—after all, they are bound to enjoy the stress-relieving benefits that come from your fitness program!

Step Five: Recognize Risk, Contingencies, and Conflict Risk

To increase the probability of success, consider the risks connected with accomplishing the goal. Risks refer to what might be lost by pursuing the goal by one method over other alternatives identified in the brainstorming process. In your 10-minute mile quest, how much higher is your risk of injury (and perhaps goal failure) if you use your old Nikes instead of spending $135 for a new pair?

Contingencies

Prepare for contingencies. Do you have an alternate location to run if you live in an area where severe weather is a possibility? Should you consider the possibility of a fitness club membership for showering and changing? What happens if a last-minute meeting comes up as you are walking out of the door to go run? Devise goals so that a large number of potential obstacles can be removed or mitigated in order to have a better shot at achieving the desired end results.

Conflict

When pursuing multiple goals managers will likely devote more time and effort to one goal than another, often trading off between quantity and quality goals. Task difficulty and interest will determine the goal selection and performance. If managers choose difficult quality and quantity goals or if they are not confident of their abilities, they can often feel overloaded and unable to improve. As a result, they will begin to tradeoff performance quality for performance quantity.[41]

One manager expressed this concept succinctly: *We list proprietary brands in our specifications to make sure our dining patrons are getting the highest quality. Last week we could not buy Ore Ida or Lamb's shoestring fries—just the distributor's private label. Instead of our*

41 Gilliland, Stephen W. and Ronald S. Lamis. "Quality and Quantity Goals in a Complex Decision Task: Strategies and Outcomes." Journal of Applied Psychology, Vol.77, No.5, (1992), pp. 672-681.

normal five-ounce portion, we served eight-ounce portions to try to head off any possible complaints.

Step Six: Obtain Feedback

Feedback clarifies messages and verifies shared meaning. Feedback makes goal setting more effective because it indicates when and where managers may need to adjust their direction or methods so that they are achieving their best.

Feedback can also provide encouragement. If managers receive messages that support their goals and their progress toward them, they are more likely to reach those goals and set higher ones in the future.[42]

Goal-setting theory states that feedback results in higher effort and performance than lack of feedback.[43] People use feedback to compare the difference between their performance and established goals and make necessary adjustments. When an individual receives negative feedback, he or she feels dissatisfied because their performance does not meet established standards. Individuals respond to negative feedback by setting higher goals than those that receive positive feedback. The dissatisfaction from negative feedback prompts them to develop more task strategies than those that received positive feedback.[44]

In the short term, negative feedback positively affects goal setting. However, at a certain point the dissatisfaction created by negative feedback can outweigh the benefits. High levels of dissatisfaction can lead to negative behavior and an increase in absenteeism and employee turnover. Even in the short term, negative feedback can be detrimental if the individual does not believe his effort ever will result in positive feedback. Negative feedback might not be appropriate when there is a lack of organizational support, low trust, a poor relationship with the feedback source, and low self-efficacy. Conversely, a positive relationship with the feedback source, a high-trust environment, support

42 Locke, E. A., Chah, D., Harrison, S., and Lustgarten, N. "Separating the Effects of Goal Specificity From Goal Level." Organizational Behavior and Human Decision Making, 43, (1989), pp. 270-287.
43 Mitchell, Terence R. and William S. Silver. "Individual and Group Goals When Workers Are Interdependent: Effects on Task Strategies and Performance." Journal of Applied Psychology, Vol. 73, No. 2, (1990), pp. 185-193.
44 Mesch, 1994.

for goal accomplishment, high self-efficacy, and rigorous criteria for acceptable performance may enhance the feedback relationship.[45]

Furthermore, the more difficult and more specific goals become, the more feedback managers need. In essence, the process reinforces itself: Setting higher goals leads to better effort and elevated performance; learning of success through feedback encourages still higher goals in the future.[46] Talk about your 10-minute mile goal with other runners, read running magazines, try an organized fun run event. Develop an informal support group that can provide constructive feedback regarding your goal.

Goal selection and establishment using the preceding steps are perhaps the most important stages in establishing what people want to do. By this time in the process:

- The goal should be identified.

- A strategy for how the goal will be accomplished should be mapped out.

- The performance goal should be challenging, flexible, and measurable.

- Issues such as time, money, and other necessary resources for goal achievement should have been considered.

- Risk and rewards relative to the alternative selected should be understood. Similarly, a well-devised strategy for contingencies that may arise should be in place.

- Finally, a support group for receiving constructive feedback from others should be assembled.

Create a Written Goal Statement

When the decisions in the steps for establishing a goal have been successfully made, commit them to writing. Review and adjust or clarify the steps as necessary. Be specific. Using the information produced in the step process, create a written goal statement that includes answers to the following points:

Who? Sam Jones.

---

45 Mesch, 1994.
46 O'Hair, 1992.

What? Adopt the goal to run a 10-minute mile.

Where? On the track at Canyon College.

When? Within four weeks of beginning my jogging program January 1. (Without a deadline, there is less urgency, resulting in laxness and the risk of losing interest.)

Why? I have selected this goal to help me begin a jogging program.

How? I will schedule my 45-minute jogging routine five days per week—just like any other appointment.

Who cares? A regular jogging program will enable me to become physically fit, reduce stress, and allow me uninterrupted time to think about the strategic direction of my resort.

Once written, the goal will have more meaning and importance to the creator. Beverly Schlegel, manager of the Shenandoah Club in Roanoke, Virginia adds, *I first became familiar with the importance of the goal-setting process in high school. Our journalism teacher pounded it into our heads at every opportunity. To this day, I still ask those questions, not only when I write, but also when I plan. This format is a major key to our success.* Once the goal is established, move forward to the physical and cognitive steps of goal setting.

Achieving the Goal

Before beginning the achievement phase of the goal there should now exist an established, written goal. The written goal statement is a declaration of the outcome one plans to accomplish. Now consider how and when to accomplish the goal. Two of the effective ways to approach the achievement of one's goals are the cognitive approach and the physical approach.

The Cognitive Approach—Visualization

The cognitive approach takes place within the mind. It is a mental procedure, visualization. The fundamental premise behind visualization assumes that the subconscious cannot distinguish between an actual experience and one vividly imagined. By concentrating on the goal and believing that it is attainable, it is likely that the subconscious mind will begin to play a role in helping with goal achievement. Sherrie Laveroni, regional vice president and managing director of the Regency Hotel in New York City, confirms the value of the visualization process: *When you set a goal, you set into motion possibility. Possibility for something better, greater. You immediately are activated to plan and imagine what could be . . . and how to make it happen.*

There are four steps involved with visualization that will prove beneficial toward the final outcome:

- Develop an enthusiastic and positive attitude. Have confidence that the goal is attainable. If not, no amount of work will be able to overcome that fault.

- Relax. Sit back in a comfortable chair and allow your body to unwind. Close your eyes and breathe easily, slowly, and deeply.

- Imagine accomplishment. Envision success in detail. Fill your mind with thoughts of achievement. Dwell on these positive thoughts and enjoy the pleasant feeling. Now, imagine a single situation where you achieve your goal. Visualize this success repeatedly. Convince yourself that the scenario exists. Repetition is important in helping convince the subconscious that the success is real.

- Reorientation. After an intense session, clear your mind. Allow time to reorient with your surroundings and resume your daily activities. This may be helpful in avoiding any possible obsession or loss of touch with reality regarding the goal.

Physical Approach—Setting Objectives

The physical approach is the doing as opposed to the thinking orientation of the cognitive approach. The physical approach includes the setting of objectives. Objectives are short-term milestones that enable managers to map out the conditions that must be met for goals to be reached.[47] Lou Krouse, chairman of the board of Stein Eriksen Lodge, in Deer Valley, Utah, shares his opinion of the importance of setting objectives: *With the Olympic Games in our back yard, our senior management team is ferocious about setting and achieving objectives. With hundreds of projects and tasks to finalize before the athletes, tourists, and media descend upon our resort area, end-result goals would just be too complex to accomplish without interim objectives.* Just as there are steps to establishing a goal, and visualizing it, there are steps in setting objectives.

---

47 Locke, 1989.

Establish the time frame. Set a period for accomplishing the goal. Evaluate how time is spent, eliminating or spending less time on minor activities to allow more time for goal-achieving activities.

Set interim goals. Break goals into a series of small stepping-stones that will lead to accomplishment of the main goal. Interim successes will help reinforce these steps and inspire you to press onward. The goal becomes more manageable and less overwhelming when goals are broken down into objectives.

Set a deadline. Regular deadlines act as powerful motivators in helping managers reach their goals. Deadlines help determine what must be accomplished and how it must be accomplished. Be as specific as possible. Set periodic checks to determine closeness to achieving the goal and reassess progress. Determine where expectations have been met, exceeded, or fallen short of the goal. If deficient, take appropriate action to get back on schedule.

Recording Progress

An important facet of goal achieving is keeping accurate records of the progress made toward goal accomplishment. Progress will likely come as slow transformation that is not readily recognized without accurate recording of daily activities. It is important, therefore, to maintain precise records. There are two basic methods for recording behavior:

Frequency Count

A frequency count involves calculating the number of times a particular event occurs. This is perhaps the easiest and most common method of assessment. For example, if you have committed to jogging five times per week in your 10-minute mile goal, a frequency count will help assess progress being made.

Time Duration

This method involves timing the length of the activity. If you have committed to jogging for 45 minutes each session in your 10-minute mile goal, you can keep track of your progress by using the chronograph feature of a sports watch.

Reinforcing

Knowing how to measure the progress of goal accomplishment, one should also establish appropriate methods for reward and discipline when accomplishing or falling short on making progress toward the goal.

In choosing to use positive (reward) and negative (discipline) reinforcers, ensure that the criteria are realistic and attainable. By establishing criteria, managers have measurable control as to what degree a reward or discipline will be administered.

It is important to experience small rewards such as positive self-acknowledgment early and frequently to help increase the likelihood of maintaining the goal quest. Similarly, discipline for non-achievement should not be so severe as to cause one to give up.

Small lapses and regressions may occur during the process. Do not permit them to cause discouragement. Rather, let the lapse become the impetus for renewed and redoubled effort toward the goal.

Goal Aids

Aids are utilized to help managers keep their goals before them at all times—ever-present but not intrusive. They are most effective when practiced on a daily basis.

One club executive uses time spent in driving to work as quiet time for reviewing and emphasizing goal aspiration. A hotel general manager does daily step exercises to the accompaniment of *I wish to be a regional vice president, I want to be a regional vice president, I will be a regional vice president*—from fantasy, to desire, to determination.

Goal Re-evaluation

Goals are likely to change with time. There is nothing wrong with that. However, the decision to change goals should be both rational and conscious. Where accomplishment was underestimated, set higher goals. Similarly, where accomplishment was overestimated, this is the time to adjust to more realistic goals (just be sure to keep them challenging). Re-evaluate. Have efforts been maximized? Was the goal attainable and realistic within the established time period? Re-evaluation means re-thinking and making necessary adjustments. It does not mean quitting.

Re-evaluation may indicate the desirability of changing an interim goal. Do so, if necessary. The aim is to achieve the goal, not to let it beat you. Tom Hale, CEO of Myrtle Beach National, a resort company in South Carolina, offered his view on the re-evaluation process: *We have to constantly re-think our interim goals and objectives. If we see that our guests' preferences are changing, we must determine how to best meet those needs—now and in the future. Often that means altering our goals and objectives to provide the level of service desired.*

Techniques for use in Managing Others Through Goal Setting

Once managers have established their goals, and have moved toward achieving them successfully, they can begin to coach their employees on goal setting. Bob Sexton, Certified Hospitality Educator and consultant from Rancho Mirage, California, had this to say: *Goal setting cannot be implemented without effective, regular coaching. I ensure that goals:*

- *Are created by those that will achieve them*

- *Have measurable mileposts along the way*

- *Include incentive*

- *Build in steps from simple to difficult*

- *Are split between objective and subjective measures*

Employees should choose and set goals for themselves using the same methods that have been described above. Managers should encourage employees to set both personal goals and those that relate to their work performance. Norm Spitzig, GM at BallenIsles Country Club in Palm Beach Gardens, Florida describes his process: *I spend a good deal of time with each member of my senior management team asking them to come up with seven to ten major goals they want to accomplish. I also have my own list—again seven to ten in number. We discuss all of the goals, eliminate those that are unrealistic or un-measurable, modify others, and adopt some as they are. We eventually agree on the specific goals.*

Managers may want to share one of their job goals as an example to help their employees understand the concept. If managers can institute a program whereby all employees set and achieve goals, their properties will run more efficiently and more productively as the staff will understand where they are going and why they are going there. John Jordan, GM of Cherokee Town and Country Club in Atlanta had this to say: *I meet with my direct reports every week in order to give each individual an hour of my undivided attention without interruption. We use forms as guides to ensure we cover all areas—accomplishments, work in progress, questions, opportunities, work ahead, and comments on the support managers need from me. We even set daily objectives to help achieve goals. I believe that for goals to be achieved successfully, they should be set democratically but implemented dictatorially by the team leader.*

Stay in close contact. After employees have begun to establish work goals, managers should review their plans to ensure they are consistent with the larger-perspective organizational goals. Managers should encourage and support their employees' goal-setting efforts. Meet with them on a regular basis to discuss progress, problems, and goal refinement.

Praise often. Words of praise go a long way with many people. If employees are not making progress, discuss reasons why, and if necessary change the goal.

Communicate the importance of the process. If certain employees are not interested in the goal-setting process, managers should explain that it is important to the property and to those employees' growth within the organization. Make sure that employees understand the importance and benefits of goal setting in all aspects of their life. Rick Thorn, manager of San Luis Obispo Golf Club in California, offers his thoughts, *I try to have goals set at the lowest levels of the organization—almost everyone is involved. Once goals are adopted, I meet with my staff on a regular basis to assess how we are progressing and use them as a basis for rating supervisors' performance. Everyone understands the importance of the process.*

Make sure employees are capable. Pay close attention to changes in employees' feelings of self-efficacy, recognizing that they are more likely to experience low self-confidence in stressful situations, where anxiety replaces motivation. Participatory goal setting can channel anxiety into motivation and increase self-efficacy, leading to greater goal commitment than possible through assigned goals.[48] Managers can raise employee confidence and reduce anxiety by providing information and training and supportive behavior.[49]

---

48   Locke, 1988.
49 Gellatly, 1992.

Allow employees to reward and review themselves during the coaching process. Managers can increase organizational commitment and performance by encouraging employees to engage in self-generated rewards and feedback during review sessions. People are more likely to accept and derive meaning from self-generated feedback than from supervisor-generated feedback.[50] Bill Koegler, director of development and planning for Oglebay Resort and Conference Center in Wheeling, West Virginia, recalled an example from his general manager days at the resort: *We'd established a creative plan to increase occupancy, but realized that the front desk wasn't pushing the plan in order to avoid the possible embarrassment associated with overbooking. We asked them to come up with a plan. They created a reward system that divided the revenue from the last room rented among the staff. Instead of six to seven empty rooms, we got down to averaging one or two.*

Choose the right time. Goals may be presented at the beginning of a week, a new project, or when quarterly reports or performance appraisals are given. If there is a time lag between the assignment of a goal and performance, additional information input that intervenes in the process may cause changes in the originally set goals and distract attention necessary to reach the desired performance level.[51]

Select the right method. During the early stages of skill acquisition, performance goals may be distracting and, therefore, counterproductive. Different types of goals (e.g., learning vs. performance) may be helpful during different phases of skill acquisition.[52] For example, if you wish to increase productivity in the engineering department, then you should assign a difficult performance goal rather than a do-your-best job, or no productivity goal.

Publicize goals. Managers can increase goal commitment to goals by making goals public rather than keeping them private. The public spotlight and pressure will help motivate commitment.

Consider using negative feedback. Managers who expect more from their subordinates often achieve better performance than those who demand less. If trust and a good relationship are present, negative feedback can help increase and motivate employee performance.

50 Locke, 1988.
51 Matthews, Linda M., Terence R. Mitchell, Jane George-Flavy, and Robert E. Wood. "Goal Selection in a Simulated Managerial Environment." Group and Organization Management, Vol.19, No.4, (December 1994), pp. 425-449.
52 Matthews, 1994.

But, this word of caution: If managers plan to give negative feedback, they should be sure to give it in a specific, non-evaluative way so that employees are challenged to work harder to achieve.[53]

Avoid goal conflict. Managers should ensure that individual goals facilitate the attainment of organizational goals.[54] If managers reward employees for a quantity goal while being asked to make a quality goal a top priority, they will commit less to both the quantity and quality goals.[55]

Summary

Managers are expected to perform a multitude of functions including planning, organizing, leading, and controlling, and perhaps most important, executing their responsibilities through others. Managers cannot expect to manage others if they cannot manage themselves. Establishing a system of goals is a valuable tool that will enable managers to do both—manage themselves and others.

Managers should recognize some of the many benefits of goal setting:

- Directing attention and actions.
- Mobilizing peak-level performance.
- Bolstering persistence.
- Developing innovative strategies.
- Providing a short and long-term game plan.
- Preventing stress and burnout.

As a first step toward goal setting, identify the problem. Specify what is to be accomplished: the job, assignment, or responsibility to be completed. Managers can use brainstorming methods to assist in identifying problems and then rank the ideas that emerge.

The second step includes creating a plan for how to accomplish the goal. Develop a list of all possible alternatives and then discard those that are unreasonable.

---

53 Mesch, 1994.
54 Mitchell, 1990.
55 Locke, 1988.

Step three lists elements to include when creating a SMART performance goal. SMART goals are those that are: specific, measurable, attainable, realistic, and timely.

Step four identifies resources such as time, equipment, money, favors, encouragement, and moral support managers may need to achieve their goals. Anticipating resource needs will strengthen plans and actions, and planning how to utilize resources can make goals more real and concrete.

Step five refers to the risk involved by pursuing the goal using one method over another, planning for potential obstacles that develop, and the eventual trade offs among conflicting goals. Trading off between quantity and quality goals is one of the most common conflicts.

Step six discusses the need for constructive feedback. Feedback makes goal setting effective because it indicates when and where managers may need to adjust their direction or methods so that they are achieving their best.

When the decisions in the steps for establishing a goal have been successfully made, commit them to writing. The goal statement is a declaration of the outcome one plans to accomplish. Review and adjust or clarify the steps as necessary. Be specific. Using the information produced in the step process, create a written goal statement that provides the answers to who, what, when, where, why, how, and who cares?

Once an established, written goal exists, managers can then move toward achievement of the goal. Two of the effective ways to approach goal achievement are the cognitive approach and the physical approach. The cognitive approach is a mental procedure, a visualization that assumes that by concentrating on the goal and believing that it is attainable, it is likely that the subconscious mind will begin to play a valuable role in helping with goal achievement.

The physical approach includes the setting of objectives that enable managers to reach their goals. Just as there are steps to establishing a goal, and visualizing it, there are steps in setting objectives:

- State the requirements and methods.
- Establish the timeframe.

- Set interim goals.

- Set a deadline.

An important facet of goal achieving is keeping accurate records of the progress made toward goal accomplishment. The fact that progress will likely come as slow transformation makes it important to keep precise records by frequency count or time duration.

Managers should also establish appropriate methods for reward and discipline when accomplishing or falling short on making progress toward the goal. Positive (reward) and negative (discipline) reinforcers, ensure that the criteria are realistic and attainable. It is important to experience small rewards early and frequently to help increase the likelihood of maintaining the goal quest. Similarly, small lapses and regressions may occur during the process. Discipline for non-achievement should not be so severe as to cause one to give up.

Goal aids are utilized to help managers keep their goals before them at all times—ever-present but not intrusive. They are most effective when practiced on a daily basis such as during the morning commute or during exercise periods.

Goals are likely to change with time and therefore should be re-evaluated. However, the decision to change goals should be both rational and conscious. Where accomplishment was underestimated, set higher goals. Similarly, where accomplishment was overestimated, this is the time to adjust to more realistic goals.

Once managers have established their goals, and have moved toward achieving them successfully, they can begin to coach their employees on goal setting.

These are some effective methods managers can use in coaching their employees:

- Stay in close contact. Find out what support employees need from you to be successful.

- Praise often. Compliments help employees feel appreciated and valuable to the goal achievement process.

- Communicate the importance of the process to everyone involved.

- Make sure employees are capable of achieving the goal.

- Allow employees to reward and review themselves. People are more likely to accept and derive meaning from self-generated feedback than from supervisor-generated feedback.

- Choose the right time. A time lag between the assignment and actual achieving of the goal may cause changes in the originally set goals and thereby distract attention away from the goal.

- Select the right method. Different types of goals such as learning goals may be helpful and more appropriate to set than performance goals when people are acquiring information and skills.

- Publicize goals. The public spotlight and pressure will help motivate commitment.

- Consider using negative feedback. But, this word of caution: If managers plan to give negative feedback, they should be sure to give it in a specific, non-evaluative way so that employees are challenged to work harder to achieve.

- Avoid goal conflict. Managers must ensure that individual goals facilitate (rather than conflict with) the attainment of organizational goals.

Summary of classifications: 2 Owners, 3 Corporate Executives, 4 District or Regional Managers, 10 General Managers, and 3 Managers.

Bibliography

Earley, Christopher P, William Prest, and Pauline Wojnaroski. "Task Planning and Energy Expended: Exploration of How Goals Influence Performance." *Journal of Applied Psychology*, Vol.72, No.1, (1987), pp. 107-114.

Gardner, M., *The Annotated Alice: Alice's Adventures in Wonderland & Through the Looking Glass* (New York: Clarkson N. Potter, Inc., 1960), p. 88.

Gatewood, R. D., Taylor, R. R., and Ferrell, O. C., *Management Comprehension, Analysis, and Application.* (Burr Ridge, IL: Richard D. Irwin, Inc., 1995).

Gellatly, Ian R. and John P. Meyer. "The Effects of Goal Difficulty on Physiological Arousal, Cognition, and Task Performance." *Journal of Applied Psychology*, Vol.77, No.5, (1992), pp. 694-704.

Gilliland, Stephen W. and Ronald S. Lamis. "Quality and Quantity Goals in a Complex Decision Task: Strategies and Outcomes." *Journal of Applied Psychology*, Vol.77, No.5, (1992), pp. 672-681.

Latham, Gary P. and Edwin A. Locke. "Self-Regulation Through Goal Setting." *Organizational Behavior and Human Decision Processes*, 50, (1991), pp. 212-247.

Locke, E. A., Chah, D., Harrison, S., and Lustgarten, N. "Separating the Effects of Goal Specificity From Goal Level." *Organizational Behavior and Human Decision Making*, 43, (1989), pp. 270-287.

Locke, Edwin A. "The Determinants of Goal Commitment." *Academy of Management Review*, Vol.13, No.1, (1988), pp. 23-39.

Locke, E. A. and Latham, G. P. *A Theory of Goal Setting and Task Performance* (Englewood Cliffs, NJ: Prentice Hall, 1990).

Maier, Norman R. F. "Assets and Liabilities in Group Problem Solving: The Need for an Integrative Function." *Psychological Review*, Vol.74(4), (1967), pp.233-249.

Mathis, R. L. and Jackson, J. H. (1997). *Human Resource Management* (St. Paul, MN: West Publishing Co., 1997).

Matthews, Linda M., Terence R. Mitchell, Jane George-Flavy, and Robert E. Wood. "Goal Selection in a Simulated Managerial Environment." *Group and Organization Management*, Vol.19, No.4, (December 1994), pp. 425-449.

Mesch, Debra J., Jiing-Lih Farh, and Philip M. Podsakoff. "Effects of Feedback Signs on Group Goal Setting, Strategies, and Performance." *Group and Organization Management*, Vol.19, No.3, (September 1994), pp. 309-333.

Mitchell, Terence R. and William S. Silver. "Individual and Group Goals When Workers Are Interdependent: Effects on Task Strategies and Performance." *Journal of Applied Psychology*, Vol. 73, No. 2, (1990), pp. 185-193.

O'Hair, D. and Friedrich, G. W. (1992). *Strategic Communication in Business and the Professions* (Boston: Houghton Mifflin Company, 1992).

Shalley, Christina E. "Effects of Productivity Goals, Creativity Goals, and Personal Discretion on Individual Creativity." *Journal of Applied Psychology*, Vol. 76, No.2, (1991), pp. 179-185.

Stallworth, H. (1990, June). "Realistic goals help avoid burnout." *HR Magazine*, Vol. 35, 6, (June 1990), p. 171.

Terpstra, David E. and Elizabeth J. Rozell. "The Relationship of Goal Setting to Organizational Profitability." *Group and Organization Management*. Vol. 19, No. 3, (September 1994), pp. 285-294.

Thompson, Jr., A. A. and Strickland III, A. J., *Strategic Management Concepts and Cases*. (Burr-Ridge, IL: Richard D. Irwin, Inc., 1995).

Zander, Alvin, *The Purposes of Groups and Organizations*. (San Francisco: Jossey-Bass Publishers, 1985).

Article 04:

Time Management for Restaurant Managers: No Time Left for You?

Article authors: Florence Berger and Edward A. Merritt

Introduction

No time for a gentle rain, no time for my watch and chain, no time for revolving doors, no time for the killing floor, there's no time left for you.

When the Guess Who stormed onto the music scene in the early 1970s declaring, *No Time*, did they guess that the *who* for which those words would ring true would be a metaphor to describe the pace faced by today's frenzied restaurant managers as well? Some 73% of the respondents to a recent survey by Day Runner Inc. say they are *insanely busy*.[56] Perhaps like never before, managers need to develop effective time management skills in order to stay afloat amid the surging torrents of information, people, and tasks bombarding them.

Statement of the Problem: Why Time Management?

Time management is putting time to the best possible use. But when one considers time management more deeply, it becomes apparent that it is not time, but him- or herself, that a manager must manage. People like to think they are masters of their own time; in reality, most are slaves to events. But time management tools alone are unlikely to make people fully productive; the key is in understanding

---

56 Gordon, Jack, Hequet, Marc. and Stamps, David." We Realize You're Too Busy To Read This, But.... Training. Feb 1997, v34 n2, p. 20-22.

time, proper planning, and priority setting.[57] Though simple in concept, time management can be very difficult to implement. The subject has been treated extensively in articles and books, but the problem of poor time management still haunts today's manager. Shelly Fireman, patriarch of Café Concepts, creators of some of New York City's most successful dining establishments including: Redeye Grill, Brooklyn Diner USA, Hosteria Fiorella, Café Fiorello, and Trattoria Dell'Arte, offered his tongue-in-cheek method for effectively managing time: *I have a 27-hour clock that I bought in a bazaar in Istanbul 18 years ago. With the three extra hours, I exercise, contemplate the world around me, and read an additional book.* Dom DiMattia, vice president for human resources, at Café Concepts added: *There's really no secret to effective time management skills. Although managers may have 100 other things going, they must stay focused on what's important and take it one step at a time and not create catastrophes or exaggerate in their minds about the amount of work they have. We all know we get the work done.*

First we will discuss some of the details of the study—including its purpose, methodology, findings, and implications and lessons learned. Second, we will begin to gain a better understanding of time management by discussing how restaurateurs manage their time, why they are managing their time poorly, and introduce a diagnostic tool for helping managers account for where their time is going. The third and final section is devoted to implementing solutions that can lead to more effective time management. Topics include breaking bad habits, delegating, eliminating interruptions, and dealing with mounding paperwork. If managers need an incentive to read further, remember that an astounding 91 percent of study participants state that time management skills increase their organizations' bottom lines by at least 10 percent.

About the Study

Purpose

Our purpose was to help restaurant managers develop better time management habits.

---

57 Macadam, Charles. "Do You Control Your Time—Or Does It Control You? Works Management. Jan 1997, v50 n1, p. 44-45.

Methodology

We conducted in-depth interviews with a stratified sample of 74 (n=74) restaurant managers located throughout the country to help us probe further into our subject of time management.

Our assumptions were that restaurant managers consider time management to be an important component in the successful operation of a restaurant (measured in terms of bottom-line profit), that managers regularly employ some type of time management system, and that their time management systems are not very effective. Furthermore, assuming those findings, we would create a diagnostic instrument to help managers pinpoint problem areas and suggest a tool kit for implementing effective changes in present methods.

Participants

This study was conducted among 74 (n=74) managers working at restaurants and restaurant companies across the United States. Typical position titles include Owner, Corporate Executive, District or Regional Manager, General Manager, and Manager. The interviews were conducted by telephone and mail.

Demographic Information

First, we asked the expert panel to tell us about themselves. The demographic and descriptive information component of the study contains six statements to determine answers to such variables as these:

- Job title.
- Length of time in the restaurant profession.
- Length of time in present position.
- Age.
- Gender.
- In which of five areas of the country they live.

Study Questions

Next, we asked the managers to tell us about their work. Participants were asked six questions to help guide the subject matter. However, interview sessions were allowed to develop on their own to uncover areas of importance. From those answers, extemporaneous focus questions were asked where appropriate to help clarify information:

- If, in addition to their primary restaurant management duties, they also have other management responsibilities.

- Number of direct reports managers supervise.

- If they use time management principles.

- If yes, their effect on the company's bottom line.

- To rate the effectiveness of their time management practices. Four categories (poor, fair, good, and excellent) segmented the responses. The parameters of the categories reflect the relative degree of time management restaurateurs practice. The poor category consists of managers' responses indicating no planning or forethought. The fair category includes managers who plan or attempt to plan, but only in a casual way. The good category includes those managers who consistently plan, using a planner and looking forward into upcoming weeks. The excellent category includes those managers who not only use a planner but also prioritize and update their schedules.

- To list any impediments to more effective time management.

Findings

Job title:

- 49% (36 individuals) of study participants hold the job title of general manager.

- 28% (21) hold a job title such as area manager or regional manager, corporate executive, or owner.

- 23% (17) hold the job title of manager.

Years in restaurant profession:

- 38% (28) have been in the restaurant profession up to 10 years.

- 35% (26) have been in the restaurant profession at least 15 years.

- 27% (20) have been in the restaurant profession 10 to 15 years.

Years in present position:

- 43% (32) have been in their present positions at least 3 years.
- 33% (24) have been in their present positions 1 to 3 years.
- 24% (18) have been in their present positions up to 1 year.

Age:

- 49% (36) are up to 30 years old.
- 27% (20) are 30 to 40 years old.
- 24% (18) are at least 40 years old.

Gender:

- 73% (54) are male.
- 27% (20) are female.

Area of the country where working:

- 24% (18) work in the South.
- 23% (17) work in the North.
- 22% (16) work in the Central region.
- 16% (12) work in the Mountain region.
- 15% (11) work in the West.

Additional management duties:

- 76% (56) do not perform additional management duties.
- 24% (18) do perform additional management duties.
-

Number of direct reports:

- 64% (47) supervise 7 or more direct reports.

- 28% (21) supervise 4 to 6 direct reports.
- 8% (6) supervise 1 to 3 direct reports.

Those using time management principles daily:

- 93% (69) use principles of goal setting daily.
- 7% (5) do not use principles of goal setting daily.

Of those that use time management principles daily (69 respondents), does time management increase your company's bottom line?

- 35% (24) say time management increases their bottom line by 20% or more.
- 33% (23) say time management increases their bottom line by 15 to 20%.
- 32% (22) say time management increases their bottom line up to 15%.

Effectiveness of time management skills:

- 54% (40) rate the effectiveness of their time management skills as poor.
- 18% (13) rate the effectiveness of their time management skills as fair.
- 16% (12) rate the effectiveness of their time management skills as excellent.
- 12% (9) rate the effectiveness of their time management skills as good.

Reasons for ineffectiveness of time management skills:

Through focus questions, we were able to categorize interview participant answers into four major categories including:

- Interruptions.
- Walk-ins.
- Unnecessary meetings.
- Paperwork.

Implications and Lessons

Findings help support our expectations. While restaurant managers realize the important role that time management plays in business success (as measured by bottom-line effect), they can become sidetracked and succumb to unexpected events of the day. Giving in to urgent incidents produces less than stellar outcomes in terms of time management effectiveness—the majority of our study participants rate poor. However, with our small sample (n=74), we cannot generalize our findings to the larger population of restaurant managers.

Our respondents are relatively new to the restaurant business. More than one third (38 percent) have been in the industry less than 10 years. This finding indicates that, at least in terms of this study, that the opportunity to reach the level of manager comes about rather quickly. On the other hand, we were somewhat surprised to find that only approximately one third (35 percent of our study participants have been in the industry for more than 15 years. Is this a hint that the restaurant business is a young person's industry? Perhaps.

The years in present position suggests a lot of turnover. Over one half (57 percent) of our respondents have been in their present jobs three years or less—a shorter time than we expected. Advancement and job switching can account for some degree of turnover. However, something is also happening at the other end to create all of the position openings. Growth and expansion likely account for some of the opportunity; however the numbers suggest, too, that managers are leaving the industry.

Almost one half of our study participants are less than 30 years old. Three quarters of our participants are less than 40 years old. These findings suggest that, at least in our study, this is a young person's business.

Where do the others go? If we consider years in the restaurant profession, the turnover, and age of respondents, it suggests that older managers are leaving the business. But why is this so? Is it the frenetic pace? Is it due to lifestyle choices? Is the restaurant business a stepping-stone to some other area within the hospitality industry? Are managers leaving the industry altogether? The findings are unclear.

Our findings indicate that it is still a *man's world* in the higher ranks of the hospitality industry within our sample population. Men outnumber women almost three to one as managers.

A significant number of participants—almost one quarter (24 percent)—describe themselves as having other management responsibilities besides their primary duties of restaurant management. We are curious to find such a large percentage of our participants with additional duties. However, these findings are consistent with another study that we have cited within the text of this paper.

The majority of respondents (64 percent) supervise 7 or more direct reports. While this number may be large by other standards of comparison, we are not surprised to find that most of our participants supervise 7 or more direct reports.

The fact that 93 percent of the study participants utilize the principles of time management on a daily basis is as we expected. We find it remarkable that managers credit so much of the importance of time management to their bottom lines (68 percent say time management increases their bottom lines by at least 15 percent); and yet over half (54 percent) of our managers rate poor in their effective use of time management skills.

Toward a Better Understanding

How Restaurateurs Manage Their Time

Overall, restaurateurs manage their time poorly. The results of a study by Ferguson and Berger[58] found that, more often than not, restaurateurs felt they lacked the knowledge of adequate time management skills. Furthermore, Merritt notes in a recent study that when faced with vast amounts of information and forced to make decisions too quickly—and with inadequate knowledge—people can be overcome by stress.[59] We feel lack of knowledge of time management strategies is a major problem affecting the restaurateur as a manager. To navigate successfully the intricacies of management, Lewis suggests time management training to help separate useful information from clutter. According to Monical Pizza Corp. president Harry Bond, with a little scrounging and a willingness to modify lessons from other industries and time-management books, restaurateurs can find a

58 Ferguson, Dennis and Florence Berger, "Restaurant Managers: What Do They Really Do?", Cornell Hotel and Restaurant Administration Quarterly, November 1984, pp. 26-36.
59 Merritt, Edward A. "Hospitality Management: A Study of Burnout." An unpublished Master of Business Administration research project, Pepperdine University, March, 1996, p. 15.

warehouse of educational and training materials for little or no money.[60] Larry Schwartz, owner of daVinci's in Sun Valley, Idaho, believes: *Time management is a matter of constant prioritization: First things first; not easiest things first. At the end of the day, I do a recap and update so important points don't get overlooked.*

Why Restaurateurs Manage Their Time Poorly

Why do restaurant managers do so poorly when it comes to time management? Mainly because they do not take the time to anticipate how their days will actually be spent. Throughout the day they become bogged down by interruptions. As stated in the Ferguson/Berger article, *They (restaurant managers) had given up so much control over their time and work space, that they constantly managed in an interrupt mode.*[61] Heidi Pustovit, general manager of New York City's Café Des Artistes, had this to say about her method of effective management: *I list 'to dos'—I find it much easier to get it all down and then edit. When I group tasks, all I have to do is copy and paste from the original list.*

But are restaurant managers alone? Not really. The day-to-day time-management problem is caused by a set of unexpected events that disturb the planned daily activities and thus change the long-term optimal schedule for managers in all types of industries. Often referred to as *interrupt mode*, this type of operating condition includes telephone interruptions, meetings, unexpected visitors, poor delegation, and crises.[62] So the question is, *How can restaurant managers become more effective in managing their time*? Read on for some answers.

Improving Time Management Skills

Improving one's own management of time requires a thorough understanding of time—its nature and demands. A study conducted by Food Management[63] revealed that in addition to regular duties, an increasing number of persons describing themselves as *restaurant managers* (21%) are managing other areas these days. In order of

60 Liddle, Alan. "Look Beyond Foodservice For Learning Tools." Nation's Restaurant News. Jun 9, 1997, v31 n23, p. 74.
61 Ferguson and Berger, op. cit., p. 33.
62 Thrampoulidis, K. X., Goumopoulos, C. and Housos, E." Rule Handling in the day-to-day Resource Management Problem: An Object-Oriented Approach," Information & Software Technology, March 1997, pp. 185-193.
63 "The Multi-Department Management Maze." Food Management, Feb 1997, v32 n2, p. 24.

frequency, the list of extra responsibilities these managers have taken over include: environmental services, linen services, engineering maintenance, transportation, security and fire services, hotel and volunteer services, mail delivery, unit assistance and pharmacy.

This reality of the restaurant-business atmosphere suggests the question, *Just how much can one be expected to do?* Apparently a lot. And, as entrepreneurs, restaurant managers tend to have high energy levels, are high in self-confidence—believing they can handle anything that exists or could conceivably come up, and are typically impatient in matters of passing time.[64] Combining increasing management responsibilities with entrepreneurial characteristics can put a manager on the road to overload and subsequent failure, unless they can find ways to mitigate the problematic conditions. Benjamin Ceasar, manager of the trendy Zuni Café, located in San Francisco, shared this technique for staying ahead: *I continually update lists on small notepads. I find that organizing to-do lists in order of priority and area of the restaurant keeps me on top of the most important issues I am facing.* One method to begin to make sense of this phenomenon is to understand more about the nature of time.

- Time exists only in the present instant.

- Time is irreplaceable. We may try to expand the hours in the day by double-booking appointments and compressing schedules, but in the end, such bursts are not sustainable.

- Because time past is gone forever, time can only be managed effectively for the future. Plans must be made now for the effective utilization of impending time.

Analyze Where Time Goes

Time—or lack thereof—is indeed the source of many managers' problems. But the solution is not finding ways to squeeze a few extra hours out of the day. Rather, restaurant executives must change the way they think about time. As recent statistics indicate, the need to escape grueling schedules is more pressing than ever. By killing themselves to accomplish more, restaurateurs are actually being counterproductive, becoming prime targets for heart disease, burnout, depression and just plain unhappiness. Effective executives should analyze where

64 Mintzberg, Henry, Quinn, James Brian, and Voyer, John, The Strategy Process, Englewood Cliffs, NJ: Prentice Hall, 1995, p. 222.

their time actually goes. They should then attempt to manage their time and to cut back unproductive demands on that time. Finally, they should consolidate their discretionary time into the largest possible continuing units of uninterrupted time.[65] *I am relentless about planning the details of my day including scheduling time periods for achieving goals and objectives—even slack, discretionary time to use as make-up time or for projects. I write everything down in my Day-Timer®. But, serving periods are dedicated to our dining guests only—no outside interruptions*, states Cheryl Hinkle, general manager of the Bridgetown Grill, Atlanta.

This is the foundation upon which time management rests. From here managers can begin to understand how best to utilize their time. The Ferguson/Berger article outlined what restaurant managers do and how their time is spent. Average restaurant managers spend 35 percent of their time in unscheduled meetings, 17 percent in desk sessions, 13 percent on telephone calls, and 6 percent on touring the operation.[66] While these percentages point out how the time is being allocated; they do not specify the importance of the activities with respect to the manager's goals. This is where managers must do their own research: record in intervals, prioritize, and categorize to determine exactly where the time goes. This process is known as time analysis.

Some of the managers surveyed already used time analysis to a minor extent. They stated that they were currently using a daily planner or a *to-do* list. However, this is only the beginning. In an effective time analysis, the manager must record the day's events in 15-minute intervals, prioritize each event, and categorize these into groups such as unscheduled meetings, scheduled meetings, and telephone calls. For practical purposes, the manager can list the categories at the top of a time log and simply record the number of the category in the 15-minute time slot. It is very important to record the function as it happens, rather than at the end of the day or at lunch. This is so because the average manager will tend to forget the quotidian events in the workday.

At the end of the day, managers should refer back to the time log and summarize what was actually accomplished toward achieving their stated goals, and how much time was spent. Although time consuming, this process is necessary to construct a more detailed picture of a manager's day and how effectively time was used to achieve goals.

65 "Caught In A Vicious Cycle?" Sales & Marketing Management. Jan 1997, v149 n1, p. 48-56.
66 Ferguson and Berger, op. cit., p. 31.

At the end of the week, the manager should tabulate the amount of time spent on each category and estimate the effectiveness of each day. This will give managers some idea of what consumes their time in a typical workday. Using the analogy of dietary habits, people often find recording what they eat over a set number of days helps expose poor eating habits they might not otherwise have discovered. The same idea is true for keeping a time log. By keeping accurate records of where time actually goes over a specified period of time, managers can discover where their time is not being spent wisely. Without keeping a detailed record, managers may fool themselves into thinking they are effective time managers.

A Restaurant Example: The Starlight Cafe

Before analyzing the time log and its features, we must first acquaint ourselves with The Starlight Cafe and introduce its staff. This medium-sized restaurant is located in a city with minimal seasonal fluctuations. It seats 100 diners in two separate dining rooms, and one private dining room seating an additional 25 patrons. Lunch and dinner are served six days a week; lunch is not served on Saturdays and dinner is not served on Sundays. The bar/lounge doubles as a waiting room. The manager, assistant manager, administrative assistant, and chef all have separate offices. The manager's office is directly behind that of the administrative assistant, while the assistant manager's and chef's offices are near the kitchen.

The restaurant staff includes Pat, the manager; Lee, the assistant manager; Sean, the executive chef; Lisa, the administrative assistant/ bookkeeper; twelve full- and part-time cooks and kitchen workers; twenty wait staff working about 30 hours per week each; six hosts; eight bussers; and a bar staff of ten. Each day Pat, the manager arrives at 8:00 AM and usually stays until 6:00 or 7:00 PM. Sean, the executive chef, works from 11:00 AM to 9:00 PM, while Lee the assistant manager arrives at 2:30 PM and works until closing.

At this point Pat has been keeping a time log for one week and is ready to summarize results in the weekly performance and allocation report. A breakdown of the various categories on the log will show managers where their time was spent. Managers must then probe further and analyze how effectively their use of time helped them achieve their desired goals.

Let's begin by investigating the manager's goal performance. We will look at the manager's areas of effectiveness and analyze performance of daily duties, determining which were absolutely necessary and which could have been delegated. The manager should ask, *Did I spend enough time, or too much time, on this or that activity—and was it realistic?*

The manager is shown as ineffective at allocating time toward the things that matter, such as daily goals. Some of these goals were not addressed, while a great deal of time was spent on other matters. The manager must take a hard look at these goals and question if they were necessary at all. Were they important enough to warrant a major portion of the day? The manager might respond that all the goals were important and had to be accomplished for effective control and management. Perhaps, but then Pat should ask whether personal attention was needed to complete these goals. For instance, did Pat have to finish the liquor inventory Thursday? Could someone else have completed the inventory? Was it so important and sensitive that it required senior management attention? Does Pat feel the need to complete the employee schedule? Clearly such duties should have been delegated to either the assistant manager or the chef; Pat has wasted valuable time doing work of others. Managers tend to do what they *like to do* instead of what they *need to do*. A manager who does not delegate effectively is not managing.

The daily effectiveness chart shows the amount of time spent on each goal. By comparing this to the relative importance or priority of each goal, the manager can decide in each case whether the proper amount of time was spent. Naturally we tend to spend more time on things we enjoy doing and to put off the tasks we do not enjoy. Because of ingrained habits, many managers have difficulty differentiating time spent on the enjoyable versus non-enjoyable goals, since both result in the same feeling of accomplishment. Only a written record will indicate how time is actually being spent; the human memory is too deceiving.

Utilizing the effectiveness chart, a manager will be able to determine which goals are more important, the daily time spent on each, and how much time was needed to complete them. Hiring two prep people, for example, may become a more important task than doing the liquor inventory. But if managers could periodically review their own activities, they could monitor time spent in relation to goal priority and make more informed decisions about those priorities. The manager would be relying less on habits and more on facts.

The manager should review the time log to analyze it for wastes of time, process gaps, and tasks that could have been eliminated, delegated, or reduced. Should Pat be opening the restaurant mail? Is planning out next week's forecast by discussing it at 8:00 AM and 5:00 PM as effective as preparing it between 5:30 and 6:15 PM? Does the value of Pat's time justify watching the technician fix the dish machine?

Ultimately, only the restaurant manager can answer these questions. We can only show managers what to look for and suggest possible changes they could make. By targeting specific areas that need to be reduced, a manager initiates more efficient time management.

An end-of-week analysis can help the manager monitor progress. Segmenting the week into daily percentages helps provide a weekly average. The manager can then track the week's performance and adjust each week accordingly.

Time logs should continue to be maintained on a random basis. It is human nature to fall back into bad habits and forget such things as conscientious time management.

Implementing Solutions

Improvement

We have now investigated the time log and its analysis. If the manager still feels there is room for improvement, we recommend a three-pronged method designed to facilitate more effective time management:

- Breaking bad time management habits.
- Learning to delegate.
- Eliminating the interrupters.

Breaking Habits

Bad habits? Few of us recognize our bad habits because we are not consciously aware of them. When a new and better practice is developed, it should be implemented as soon as possible. This reduces the chance of the new practice being lost again to the subconscious mind. The new practice should contrast with the old so as to obviate the need to perform the old. Furthermore, when initiating a new practice, the manager must commit to following through on implementation. An announcement of the change will usually suffice to make the manager duty-bound. And once begun, there should be no excuses for not utilizing the new practice.

Procrastination. The human failing most closely associated with poor time management is that of procrastination. Everyone procrastinates to some extent; there is always something one would rather do than a distasteful task. Procrastination is something to be recognized and faced. You can fight your tendency to procrastinate by following these guidelines:

- Do not try to do it all at once.

- Start anywhere.

- Start imperfectly.

- Start even when you are not in the mood.

- Work no more than 15 minutes at a time.

- Do not avoid or delay the most difficult problems.

- Realize that unpleasant tasks do not get easier over time.

- Schedule a *Crazy Day* whereby you work through time-consuming details.

- Take the *drive yourself nuts by doing nothing* approach.[67]

No closure. Another bad habit practiced by managers is not completing a task or a decision the first time. Each time a manager picks up an unfinished task, they must re-familiarize themselves with it again. This not only wastes time but in many instances reduces the quality of the task accomplished or the decision made. The manager's original ideas about the task might not be recalled to assist in the final execution. An effective manager follows through with an initiated task until it is accomplished.

Ineffective communication. Task lists are communicated to the staff

[67] Spencer, Margaret S. "Overcoming Procrastination: How To Get Things Done Despite Yourself." Law Practice Management. Apr 1997, v23 n3, p. 51-53

in many forms: Extemporaneous verbal directions, scribbled notes, and elaborate lists and charts. Effective communication strategies vary in part with the characteristics and conditions of the job at hand. Whatever strategy is most appropriate, a manager should take time to ensure expectations are clear so that the staff will know what is expected of them.

Sweating the small stuff. Some managers are able to face crisis after crisis with complete calm. They make handling difficult situations look simple. However, most managers should negotiate around the small speed bumps that occur during the day, so that there is enough energy left to deal with real crises. One strategy is to determine what causes managers to blow things out of proportion in the first place. Misplaced perfectionism is many times at the root of this problem.

Just say *no*. Managers should prioritize their work and distinguish between the important issues that they must handle and the urgent, squeaky-wheel issues that crop up during the day. Often, restaurateurs will over-commit to their bosses, customers, employees, or others, only to find themselves hopelessly behind in their work. When managers cannot say no, they should try compromising. Saying *yes, just not now* may buy the manager the amount of time necessary to work the request in with other tasks and projects and follow-through.

Relying on technology for shortening deadlines. Reynolds[68] warns against the management practice of compressing two weeks' worth of work into one week by relying on available technologies to make the work go quicker. While equipment such as computers and cell phones can increase productivity, the availability of such technology does not necessarily translate into a sustainable competitive advantage. The restaurant industry has adjusted its ways of doing business right along with other industries. The timesaving provided by such devices has created a new benchmark. Deadlines are shorter and expectations are higher than ever before.

Plug time leaks. Restaurant managers should be relentless in their quest to manage smarter. And, part of managing smarter is learning the difference between just doing and true managing. True managing includes avoiding over-supervising, avoiding excessive attention to low-yield projects, and working like a craftsperson for more than simply the money.

68 Reynolds, Dennis. "Mitigating Managerial Burnout—Recognize the Symptoms and Take Remedial Action." Trumpet. Fall 1993, p. 12-13.

Delegating

Throughout this discussion we have emphasized the importance of delegation. We will now describe how managers can delegate effectively. Where does this process begin? Analysis of the time log should initiate the first step. Before delegating tasks, managers must identify where their time is being spent and which tasks could be performed by someone else.

Reasons for Delegating:

- Delegation allows more time for thinking and planning.

- The person closest to the activity should be better able to make decisions than a distant superior.

- Delegation tends to encourage initiative of subordinates and to make effective use of their skills. Initiative, in turn, improves morale.

- Delegation tends to reduce decision time, as it eliminates recommendations going toward the superior where the decision is made and subsequent downward communication.

- Delegation develops the skills of subordinates by permitting them to make decisions and apply their knowledge gained from training programs and meetings.

However, the manager must realize that delegation involves the transfer of authority and decision-making, not of actual responsibility. James Ippoliti, owner and general manager of Hooligans Café in Liverpool, New York, had this to say about delegation: *With 85 employees, I have to delegate. We assign department managers by area and empower interested service staff to take on additional duties such as closing and inventory control. While it's a great help to the managers, it also becomes a track by which our service staff can move up.*

Delegating Principles

Levels of delegation. Delegation is not an *all or nothing* situation. There are different levels of delegation, and a manager must determine to what degree they want to delegate authority. An effective manager understands that some tasks to be performed by others require only fact finding, while others may be followed through to completion. Here is a list of some of the various degrees of delegation:

- Investigate and report back. The subordinate gathers facts for the manager. The manager then takes appropriate action.

- Recommend action. The subordinate recommends action based on fact-finding or specialized knowledge. The manager evaluates the recommendation and takes appropriate action.

- Advise of action planned. The subordinate makes decisions based on investigation. The manager evaluates the decision and approves or disapproves the decision.

- Take action; advise of action taken. The manager gives subordinate control over decision taken. The manager requests to be kept informed as to the action taken.

- Investigate and take action. The manager allows the subordinate full control over decision and supports the decision.

When delegating, the manager should be aware of certain limitations or rules of delegation. First, the delegating manager must follow through and find out the results. This is important not only for the task itself but also for the manager's understanding of subordinates' capabilities.

Delegating managers also need to set standards of performance so that subordinates can track their progress toward completing the task. Managers must also develop ways by which to monitor subordinates' progress. Such monitoring may take the form of written reports or discussion in meetings.

The delegating managers relinquish many operational tasks. Although this gives managers more time for *managing*, they are still responsible for the smooth running of the overall operation. By setting levels of operating performance, the manager can monitor the operation and be alerted to changes. *Spread the work around. Let people know exactly what you expect. Follow up. It works—but only if you are organized. I come in about one-half hour earlier than expected so that I can get a sense of what needs to be done*, states Lisa Rinehart, manager of The American City Diner, located in Bethesda, Maryland.

To Do or to Delegate

You now know the degrees of delegation as well as its advantages and limitations. Where do you go from here? Time log analysis should give managers a clear idea of how their time is being spent. Using the above guidelines, managers can then decide which tasks they must do and which can be delegated.

Marilyn Moats Kennedy[69] suggests that the manager segment tasks into three categories to help eliminate activities that clog one's day. In the first category is work that can only be prioritized and done by the manager. In the second is work that can be delegated immediately. In the third is work that someone else could (and should) be doing when there is someone capable of accomplishing the task. The manager should understand subordinates' capabilities so that work in the second category can be delegated and accomplished immediately. The nature and amount of work in the third category will identify the staff's training needs. As training progresses, the manager will have more time for *managing. I concentrate on utilizing my strengths. By recognizing what I am not good at doing, I can delegate to someone that has talent in those areas*, states Jennifer Irwin, owner of Just A Taste restaurant in Ithaca, New York. Once these two categories of work have been addressed, the manager can concentrate on eliminating the *interrupters*.

Delegation Questions

Before automatically delegating to others there is a series of questions one should ask to help measure the appropriateness of the planned delegation. Here are the questions to ask:

Questions:

Should I delegate to one person?

Should I delegate to a group?

When to delegate to an individual:

• They have pertinent information or appropriate skills.

• You need for them to comprehend and embrace the task.

• They can grow personally or professionally.

69 Kennedy, Marilyn Moats. "Rightsizing Your Job." Across the Board. Feb 1997, v34 n2, p. 53-54.

- Time is not a critical factor.
- The conflict risk is low.

  When to delegate to a group:

- The interaction will add clarity to or help structure the problem.
- Interaction will help increase motivation.
- Conflict may lead to better solutions.
- Time is not a critical factor.
- Excessive conflict risk is low.

  Questions:

  Should I delegate decision-making authority to the group?

  Should I participate with the group?

  When to delegate:

- The group can perform competently and your time will be saved.
- The group's autonomy will increase their drive to perform well.
- The group has adequate information and talent to accomplish the task or project.

  When to participate:

- No one else can provide the necessary leadership.
- The group needs information only possessed by you.
- Your presence will not disrupt the group process.
- Your time will be spent productively.

Eliminating Interruptions

Customer retention and business expansion are primary foci of most restaurant business plans. However, for many restaurants, actual work effort devoted to retention and expansion has fallen far short of goals. The primary reason for the lack of follow through on retention and expansion efforts stems from one of the ongoing dilemmas of time management: Critical activities often push aside the vital but non-critical activities of retention and expansion.[70] The day-to-day running of the restaurant gets in the way of primary goals and objectives. *In the day-to-day, you never know what is going to come up*, states Mark Marotto, owner and manager of Marotto's restaurant in Kenmore, New York. *I plot, prioritize, and color code the daily, weekly, and monthly routine; but I have to schedule for the unexpected, too. At times, I have to 'just do it'—get rid of all the clutter to see the top of my desk.*

The Phone Went Dead

What can be done to eliminate frequent and unproductive interruptions in the workday? A well-trained assistant is the manager's first and most effective line of defense. The Ferguson/Berger study noted telephone calls as the most serious interrupter of all.[71] In fact, a recent survey found that the majority of small-company managers spend one to three hours a day on the telephone.[72] By screening calls, the assistant can prevent the majority of these interruptions for the manager. Since occasional emergencies and other situations do arise, the assistant should be able to distinguish important calls and be aware of key individuals the manager should speak with immediately. Another option is for assistants to take messages, thus allowing managers to fit return calls into their own schedules.

If managers become involved in fruitless phone conversations and the callers will not hang up, managers can experiment by using the *radical termination method* in which they hang up in the middle of one of their own sentences. Most callers will blame the disconnection on the phone company rather than assume that the manager was being rude. After all, *who hangs up on him- or herself?*

I Only Need a Moment

The next most serious interrupter in the manager's workday is the unscheduled meeting or *walk-in* visitor. According to the Ferguson/Berger study, restaurant managers spend three and one-half times

---

70 Phillips, Phillip D. "Business Retention And Expansion: Theory And An Example In Practice." Economic Development Review, Summer 1996, v14 n3, p. 19-24.
71 Ferguson and Berger, op. cit., p. 30.
72 Caggiano, Christopher. "All Talk No Action?" Inc. Jul 1997, v19 n10, p. 104.

more of their day on unscheduled meetings than other managers (35 percent versus 10 percent).[73] Such meetings take up more of a restaurant manager's day than any other single activity. Consequently, they must be reduced to the point where the manager is once again in control of the workday. Again, the assistant can screen visitors and schedule meetings with the manager at a more convenient time. If the visitor insists on seeing the manager, the manager should come out of the office and meet the visitor on neutral ground, thus preventing the guest from sitting down and tying up a long period. Should the visitor persist in idle conversation—watch for nonverbal signs at the start, such as leaning against a desk or a doorway and rocking back and forth—make the visitor aware of time limitations. As a next step, the manager can begin on-the-floor rounds, thus letting the visitor know cordially—but unmistakably—that time is finished. If that fails, a trip to the restroom will likely do the trick.

A Desk in the Rafters?

While an open-door policy is valuable for promoting open communications, the manager must have some uninterrupted work time. Many managers now find that it is beneficial to have a second office or a hidden retreat where they can work uninterrupted for extended periods. Although a second office is not common in the restaurant where space is usually at a premium, a desk or a table in the attic or the basement would work. If this is not possible, the manager should spend certain mornings working at home.

Meetings

Scheduled meetings also proved to be a time user for the restaurant manager. The Ferguson/Berger study determined that restaurateurs conducted an average of 2.4 meetings lasting approximately 46.2 minutes long each per day.[74] This accounted for 29 percent of the entire day. We feel that meeting time could be reduced through planning and prioritizing the issues for meetings using the following strategies:

- Each time a meeting is held, a record of the time spent per person and the hourly salary of the persons attending should be kept. This can be tabulated to determine the total cost of the meeting and compared to the actual results or outcome of the meeting. If

73 Ferguson and Berger, op. cit., p. 31.
74 Ibid., p. 31.

someone other than the manager calls the meeting, that person should be given a copy of the cost and analyze its impact of it on the daily operating performance. The astute manager will be able to determine if the benefits derived from the meeting outweigh the costs. The probable outcome will be fewer, more productive meetings.

- Be aware of meeting attendees with compound agendas. When a person has multiple issues, a list-making strategy can be employed. Taking brief notes forces the speaker to be clear and specific. Ending a rambling conversation positively, yet firmly, is a critical skill to develop.

- All too often, meetings are held on an open basis in order to receive as much input as possible. Sometimes this can cause them to become aimless and unstructured chat sessions instead of information forums. To reduce the chance of meetings from getting out of control, the manager and staff must be well prepared in advance. This task is in the control of the manager who can set up time limits and detailed agendas to follow, and assign persons to comment on certain topics.[75]

- Once the agenda is complete, the meeting should cease. If there are topics that have been addressed outside the agenda, the manager should schedule those topics on the next agenda. If the topic is of extreme importance, it should be discussed with the appropriate people after the meeting concludes. This way, people that will not be involved can return to their own tasks and not have their time wasted in a costly drain of resources. Before the meeting is adjourned, the manager should present a briefing as to the issues and responsibilities for the next meeting so each person will be prepared.[76]

Michael Furtado, regional manager of California Pizza Kitchen shared these ideas on meetings: *Monday staff meetings work well. We can communicate prior week results while events are still fresh on our minds. It also gives us an opportunity to make necessary adjustments for the upcoming week. Everyone is involved. I always keep a pad handy so I don't forget to note important issues.*

75 "How To Save Time At Meetings." Management-Auckland. Nov 1996, v43 n10, p. 18.
76 Struebing, Laura. "Does Your Company Invest Your Time Wisely?" Quality Progress, Dec 1996, v29 n12, p. 10.

Are Attendees Contributing?

The manager should also be aware of other peoples' time. How often have you been asked to attend a meeting that wasted your time? Often a copy of the minutes is as informative as the meeting itself. Keep this in mind whenever you schedule a meeting. Require attendance only of those who will be contributing to the agenda and ask others if they would like to attend. This will allow others to evaluate how the meeting will affect their time and will prevent anyone feeling overlooked.

If the meeting is informal, of short duration, and consists of only a few persons, the manager may elect to hold a stand-up meeting. When required to stand throughout the meeting, people tend to say only what really needs to be said. This will help ensure that the meeting does not go into *overtime*.

Mounding Paperwork

Incoming paperwork is another problem faced by the restaurant manager. One day's absence from the desk can result in a stack of correspondence and memos that takes two days to sort and answer. People seem to take advantage of the manager's day off to overload him or her with unusual amounts of material. This perception is true in a sense because throughout a working day, the manager is constantly sending verbal replies to the queries of others.

The manager can eliminate a large portion of wasted time by reviewing all incoming paperwork. Shelly Branch focuses on Marriott International's CEO, Bill Marriott, who has a long-standing policy of handling *one piece of paper just once* before routing it or throwing it away.[77] Expanding on the Marriott method, Branch recommends that while managers review the paperwork, they should organize it into three categories: one that requires action, one that requires reading, and one that should be thrown out. When going through the first group (action category), the manager should respond to each one individually. Action should be taken before the next one is read. The second group (reading category) should be separated into two piles: those that require passing on and those that need filing. The third group should be discarded. The emphasis is on handling each piece of paper one time only. Nicole Melvin, restaurant manager of The Heritage House in Cincinnati, Ohio, shared her secret for keeping up to date with industry reading: *I scan*

77 Branch, Shelly, " So Much Work, So Little Time.", Fortune, Feb 3, 1997, v135 n2, p. 115-117.

the industry magazines for articles of interest and toss the rest. If I don't, they'll build up into a pile a mile high that I'll never get through.

Writing Reports

Sometimes reports submitted to the manager are of poor quality and too lengthy and need to be re-written. One study found that some department heads spend up to 40 percent of their time just in writing.[78] This writing process should be a tool for productivity, but is often a blockage: Writers waste time producing poorly written, laborious texts that waste even more time for managers. Here are some strategies that can help alleviate the restaurateur's burden of revising shoddy, long-winded reports:

- Have the person responsible redo the work.

- Set an atmosphere of excellence to help minimize problems in the future. Make it clear that you expect smart, simple, and short reports.

- Make sure the staff person understands the job requirements and timetables.

- Make sure people are not over-committed. Staff people have a tendency to say *yes* to every demand. Over-commitment leads to unfinished and sloppy work.

- Give or bring in an expert to give a one-day seminar on writing memos.

Spam

What about junk mail and e-mail? Once a manager is on one mailing list, amounts of spam seem to increase proportionally. A program or assistant can eliminate most of this problem also by opening all mail and forwarding all the important pieces. This can then be roughly sorted by the manager in order of importance and be dealt with appropriately. Another trick would be to use different forms of the restaurant or manager's name when subscribing to publications, ordering them through vendors, and other correspondence. This will identify the

---

78 Neff, Richard E. "CEOs Want Information, Not Just Words So... Write Smart, Simple And Short. Communication World. Apr/May 1997, v14 n5, p. 22-25.

source of the incoming mail and will help the sorting process in terms of importance.

Limited Support

It's no secret that in most cases, only large, high-volume restaurants can afford an administrative support staff. Typically, restaurateurs operate in a self-contained mode. Here are some tactics managers can consider for dealing with interruptions when they do not have other staff members to whom they can delegate tasks:

- Use voice mail to screen calls. Return important calls in groups.

- Move the telephone or turn the ringer off so you cannot hear it ring.

- Use e-mail or messaging to help eliminate unnecessary calls.

Summary

In this article, we have shown the manager how to break old habits, how to delegate tasks, and how to eliminate interrupters. With proper implementation, we are confident that even the worst time managers will benefit from these techniques. It all begins with the time log and a proper analysis of how time is spent. Though itself time-consuming, the time log will produce lasting benefits of better habits, more effective delegation, and fewer interruptions.

Where Managers Go From Here

Managers must use the freed time to attend to more important tasks and projects including: planning, organizing, being creative, and leading. Managers must be prepared to take these new blocks of time and use them to plan for the future.

Hints for Effective Time Management

- To do list. Maintain a daily list of things to do; make a new one each day. Use a clipboard, a yellow pad, a daily planner, an app— whatever works.

- Quiet time. Schedule quiet time for thinking, planning, and reflecting.

- Slack time. Schedule slack time as a buffer.

- Togetherness. Group similar tasks.

- Scheduling. Vary your work schedule to include off-peak periods and work done away from the restaurant.

- Time matters. Instill a climate of discipline in which everyone respects the keeping of time.

- Strengths. Concentrate on your personal strengths.

- Industry publications. You cannot possibly read all of the industry magazines and blurbs; and you would probably be better off to stop trying.

- Notes and reminders. Keep a notepad handy.

- Avoid over-supervising and micro-managing. Let people make (and learn from) mistakes. Ensure that employees are capable and know their permitted bounds for decision-making.

- Set short- and long-term goals including deadlines for each goal.

- Set priorities on a daily basis. Rank tasks in order of priority of importance.

- Work smart. Avoid excessive attention to low-yield tasks or projects; delegate to others.

- Avoid over-committing yourself. Do what you do well—like a craftsperson.

- Distinguish among *nice* to do, *important*, and *urgent*.

- There is no perfect time. *Just do it* and thereby avoid procrastination and perfectionism.

- Prioritize. Do first things first including unpleasant, distasteful, or dreaded tasks.

- Empower others. Encourage and empower team members to solve their own conflicts.

- Screen door. Control interruptions (phone calls, meetings, drop-in visitors, etc.). Move from an open-door policy to a screened-door policy.

- Utilize, but do not waste time with computers. Wasting time includes activities such as re-configuring programs, on hold and on line time with technical support, and clearing out cluttered storage.

Article 05:

Assessment as a Predictor of Income

Article authors: Edward A. Merritt, Dennis Reynolds,
and Florence Berger

Abstract

Assessment centers are one of the fastest growing selection methods used in industry today. However, they are underutilized in hospitality and academe (Lowry, 1994). The hospitality industry can use assessment centers to enhance both employee selection and professional development. Hospitality educators can use assessment centers as a development tool in producing graduates who meet the needs of organizations, and also in evaluating administrative and teamwork skills.

In this study, we described the assessment center process used in the graduate hospitality program at Cornell University and found that leadership skill best predicted total income upon graduation.

Introduction

Since their first application in the 1950s, assessment centers have been used in numerous organizations for assessing executive talent. In the assessment process, typically top-level managers observe employees to gauge management expertise for the purposes of selection, early identification of managerial talent, development planning, identification of training needs, promotion, and management succession (Spychalski, et al., 1994).

Universities have begun using assessment centers as well. At Texas A&M, the University of Maine, and throughout the Pennsylvania university system, the assessment center technique has been used to evaluate students in various colleges (Wendel & Joekel, 1991). Baldwin-Wallace College in Berea, Ohio, has used assessment centers to help students develop management and career planning skills (Rea, et al., 1990). John Carroll University and Glasgow Caledonian University in Scotland have used assessment centers at the undergraduate level in management education (Extejt, et al., 2001; Dalziel, et al., 1993).

Though the use of assessment centers has not been widespread in education, rudiments—case studies, role-plays, and in-basket exercises—have been used in the classroom (Wendel & Joekel, 1991). Michigan State University has used assessment centers in their hospitality business program and Cornell University uses an assessment center each year for its incoming Master of Management in Hospitality students.

Research Statement

The focus of this study was the relationship between management skill areas as evaluated by an assessment center and total income upon graduation.

Importance

A review of the literature indicated that there was a lack of consequential hospitality research in this area and the impact of these variables was unknown. This study, therefore, became an initial step in management research in suggesting a positive correlation between leadership skill and total income. Moreover, the findings suggest that schools may be able to increase the value of their programs to students by including leadership skill development in their programs.

Scope

This was a study of students in a master of management in hospitality program. The population of interest was the 55-member class. The unit being analyzed was the individual student. Students took paper-and-pencil tests and industry executives observed and rated students' behavior.

While certain results may provide insight, this study does not propose to be generalizable to a wider population.

Review of the Literature

Assessment Centers have been found to be valid, cost-effective, and are viewed as credible by managers and participants (Adler, 1993). Schmitt, Gooding, Noe, & Kirsh (1984) compared various selection methods and found that assessment centers are better predictors of job performance than the other methods and have high criterion validity (Chan, 1996) regardless of educational level, race, or gender (Schneider & Wallich, 1990). Moreover, assessment centers are seen as being fairer than paper-and-pencil tests because candidates are evaluated on how they act in situations that a manager would commonly encounter (Thornton & Byham, 1982).

Within universities, assessment centers provide educators with a credible method for determining skill development and assist in other ways: they can bring realistic business situations into class, provide for industry and education partnerships, assist in revising the managerial curriculum, aid in counseling students, and based on the management competencies literature (e.g., Bass, 1981; Boyatzis, 1982; Mintzberg, 1975) and interviews with executives, they can produce a significant impact on more skills than participation in a development program (Extejt, et al., 2000).

One study found 44 percent of organizations used assessment centers as part of their graduating student recruitment (Keenan, 1995). Such a high degree of use by organizations (IRS Employment Review, 1992) gives universities opportunities to prepare students for these real-world situations.

The primary drawbacks to using assessment centers include time, coordination required, and cost over testing alone (Hoffman & Thornton, 1997). Moreover, when using assessment centers as a selection tool within organizations, unsuccessful candidates showed a decline in self-esteem and need for achievement (Fletcher, 1991).

McEwen & McEwen (1995), Scherer (1990), and Dulewicz (1991) determined that it is difficult to measure management skills with paper-and-pencil tests alone. Assessment center exercises have been found to be more successful than aptitude tests in predicting management success (Rea, et al., 1990). More than 50 validation studies (Dulewicz, 1991) indicate that assessment centers predict future performance or success better than other assessment tools.

Methodology

Independent Variables

We used test scores and five management skills which were evaluated during the assessment center—written communication, presentational speaking, group process, leadership, and creativity—as our predictor variables. Additionally, students were segmented on the basis of personal and environmental demographics.

An overview of the six skills that were assessed is provided in the paragraphs, which follow. It was assumed that students would aspire to becoming general managers. Therefore, exercises were focused toward that end.

Area One: Standardized Tests

The program began with students completing four standardized tests measuring 1. Critical thinking ability, 2. Stress management skill, 3. Time management skill, and 4. Supervisory skill.

Area Two: Written Communication

This area measured students' competency in two ways 1. Communicating information clearly and directly by analyzing a profit and loss statement, and 2. Maintaining a positive guest relationship while communicating essential information.

Area Three: Presentational Speaking

Participants were asked to put themselves in the GM's position and inspire a group of new employees. Each person was assessed on the effectiveness of his or her organization, development, ability to relate to listeners, and delivery skills.

Area Four: Group Process

The Group Process session provided an opportunity for students to discuss key organizational issues in small group settings such as service quality and guest services. Participants were asked, for instance, *What would you do when an important guest has a heated conflict with a key employee?*

Area Five: Leadership

Few skills are as important to senior managers as effective leadership. In this exercise, each student served as leader of a five-member team. The leader was given a specific task and asked to facilitate the development and presentation of a strategic plan. The leader was also charged with engendering the full support of the group.

Area Six: Creativity

Leaders in the next century will be those who develop innovative solutions to pressing problems and who approach daily challenges with entrepreneurial perspectives. In the creativity exercise, students created a commercial advertising the organization's hotel of the future.

Follow Up

Goodge (1995) found that for an assessment center process to work, it must be incorporated into a management development plan. Feedback provided during the individual interview sessions and in a comprehensive summary report following the session was used as a basis for students' professional development efforts.

Dependent Variables

We used job offer data upon graduation in determining our outcome variable, total annualized income for year one (including signing bonus, base salary, commission, and performance bonus). Additionally, students were segmented on the basis of personal and environmental demographics such as industry, position, and position focus. Data were available for all 55 master's program graduates.

Research Goal, Nature, Question, and Hypothesis

The goal of the study was to detect relationships that might exist among the independent and dependent variables rather than to establish cause-effect relationships. Therefore, the type of study suggested a one-shot investigation correlational design instead of an experimental design (Campbell & Stanley, 1963). A significance level of $p < 0.05$ was adopted to determine whether relationships existed (Schmitt & Klimoski, 1991).

Research Question and Hypothesis

Research Question: Do management skill area(s) predict total income?

Research Hypothesis: Higher ratings in management skill area(s) will predict higher total income.

This hypothesis reflects the relationship between assessment center ratings predicting organizational success suggested in the literature review from more than 50 validation studies (Dulewicz, 1991).

Analysis and Results

Model Formulation

We performed the steps in model formulation. Overall, the majority of the scatter plot pairings suggested good linear relationships with few gaps in the data. A linear regression was therefore identified as a possible method for analysis.

Following this preliminary inspection, step-by-step and hierarchical regression were used to assist in the development of a model which would be based on theory from the literature, simple and straightforward, and demonstrate good fit.

Diagnostics

We performed graphic and statistical diagnostic tests to help ensure soundness of results. Remedial techniques were examined where data did not fall into accordance with the regression model's conditions. The model was determined to demonstrate goodness of fit, be appropriate from which to make inferences, and explained 31.6 percent of the variance.

Findings

Significant support was found for the research question and hypothesis that students who scored higher ratings in leadership received higher total income job offers upon graduation. We did not find significance for any of the other management skills assessed (either alone or bundled) as predicting total income. Implications for application suggest a direct outcome supporting the value of schools including leadership skill development in their programs, higher leadership skill equals higher total income.

Limitations

1. The goal of this study was to detect relationships rather than to establish cause-effect (as in experimental design). The study design therefore, can only suggest bases for correlations.

2. This was the first time that a study of this type had been conducted in this fashion. Additional studies in this area of organizational behavior would have helped suggest hypothesized relationships more precisely.

3. This study included only one class of 55 master's program students. While findings provide insight into relationships that may exist, additional numbers of students, classes, and/or programs may have added to the validity of the findings.

4. The cross-sectional rather than longitudinal nature of this study may be a limitation. It could have added validity to follow the students beyond their first year of total income to determine whether the positive correlation held.

5. The literature identified more than 50 studies indicating assessment centers' proficiency in predicting success better than other assessment tools. We selected only one measure of success in using total income as our dependent variable.

Areas for Future Study

1. Replication. Since this was the first study of its type, additional information from more participants in other studies would help enhance the validity of the findings.

2. Experimental Design. The findings suggest that a future study using experimental design could help enhance the study's validity. Experimental design could also become a next logical step in determining cause and effect.

Concluding Remarks

This study achieved three worthwhile purposes: First, it enabled us to gain insight into management skills and how they relate to total income. Second, it was possible to utilize theoretical foundations and rigorous methods to investigate a hunch, which suggested relationships among management skills and total income. Third, it was possible to develop a model, which can be used to measure leadership in determining how it may relate to total income.

References

Adler, S. (1993). "Assessment Centers in Human Resource Management," *Personnel Psychology*, Vol. 46, No. 2, pp. 447-451 paraphrasing a statement from George Thornton's book, Assessment Centers in Human Resource Management.

Campbell, D, & Stanley, J. (1963). *Experimental and quasi-experimental designs for research.* Chicago: Rand McNally College Publishing.

Chan, D. (1996). "Criterion and Construct Validation of an Assessment Centre," *Journal of Occupational and Organizational Psychology*, Vol. 69, No. 2, pp. 167-182.

Dalziel, S., McDougall, M., Barclay, J. and Nimmo, R. (1993). "Introducing Development Centres into Management Education: The way forward?," *Management Education and Development*, Vol. 24, No. 3, pp. 280-294.

Dulewicz, V. (1991). "Improving Assessment Centres," *Personnel Management*, Vol. 23, No. 6, pp. 50-61.

Extejt, M.M., Forbes, J.B., Smith, J.E. (2000). "Evaluation of a Multimethod Undergraduate Management Skills Development Program," *Journal of Education for Business*, Vol. 71, No. 4, pp. 223-234.

Fletcher, C. (1991). "Candidates' Reactions to Assessment Centres and Their Outcomes: A Longitudinal Study," *Journal of Occupational Psychology*, Vol. 64, No. 2, pp. 117-128.

Goodge, P. (1995). "Design Options and Outcomes: Progress in Development Centre Research," *The Journal of Management Development*, Vol. 14, No. 8, pp. 55-60.

(1992). "Graduate Recruitment Survey: Vacancies, Salaries and Prospects," IRS *Employment Review*, November, pp. 2-11.

Hoffman, C.C. and Thornton III, G.C. (1997). "Examining Selection Utility Where Competing Predictors Differ in Adverse Impact," *Personnel Psychology*, Vol. 50, No. 2, pp. 455-470.

Keenan, T. (1995). "Graduate Recruitment in Britain: A survey of Selection Methods Used by Organizations," *Journal of Organizational Behavior*, Vol. 16, No. 4, pp. 303-318.

Lowry, P.E. (1994). "Selection Methods: Comparison of Assessment Centers With Personnel Records Evaluation," *Public Personnel Management*, Vol. 23, No. 3, pp. 383-395.

McEwen, T. and McEwen, B.C. (1995). "Assessment Center: A Technique for Evaluating Administrative Skills," *Journal of Education for Business*, Vol. 70, No. 6, pp. 362-371.

Rea, P., Rea, J., and Moomaw, C. (1990). "Use Assessment Centers in Skill Development," *Personnel Journal*, Vol. 69, No. 4, pp. 126-131.).

Scherer, G. (1990) "How Candidates Perceive Assessment Centers," *The Police Chief*, Vol. 57, No. 2, pp. 33-34.

Schmitt,N., Gooding, R.Z., Noe, R.A., and Kirsh, M. (1984). "Meta-Analysis of Validity Studies Published Between 1964 and 1982 and the Investigation of Study Characteristics," *Personnel Psychology*, Vol. 37 No. 3, pp. 407-422.

Schmitt, N., & Klimoski, R. (1991). *Research Methods in Human Resources Management*. Cincinnati, OH: South-Western Publishing.

Schneider, G.T. and Wallich, L. (1990). "Assessment Centers as Avenues to Administrative Career Advancement," *Planning and Change*, Vol. 2 No. 4, pp. 225-238.

Spychalski, A.C., Quinones, M.A., Gaugler, B.B. and Pohley, K. (1997). "A Survey of Assessment Center Practices in Organizations in the United States," *Personnel Psychology*, Vol. 50, No. 1, pp. 71-90.

Thornton, III, G.C. and Byham, W.C. (1982) *Assessment Centers and Managerial Performance* (New York: Academic Press), pp. 127-132.

Wendel, E.C. and Joekel, R.G. (1991) *Restructuring Personnel Selection: The Assessment Center Method* (Bloomington, IN: Phi Delta Kappa Educational Foundation.

Article 06:

Strategies for Increasing Hotel Room Sales

Article author: Edward A. Merritt

Summary

The focus of this article was written primarily for limited service lodging properties. This article identifies and discusses 15 proven techniques, which can be implemented to increase hotel room sales. It also includes ideas for fine-tuning or overhauling the room sales strategy.

Strategies

1. Price room rates according to selling point. Inspect rooms for uniqueness, room size, features, location, and guest requests. Categorize these elements as a basis for room rate differential from which to sell.

For example, a down (ground floor) and out (outside corridor), end room, with oversized parking in front of the room door, Jacuzzi tub, overlooking a wooded stream, which is the most-often requested room would sell for more than an upstairs room located farthest away from the stairs. Creating a variety of room rates allows for creative up selling by the staff. Moreover, a variety of room rates allows for a basis of negotiation when booking a reservation.

2. Spruce up. Examine the property from a guest's point of view for outside curb appeal. Are potholes filled? Has the parking lot recently been slurried and/or seal coated? Has the concrete been recently pressure washed? Are the parking lot stripes fresh? Are all light bulbs

all shining? Is the grass freshly trimmed? Are the flowerbeds alive with annual color? Are automatic timers for signs and lights set for the correct times? Are windows clean? Is the pool sparkling clear? Are room doors freshly painted? Are room numbers visible? Are doormats fresh?

3. Draw guests in with price. Not all properties want to compete on price. However, if the drive is to sell rooms, price is an effective motivator. Consider a changeable letter board (inexpensive) or an electronic sign (expensive, but distinctive and easy to change), which can display a message. Advertise the lowest possible price. Use price as an opportunity to upsell on the basis of features. As occupancy increases, consider raising rates. This is especially true if, for example, the property's walk-in traffic increases after 6 p.m. (with an average 20 requests) and you have just 15 rooms left to sell at 4:30 p.m.

4. Empower guest service agents to negotiate price. Travelers expect to be able to negotiate. This ability to negotiate is especially true when travelers notice that parking lots have few cars at 10 p.m. at other competing properties. The idea in this case is that any rate above variable costs (costs for housekeeping, electricity, amenities, and laundry) contributes to profit. Note that fixed costs (items such as mortgage, real estate taxes, salaried employees, etc.) do not change based on occupancy. If a property calculates its variable costs at $18.50 per room, then any rate above $18.50 contributes to profit (helps pay for fixed costs). Set the parameters; clerks negotiate within those parameters. Bonus guest services agents on room sales over base sales price and/or numbers of rooms sold.

5. Allow options for the breakfast question. Many limited service properties have a tough time deciding whether to add eggs and meat products to their complimentary breakfast. Consider continuing with continental breakfast being complimentary, but perhaps adding a modest charge for the option of eggs and meat products.

6. Sell to the local community. Advertise the property to the local community in the Shopper as an extra bedroom. Give locals a special rate to encourage them to use the property when out-of-town guests come to visit. Consider blast emailing last-minute bargain rates when sales fall short of forecast. Use other forms of social media to create and maintain awareness.

7. Examine the number of tasks that guest service agents provide. There is always a balance which must be maintained between labor cost and guest service. At some point, however, the property loses room sales when clerks are trying to perform too many functions.

Consider, for example, the incoming phone reservation, which is missed because the clerk on duty is taking another reservation, cashiering, night auditing, providing room service, rebooting the television, replacing an air conditioner, performing wake-up calls, taking a message, walking security rounds, room clerking, running the phone console, issuing a key card, or giving directions to the local diner.

8. Choose a market niche. In which market does the property compete? Successful operators know their market niche and stay within their bounds. There has always been a margin for properties to cross over into competing territories ever since Holiday Inn merged concepts of full-service hotels with limited-service properties. However, a $99.00 rate likely does not warrant custom toiletries and triple-sheeted beds. The limited service category emphasizes basic room accommodations and minimal public areas.

Therefore, consider competing on the basis of providing the best value instead of the most amenities. Value is a function of three variables: Quality, price, and service. As such, value can be affected positively, neutrally, or negatively by adjusting any one or more of those variables. For example, raising quality or service increases value. Raising price lowers value. The effective property owner experiments with the right mix of variables in providing a high overall value in the market to customers. Motel 6 and the early days of the original Volkswagen Beetle revolutionized their industries by utilizing these principles.

9. Re-examine operating affiliation. Is this an independent or a flagged property? If independent, a property may benefit from the advertising, name recognition, centralized reservations system, and operating support of an established brand. On the other hand, location, operating conditions, demand, and market may suggest re-thinking the expenses involved in maintaining a flag relationship. The bottom line— does a flag affiliation offer you a net gain (advantage) or a net loss (disadvantage)?

10. Establish a program of total quality management. All employees should have an opportunity to be involved in a program to incrementally

improve operations at the property. The function of a total quality management program is that operational challenges are addressed at the lowest possible level within the organization, which can yield operational savings, increased employee satisfaction, as well as increased guest satisfaction.

W. Edwards Deming, a well-known US-based consultant, was instrumental in helping automobile manufacturers Datsun (Nissan), Honda, and Toyota in Japan develop their once cheap cars from the 1970s into world-class quality cars by the 1980s. More recently, Hyundai has followed a similar path from cheap to world-class quality. The idea is that every employee within the organization is charged with making one small positive change to his or her workplace. The change may favor the organization, the employee, or the customer. The same can work at any property—no matter how small.

11. Mine demographic data from registration cards. Watch for patterns and useful information among variables such as zip codes, e-mail, company, number in party, arrival days and times, and special requests. For example, zip code patterns suggest areas for advertising. E-mail addresses allow communication with guest history easily, quickly, and almost without charge. A recurrence of a particular company would allow you to investigate the possibility of creating special rates and/ or bill-to accounts. Number in party and special requests can assist in providing an adequate number of no-smoking rooms, rates for late checkouts, rollaway beds, daytime rates, etc.

12. Become a female-friendly property. One fast growing sector of the lodging industry is single female travelers. Tap into this market by making subtle adjustments to operating standards. For example, clip and maintain all hedges no higher than hood height. This helps provide additional security by reducing hiding places and shadows. Ensure that parking lot and walkway lighting maintains lighting conditions to a minimum of dusk illumination. Change remote corridor entries to operable only with room keys (and remove door props). Position security cameras throughout public areas. Review the amenity package. Review lighting quality and amount in the bathroom and dressing areas.

13. Book returns at check-in and check-out. Train guest service agents to ask about return reservations at check-in. For example, it is normal for clerks to maintain a friendly conversation with guests during

the check-in process. Use these conversations to discover opportunities for advance bookings:

Guest Service Agent (GSA): *Where are you headed this morning?*

Guest: *We are driving up to Wyoming to visit Yellowstone for 10 days.*

GSA: *Would you like to reserve a room now for your return trip home?*

Clerks should be paid bonuses for booking gains such as these. Similarly, clerks should inquire about future reservations at check-out.

GSA: *Do you get out this way often?*

Guest: Yes. *I have a consulting contract with ABC Manufacturing. I am here every month from the 25th through the 30th.*

GSA: *Can we book some future reservations dates for you while you are here and we have all of your information in the system? That way it will be all taken care of for you, the rates will be set, and you won't have to worry. You can always let us know if something changes.*

Cha-ching!

14. Offer special and/or customized business packages. Operators are always searching for ways to raise their average daily rates (ADRs). Traditional thinking suggests that frequent business travelers expect discounted rates. Maybe not. Consider this alternative strategy by example: Business traveler Smith stays at the Shady Rest Inn. The rack rate at the Shady Rest is $90; The ADR is $75; and Smith pays $80 for a room. Smith pays with a Corporate American Express card. Over time, the operator, has come to know Smith and has discovered that Smith's company will pay up to $100 per day for a room. The operator bundles a value-added business package for Smith with the following daily features: Best room available at check-in, two complimentary drink coupons for the manager reception, complimentary full breakfast, Wall Street Journal, USA Today, and free movies. Smith pays $95 per day.

Let's examine the impact of the deal:

Smith's rate increases from $80 to $95 ($5 over the rack rate and $20 over the ADR).

Smith's company continues to reimburse the expense, since the rate is within the allowable range.

Smith gets the best room available at check-in, which, arguably, costs property $0. Smith values the room premium at $15.

Smith gets two drink coupons, which costs property approximately $3. Smith values the coupons at a street value of $6.

Smith gets a full complimentary breakfast, which costs property $2 above the free continental breakfast. Smith values the breakfast at $7.

Smith gets a Wall Street Journal and USA Today, which costs property $3.50. Smith values the papers at $3.50 plus a convenience factor.

Smith gets free movies, which, arguably, cost the property $0. Smith values the movies at $7.

The result is a win-win situation for both Smith and the property. Smith is rewarded for being a frequent guest at the perceived value at $36.50 per day. Property receives $9.50 per day more after expenses. Think about this example when considering frequent guests.

2. Consider minimum stays and drastic rate deviation during special events. For example, the Big Cliff Lodge rack rate is $85; The ADR is $79. During homecoming weekend at the nearby university, demand is such that the property charges $100 per day with a two-night minimum. This rate and minimum stay hold until 15 days before the event. Inside of two weeks, the property first drops the minimum stay and then the rate in order to help ensure a sellout. Three days before the event, the rate increases to $150, but no minimum stays on remaining rooms. The community accepts the policy due to market conditions. Consider opportunities for implementing similar strategies.

Article 07: James A. Collins Interview

Article author: Edward A. Merritt

Summary

The following article consists of a transcript of Dr. Ed Merritt's interview with James A. (Jim) Collins. Jim and Carol Collins are founding and longtime major patrons of The Collins College of Hospitality Management and Cal Poly Pomona University.

This interview is from 2010 and occurred during the Frank Lectureship Series held at The Collins College. Jim Collins discusses his life and leadership philosophy. This interview was conducted live in front of a standing-room-only audience of approximately 150 attendees. The transcript is written in conversational English format.

Merritt: Thank you and welcome everyone. I know that all of you are quite interested in hearing the Jim Collins Story, so we will get right to it. *[Laughter]* Well, Jim, it's great having you here with us at the Frank Lectureship Series. Thank you so much for coming, and we're delighted that you're here.

Collins: Well, thank you.

Merritt: We'd like to record this session, if it's all right with you, to share it with those who couldn't be with us. Is that okay?

Collins: Sure, fine.

Merritt: Great. What I thought we'd do tonight is talk about some of your story. I've heard bits and pieces of it, and others have, too, and we all enjoy hearing from you so much. Tell us about your background and your college days.

Collins: Well, let's see. Where do we wanna begin? I came out of the Navy in 1946, and I had had 50 college units in getting ready for pre-flight down in Pensacola, to fly an airplane for the Navy. But anyhow, I put in an application and got accepted at Berkley and UCLA. And by the way, it was easy to get into in those days.

[Laughter]

I wouldn't have made it today, but I got accepted, and I decided to go to UCLA. And everybody wants to know, *Why did you pick UCLA instead of Berkley*, and that's because my mother could do my laundry on the weekend. And that's it.

[Laughter]

That may sound funny, but it was a good reason, I gotta tell ya. But I started in the fall of '46 at UCLA, and I wanted a degree in engineering. And after about three years there, five of us guys decided to go to Berkley, because we wanted a degree in civil engineering, and UCLA only offered mechanical, electrical, and general engineering. So we sauntered up to Berkley in the fall of 1949, and I took about 18-19 units up there. And then, UCLA gave me a degree in January, 1950, in civil engineering, because I had the courses, which I had to get up in Berkley. But anyhow, that's the story.

I guess the fun thing was that I had done a lot of surveying in my time, and my dad, by the way, was a civil engineer, my brother-in-law is a civil engineer, and my uncle is a civil engineer, so. And I didn't have academic counseling in those days. If I'd had academic counseling, I never would've become an engineer, I tell ya.

[Laughter]

But I started working, for the first month out of school, in January 1950, with the Department of Water and Power, on a survey crew. And I wanted to get into construction. My option in civil engineering was construction, so I ended up getting an interview with a small company in Pasadena, called Feiston Company. And I went for the interview, and Mr. J. Feiston was running the company as the CEO, and he was an architect, and his son-in-law had graduated as a mechanical engineer from Cal-Tech, and they interviewed me for the job. Only the two of them ran the company. It wasn't a big company.

But they said, *How much are you getting paid at the Department of Water and Power?* I said, *$275 a month.* They said, *We'll start you at $275.* So I went to work in February. But the thing that makes this a fun story to tell is the fact that, all we did at Feiston Company was build Catholic churches. So for two years, I was building Catholic churches from San Diego to Santa Barbara. And I have to tell ya, in case you don't realize, this is a good thing to do.

[Laughs]

Merritt: That must have been a great opportunity.

Collins: A very good thing to do. But about two years into the church building business, my father-in-law had a 10-acre plotted out on a corner on Sepulveda, and he wanted to take an empty building and make a coffee shop out of it. And the reason he did was because he had an 18-pump gas station, he had 110 spaces in a trailer park, and nothing to eat for the people in the trailer park, and nothing to eat for the people on Sepulveda. And by the way, the 405 freeway was not there at that time.

So anyhow, he had me look at this building, and I said, *I can remodel it into a coffee shop.* I'm half way through, and the Edison man came by one day to figure out what kind of connected load I was gonna need for this coffee shop, and it turned out to be a 40 amp panel. And as he's getting into his car—this is the best part of the story—he said to me, *Have you got time to take a ride with me tomorrow?* And I said, *Sure.* I was about 25 years old. And so he picked me up and we drove out Foothill Boulevard to E Street in San

Bernardino, and met a couple of brothers, Dick and Maurice (Mac) McDonald, running a 15-cent hamburger stand, the only one in the world. It's still out there.

And at noontime, I wanna tell ya, it was just packed. And the hamburger was 15 [cents], a cheeseburger was 19 [cents], a milkshake was 20 [cents], cold drinks 10 [cents], coffee 10 [cents], French fries a dime. And that's all they had. No seats inside, no seats outside, just eat it in your car, or take it with you. That's all you could do. So I got back home that night and I called my father-in-law, and I said, *Have you got time to take a ride with me tomorrow?* And he said, *Sure.*

[Laughter]

And I put him in the car and drove out Foothill Boulevard, again, all the way out Foothill to E Street, San Bernardino, at noontime. This place was doing a fabulous business. So we looked at each other and said, *Yeah.* And so, right in this middle of this deal, I told the equipment company, I said, *Stop.* And I hired a hotel supply outfit to convert this building to a hamburger stand. And in—let's see, the 29th of September in 1952, I opened up a 19-cent hamburger stand. And just to make it easy for you, McDonalds was cutting a ten-to-the-pound hamburger in San Bernardino for 15-cents, and I cut my plate bigger at nine to the pound, and raised the price four cents.

[Laughter]

But after the first year, our business was booming because there's no self service out there, and everybody wanted to get fast food, and there wasn't any fast food around, and McDonald's hadn't done anything to expand yet, the brothers had just the one store out there in San Bernardino. And so, at the end of the first year I checked it out, and we had averaged $0.51 per customer, and we had done about $419,000.00, which doesn't seem like much, but that's still over 800,000 customers a year.

Merritt: That is an incredible number.

Collins: So anyhow, it was just a wonderful. And by the way, my pay went up a lot from $275.

[Laughter]

Merritt: I would guess that it did.

Collins: So anyhow, that was really a great start. Why don't you ask some more? I don't wanna take too long here.

Merritt: Will do. About 1955, you had become Carnation's largest customer. Can you tell us more about that?

Collins: For a single stop, yes.

Merritt: For a single location delivery?

Collins: Yeah.

Merritt: Can you tell us how you were able to leverage that relationship and expand the business?

Collins: My buddy, who was a salesman, Dale Trinkle, fabulous guy, and it was in about late '56, the hamburger stand around the corner came up for sale. The lady that owned it with her husband, he had died of a heart attack, and her father, who was named Carl, from Salt Lake City, who had the drug stores. So she said, *You're gonna have to come down and meet with my dad.* And so, I came over. It was just around the corner. It was only about three miles away. And so we talked and then they wanted $35,000.00.

And oh, my father-in-law wouldn't let me have a second hamburger stand. He thought, well, he'd been through the depression, and one was enough. So anyhow, he was away for two weeks, and I made a deal to buy this, and I didn't have any money. And the Carnation guy said to me, *Look, Jim, you're our largest single customer. You use over $10,000.00 of our product every month. So just don't pay me for the next* *three months, and then when you get the money you can pay me back, no interest or anything.*

[Laughter]

So I—you know, things were different then. I mean, here's a guy with a handshake that I was doing business with and said, *Don't pay your bill for the next three months.* So anyhow, I bought Hamburger Handout Junior, and it was very successful, again. So that's how I got the second store.

Merritt: That's a great story. At about the same time, you had a friend named Dale that was coming up with a concept called Sizzler. Can you tell us about that? About 1958, I believe.

Collins: Yeah, well, actually, Dale Johnson was his name, and he was a good friend, and he was looking around for something to do. And the lead article, in the left hand column, on the front page of the *Wall Street Journal* read, *Tad's $1.09 steaks, New York, Chicago, San Francisco.*

Merritt: Tad's Broiled Steaks.

Collins: And good old Dale, because he's a friend of mine, he didn't fly. So anyhow, we got in a car, after this article, the next day, and we drove to San Francisco and went to Tad's, and had a $1.09 steak. And it was—it wasn't very good, as a matter of fact.

[Laughter]

They were not using very good meat. Well, anyhow, to make a long story short, in 1960, in January, Dale Johnson took the trailer sales office in front of this trailer park, and he had about 25 seats inside, and under the umbrellas outside another 30 seats, and he opened up Top Sirloin Steak - $0.99, New York Steak - $1.09. And he had coffee and cold drinks, and I guess some baked potatoes and—I don't think he had any French fries, but I loaned him a 60-cubic-foot stainless steel refrigerator. I gave him a 15-pound Hotpoint fryer, and a five-foot gas grill, and I even bought the fixtures for the ceilings.

We did wagon wheels for this steak house that he opened up. And I didn't pay much attention, but he was on the same corner with me.

But in 1967, he walked in the door, and by then he had gotten up to four company stores, 160 franchise stores from New York to Hawaii, and he says, *Jim, I'm gonna retire and play golf every day.* And he loved golf. He wanted to play every day. He says, *I'm gonna sell this to you.* And two fraternity brothers of mine and I, we bought it a third apiece, for $885,000.00. Nothing down on a 10-year, six-percent note. So then—and you know, and the one lesson you wanna learn here is, anytime you can do a favor for somebody, just do it, because it'll come back and repay you many times over.

And every time in my life where I've done somebody a favor, it's come back and really done great things for me. So anyhow, I think that's one of the real pure lessons that I could pass on to you.

Merritt: That's a fascinating story and a great lesson. If we can back up, I want you to talk about the days when some of your friends in the hamburger business started selling chicken.

Collins: Yeah. Carnation was sending people from Seattle, Portland, Northern California, and Austin, Texas in, and they'd stay a week and work with us in the hamburger stand, and then they'd go home—and this was back in '54/'55. Anyhow, this one lady, Mrs. Burke, in northern California, called Burke's Drive-In, she had four hamburger stands. And she put Kentucky Fried Chicken on the menu in 1959. And I'm out visiting her, and it's February, 1960, and she said, *What do you do with chicken?*—oh, she thought the chicken was great. And I said, *I don't want any chicken in my hamburger stand.*

Anyhow, so what are we gonna do? She says, *What are you doing tomorrow?* I said, *Just frying hamburgers.* She says, *No, you're not.* And she was much older. You know, I thought she was a really old lady. She was about 65, and I thought—I can't even think back that far. But—

[Laughter]

But she called over to the airlines and bought two tickets. And when we got on the plane that night, we didn't land until 6:00 AM the next morning, in Louisville, Kentucky, because it was a propeller plane. There were no jets, so it took a long time to get there.

Merritt: I see.

Collins: About 12 hours, as I recall. But anyhow, the driver picked us up. There was snow on the ground, about four inches deep. School was out because of the snow. They don't have much snow in Louisville, but anyhow, the Colonel and Mrs. Burke took me over to the colonial mansion that he had there in Shelbyville, and I stayed for three days. And when I left there, I signed up for Kentucky Fried Chicken in my four hamburger stands. And so, I started selling the chicken in 1960, and it was fabulous, but it started off very slow.

And we didn't have, really, a great take home chicken—just so you know, in 1960, there were no take home chicken stores in the whole of the United States. And in 1961, the first one, take home chicken store, opened in Georgia. And so, I had the chicken in my hamburger stands in about—let's see, I'm trying to think, now—1962, I guess. And it went on from there, but it wasn't until '64 that I had one that would really—had a bottom line, where it'd make some money. But it just kept getting better and better. And by 19 oh, I don't know, but I was gonna say 1990/1991, we had in the United States here 209 Kentucky Fried Chicken stores. And even today, we sold those stores to Pepsi for Pepsi stock, but we have 119 Kentucky Fried Chicken stores in Queensland, Australia, and 27 Sizzlers.

And the chicken stores in Australia are almost the best in the whole world. They do two and a half times as much frying there, $2.5 million a year per store, compared to the ones up here that do a little over $1 million a year per store. So we're very pleased our sales in Australia this year will be about $350 million, believe it or not.

Merritt: Remarkable.

Collins: Incredible, yeah. Just incredible. So anyhow, good story.

Merritt: That's a great story. But let me back you up just a bit, because you've got a lot more to tell us. If we go back to when you first had a warehouse, you'd been working with the Colonel, and you formed a relationship with him that would go on for a long time. You became his agent. Can you tell us about that?

Collins: The Colonel? When I met him in 1960, he had a secretary and a bookkeeper, and two other employees, and he was really under-staffed. And by the way, as great of a cook, and as good as he was with seasoning and recipes, he wasn't the best in business. But anyhow, in 1961 and '62, he would call me up the night before and say, *Jim, I got this lady out in such and such, she's gonna open up her take-home chicken store tomorrow. Could you go over there and show her how to cook the chicken, make the mashed potatoes, gravy, and the coleslaw?*

And I would do that, and it'd take me about a day or two to do this, and I did this over and over. And finally, I learned from the boys in Chicago, that they had the same deal with the Colonel—Colonel Sanders. So when I had the Colonel with me in Portland, Oregon, I said, *Colonel*—this was 1962, yeah, '62, I said, *Why don't you let me be your representative in Southern California, from Santa Barbara—no, no, San Louis Obispo to San Diego? I'll open the stores for you. I've got a warehouse. I've got a trader. I've got a construction guy. We can get these people in business, and you don't have to worry about it at all?* He said, *That's a deal.*

And so, he didn't believe in attorneys, so we had to sit down and write out this two-page agreement, which I still have in my file. And it was just fabulous. And from 1962 until 1968, I was able, along with all of my team, to open up three—240 Kentucky Fried Chicken stores, and I currently own 33 of those, and the rest of them are all franchisees. And by the way, they all did really well and made a lot of money. So I don't wanna make anybody feel bad, but the chicken business has been good to everybody that got in early, you know, really good.

Merritt: About 1963, you noted a produce stand down in Orange County.

Collins: It was even before that. It was in the late '50s. We were making a lot of money, and down—the farms down on Rosecrans and Vermont, I think, were—anyhow, yeah, Rosecrans and Vermont, these three guys from Japan had a produce market that was so successful that they were selling out every day, this fresh produce. And it was just a really great thing that they were doing. So my father and I were looking, and he wanted to expand the property where we were on these 10 acres, and put in a market and a produce stand. So we got these guys and said, *Look, you guys come up and you do the same thing here. We'll put up the building, and you run it.* One lesson learned. I lost $40,000.00 in about five months, and throughout the year, was also building our new house.

[Laughter]

But it was just interesting. We—they bought—when we'd go to—when I'd go to market at 2:00 AM in the morning, and they—and the guy would come say, *You need 200 boxes of apples.* And he says, *At $0.05 a pound.* And they'd say, *But, if you take 500 boxes, we'll give them to you for $0.04 a pound.* And every night, for as long as I can remember, I was going to the hog farm with a truckload of produce that was not sold. And it was just a disaster. And it's interesting, when you have someone that doesn't have any skin in the game, be careful, and you learn a really good lesson.

They didn't have any of their own money in it, and they ran it differently, and that's another great lesson to learn, by the way, you know.

Merritt: That's a great story with another terrific leadership lesson.

Collins:　And you're very kind.

Merritt:　It is wonderful for everyone here to be able to hear your stories.

[Laughter]

Collins:　I was remembering while driving out here, you know, the last time that I did this for Richard Frank was in 1990, and I'll bet you half the people in the room weren't born yet.

[Laughter]

Merritt:　Colonel Sanders sold the company toward the mid-'60s. Can you tell us how the new company, and you were affected?

Collins:　You know, the Colonel sold the company in 1962, and he—I have a copy of—you know, he sold it to a gentleman from Nashville, Tennessee, Jack Massey. And the fellow that made the introduction, John was a good friend, and he was working—helping the Colonel. And they paid the Colonel $2 million for the company. They paid him $500,000.00 down, and the note for a year—two to three year note, at six percent, for—and paid $500,000.00 a year for the next three years. They brought some expertise and some business sense to the thing, and it started going really well.

As a matter of fact, Mr. Massey, when it was a private company, he put me on the board of directors, after he bought it. So I had a little fun there for about a year and a half. And then, at about—well, I'm exaggerating, but about—in '64, I guess it's '64, he decided to take the company public. And he says, *Jim, we can't have franchisees sitting on the board of a public company.* And I understood that, and so I got moved off the board. But they had a very successful offering on Kentucky Fried Chicken going public. And because they had money, they moved forward there and built a lot of new stores. And the company ran really well after that.

By 1969, Jack Massey and my friend, John had stopped talking to each other.

Merritt: Oh?

Collins: This is not good in a franchise organization, you know. And Mr. Massey's the best businessman I think I've ever known. And John, who was an attorney, and his father was Colonel Sanders' attorney, that's how the Colonel knew him. He'd known him since he was about five years old. So anyhow, they sold the company to the Heublein people who make the A.1. Sauce.

And then, about a year later, A.1. sold out their deal, which included Kentucky Fried Chicken, to Del Monte, out here in California.

Merritt: Sure.

Collins: And then, after that, I guess it was—I'm trying to think of the tobacco company who bought Kentucky Fried Chicken. Let's see, it was—no, it wasn't. It was—

Merritt: Maybe RJ Reynolds.

Collins: Yeah, yeah, RJ Reynolds.

Collins: Yeah. Anyhow, again, you're looking at really big companies with a lot of money. And they just took care of the franchisees in the very best way. It was a good time, a good era. And everybody was building more stores, and everybody was really successful in that time, yeah.

Merritt: Along the way, did that affect your agent agreement that you had had with the Colonel?

Collins: Oh, gosh. You know, this is my favorite story, I guess. We had about 33 chicken stores, and we had four company Sizzlers, and we were the franchisee in chicken, with a franchise agreement in Sizzler company. We bought it from Dale in 1967. And it's now 1968, and we wanna go public.

So we put this thing together, called it S1, and Collins Foods International, and I called my friend John, and said, *John, I've got 33 franchise agreements here in 33 corporations.* And by the way, so that you understand, each corporation had a different tax rate. And when you put them—and today, you can't put them all—you put them all together by law. Back then, they were brother and sister corporations. Each one of them paid their taxes separately, depending on their earnings.

But anyhow, he says, *Jim, we don't want any more public franchisees. We have one in Atlanta, and we have one in Toronto, and we have—the boys at Pennsylvania, the Ginos, and that's—we don't want any more, so I'm not gonna do it.* So when I called him again a couple of weeks later and asked again, he said, *No, I'm not gonna do it.* Anyhow, the year before this happened, in about 1967, he and Jack Massey came to L.A. They wanted to buy my—the contract that I had, this being an agent for the Colonel. They wanted to buy it for two—they offered—they said, *$2 to $3 million, that's the range we'll give you for it.*

And I said, *You know, the Colonel didn't charge me for that, and I didn't pay anything for it, so basically, it's not for sale.* Well, anyhow, about the third time around on this going public in '68, I got a call from the attorney in Louisville, and I knew him really well, Don, Don Grier. And he said, *Jim, you wanna know how to get those franchises transferred? 33 of them?* He says, *Call John and tell him you'll give him the contract he tried to buy last year for $2 to $3 million.* Well, I thought about it over night. And by the way, that contract was giving me more than $40,000.00 a month, so it was—it had some value.

But anyhow, I called up John the next day, I says, *John, come on out here and I'll give you that contract you tried to buy last year, the agent contract.* And he said—he got on the plane and he came out, and we met at Gibson Dunn's law office in Beverly Hills. And we stayed there from noon until midnight, signed it all up, and walked out the door. And then—and we made the deal, and he transferred the franchises. And on the 15th of November, 1968, Collins Foods became a public company. So anyhow, but—

Merritt: What a story.

Collins: A lot of fun, but you never know sometimes. You know, that was a hard decision to make, but it turned out to be exactly the right one, by the way.

Merritt: Well, we've talked about Sizzler, and we've talked about chicken. Tell us about London Bridge Fish and Chips.

Collins: London Bridge Fish and Chips. One of the friends of mine, Bill Freemont, he and Keith Ferguson, the ice fishing guy, they had started a little chain called London Bridge Fish and Chips, and they had about seven stores. And it was January 1969, and Bill said, *Why don't you buy this from us and really go?* So we said—we thought we were pretty smart, right? We had all this new money from going public, and so—and we bought it from them for stock. Collins didn't pay any cash for it, we just bought the thing from him. And it wasn't a week later that John called me on the phone and said, *Jim, we are now doing fish and chips, and we want you to be the franchisee for California.*

And I said, *John, I'm with London Bridge Fish and Chips for two weeks now.* And so, that took care of that, but—

[Laughter]

There's a lesson to learn here, and let me tell you what it is. This is a great lesson to learn. If you've ever had Kentucky Fried Chicken, or any kind of Chicken, it's good when it's hot, it's pretty good when it's warm, and if you take it out of the icebox the next day, that cold chicken, it isn't bad. Now, if you go to fish, and begin with when it's hot it's good, when it's warm it's no good, and when it's cold it's terrible.

[Laughter]

We would—we put drive through windows in these London Bridges that we built, and—thinking that everybody would take it home and eat this chicken, well—the fish, I mean. And, of course, fish, by the time you get it home, it's probably warm and not worth having. And so, we finally—after about, oh, maybe two years, we locked them all up and walked away.

Merritt: Sure.

Collins: But what a—you know, and you think you're smart, and you think that what you're doing in chicken you can do with fish. Well, it's not true at all, of course. And so, anyhow, we—another lesson learned.

Merritt: Costly but valuable.

Collins: Yeah, didn't break the bank, so that's—

Merritt: So, there you go. You told us about opening some chicken stores in Australia. Tell us about how you selected the cities and the area.

Collins: Well, in 1967, my friend, Bob LaPointe, was sent to Australia to open up some chicken stores, Kentucky Fried, in Sydney. And when he came to L.A., he was on his way, and I said, *Look, we've got a warehouse. We've got seasoning, the Kentucky Fried seasoning. If you need anything, you call me.* Well, he went on down to Sydney, and he opened up four stores in Sydney, Australia. And so, one day the phone rings, and it was probably June of '68. And he said, *Send me ten cases of seasoning on the Pan Am flight tonight at 8:30 PM.* He knew what he was talking about.

And I said, *Done.* And I said, *By the way, what's happening with Kentucky Fried Chicken in Sydney?* He says, *Jim, I've got*—these were little storefronts, maybe 20 feet at the most, and he says, *I've got four storefronts down here. They're lined up around the block, and I can't cook chicken fast enough.* I says, *Bobby, this is your friend. Don't do that to me.*

[Laughter]

So the next day, I got on the plane and I went to Australia. And we flew from Sydney and went down to Melbourne. And then we went across the bottom at Adelaide. And then we went west off to Perth on the west coast. And then we went, nonstop, from Perth back to Brisbane, and then from Brisbane back to Sydney, and then I came home again. So, I'm dealing with my friend John, now, remember, in the fall of 1968.

Merritt: Sure.

Collins: And I'm sitting there, and we're about all done, and I said, *By the way, John, I wanna open up—I want some territory. I want half of Sydney, or half of Melbourne, in Australia, for Kentucky Fried Chicken.* He says, *Jim, I've got commitments. I've got this. I've gotta save space for the company.* He says, *But if you want Queensland, or you want south Australia, with Adelaide, or you want western Australia with Perth, your call.* So I had to think about it. And let me tell you how you make really strategic decisions. I thought about it that night. Bob LaPointe's down in Sydney, and the closest city to Sydney is Brisbane, not Adelaide, and certainly not Perth.

So I called John back the next day, and I said, *Hey, we'll take Brisbane, Australia, you know, or the whole state of Queensland, with Brisbane as the capital city.* And he says, *But you've gotta make a deal with me, you've gotta sign a contract to open up 20 stores in five years.* And I said, *Done.* And we signed off, and today we have 119 stores down there, and the hottest selling ones. It was a fun thing to do, and we ended up in—and Queensland, by the way, for those of you who don't know, from Perth—or excuse me, from—Perth?—from Cannes, at the top of Queensland, this coastline down at the bottom coastline is 1,200 miles long.

Merritt: Goodness.

Collins: And there are so many cities, Northampton, Townsville, Mermaid Beach, and all of them down there, Southport and so forth, of our 119 stores in Australia today, about—more than 40-percent of them are on that coastline, that 1,200 mile coastline. Well, they don't have any coastline to speak of in south Australia, with Adelaide, and they have only the one major city, Perth. They don't have much in western Australia, either. My two buddies that took south Australia and western Australia each have 55 stores, and we've got 119. So—and I picked Queensland because I wanted to be close to Bob LaPointe.

Let me give you an example. When we got ready to go, we opened up our first store down there on July 15th, 1969. And last year, when I was down—I've been there 47 times. We went down while we were celebrating our 40th anniversary last year, on the 15th of July. Anyhow, but I said, *Bob, we gotta get started down there.* We go and open the store up in '69. So I sent him a check for $50,000.00, and when we got there in about March of 1969, he had the store half built. So we finished it and opened it, the mayor came, and it was an instant success, because again, there wasn't any chicken in Australia yet, and there wasn't really any take-out food down there.

And by the way, one of the lessons you need to find out, and that is that every restaurant, full service restaurant that's come to Australia, it doesn't matter who it is, Denny's all the way through all the really good ones, Red Lobster, Olive Garden, and the rest of them, have all opened up five, six, seven stores that closed up. And the reason that they do is because the labor laws down there are such that you pay time and a half on Saturday, double time on Sunday, everybody, from day one, gets four weeks holiday every year. And so, you've got a situation down there where you—if you have a full service restaurant, you don't make it.

In Australia today, there're 700 McDonald's. There're 550 Kentucky Fried Chicken stores. And this is a country with only 22 million people. And those are the only two chains that have really knocked them dead. And the reason we're able to do it, and McDonald's, is because we have a limited service. Our labor cost is not a big item. But in the full service business, it's tough. And when I was down there in '67/'68/'69, the hotels, the only place you could eat on Saturday and Sunday was in a hotel, and they put a surcharge on the menu down at the bottom for extra labor on the weekends, just because it was so high priced.

Merritt: Good grief.

Collins: But anyhow, yeah, we had a—we've had a great time in Australia. You know, we have 7,000 employees down there now, counting our part-timers, so it's been a—it's interesting. You went down on a lark, okay? And then today, it turns out to be a smart move. I just want you to know, you know.

Merritt: That's quite a lark.

[Laughter]

Collins: Yeah. You don't always have to be smart, you have to be lucky sometimes.

Merritt: You've had a great and long-term relationship with both UCLA and Cal Poly Pomona. Can you tell us about your philosophy about giving back?

Collins: Hey, you know, I'm involved in three capital campaigns right now, or maybe four. But anyhow—and I owe a lot of money on all of them, but when you get my age, you're not really getting old. But then one of the things I have the most fun in is being in the philanthropic area, where you get a chance to give back. And so, anyhow, my kids watch me and hopefully they'll do that, too. But we are finishing up a campaign to remodel Pauley Pavilion at UCLA. It's a $100 million campaign. We've raised about $67 million, and we're coming along fine.

The YMCA in Westside, we—I've been on the board there since 1960, and we've got a $20 million campaign, and we've got $14 million raised on that, and we're finishing up on that. And then we've got a campaign out here, and we've gotta get going on that, but we wanna build a new building right over here, and so we've gotta get that $10 million in the bank and go with that. But anyhow, but I want to tell you that I look forward to doing these kinds of things, and I really enjoy it. And Carol, she worries about me, but I'm fine.

[Laughter]

But we're keeping bread on the table at home, too, okay?

Merritt: I'll bet you are.

[Laughter]

Well, Jim, I want thank you so much for being with us tonight. It's just wonderful having you here. And thank you so much for caring so much about us.

Collins: Okay. I love it. I wouldn't change it. Thank you.

[Applause]

Merritt: I'm going introduce Sasha, who has a small gift for you, if you'll stand up.

Collins: Oh.

Sasha: Hello Mr. Collins. On behalf of The Collins College, I would like to present to you a token of our appreciation for all that you do for and mean to us.

Collins: Oh, thank you, thank you. Oh, thank you.

[Applause]

Merritt: Thank you, Sasha. And, once again, thank you to our founding patron, the one and only, Jim Collins.

Collins: Not at all.

Merritt: And Richard and Mary-Alice Frank thank you for hosting a wonderful evening. Thank you so much for everything you do for the Collins College.

[Applause]

Merritt: I know we have a number of friends waiting for us at the Restaurant at Kellogg Ranch, so let's walk over together and continue the celebration.

[Crosstalk]

[End of Audio]

Article 08:

Green Point Resort and Spa Strategy

Article author: Edward A. Merritt

Primary Strategic Issue

How can Green Point Resort and Spa overcome the perception that it has become passé and regain its place among the elite resorts and spas in the world?

Situation Analysis

Green Point Resort and Spa was originally completed in 1928, and for approximately its first 20 years of existence it reigned as a leader among American resorts as the place for stars, professional athletes, corporate leaders, and other high profile people to relax and luxuriate.

The gentle, private, and well-manicured image of Green Point began to change when international investors acquired the resort from the family and limited capital investment to a bare minimum (from approximately 10 percent of gross income to two percent or gross income). Over the past 10 years, new and more modern resorts, with greater space and amenities for corporate functions, have been built to compete with Green Point. In 2009, Ashton Recreation, which owns other premier resorts in the United States, purchased Green Point and immediately began a $250 million renovation and expansion of the facilities. The first phase of the plan is scheduled for completion in the Fall of 2016. A second phase, which includes building new resort villas that will sell between $900,000-1.2 million, is scheduled to begin in 2016.

Since Ashton took over, Green Point has continued to see its revenues slide. However, it has stayed competitive by dramatically slashing its average daily rate (ADR) for room stays. Most of the revenue decrease has been attributed to the extensive construction for the renovation.

So just how far has Green Point fallen in public perception? Following are some research highlights. Note that Green Point had been appeared consistently (every period) on each of these ratings sites for the previous 10 years:

- In *Golf Mecca's* 2014 ranking of notable resorts, Green Point did not make the list that totaled 70 resorts and included local direct competitor The Four Seasons. Three other Ashton properties did make the list.

- In *Golf Worldwide's* 2013-14 ranking of America's 100 best golf courses, Green Point did not make the list.

- When *Dollars* highlighted the best places to vacation for golf in 2014, another local competitor, The Ritz-Carlton placed first. Green Point was not mentioned. Green Point also was not mentioned in the best places to vacation for spas.

- *Host Traveler* ranked its top 50 spas in 2012 and 2013, and Green Point did not make either list. However, two of its competitors, Williston Resort and The Stockton Inn ranked 5th and 8th both years. Ashton's Ismo Island Resort Hotel & Spa was ranked 3rd in 2014.

- In *Leisure's* 2014 ranking of the world's best 50 spas, Green Point was not on the list.

- In the fall of 2014, *Spa* magazine published the results of a readers' poll that ranked the favorite spas, and Green Point was rated as a second tier resort.

- SmallConference.com released its 2014 Gold Awards and Green Point did not make the list. However, direct competitors—Deerwood Resort, Sawgrass, Hotel del Coronado, Cavalcade, and Paradise Point Resort & Spa—and other Ashton properties—Tiftway Resort and Spa, Grand Coral, Doheny, and La Escondito—earned Gold Key awards. There were 100 total Gold Key winners.

- In *America Today's* top 100 tennis resorts of 2014, Ponte Valley, topped the list, and Green Point ranked 71. La Keene ranked 18 and Jumash Inn was 69.

Assorted comments from former guests in major media outlets:

- *The resort was under construction and was preparing for a golf tournament, which prevented us from playing on the grass (tennis) courts. We were not informed of this inconvenience prior to arriving at the resort. We also self-parked our vehicle and we were charged for this privilege daily. Also we were charged a daily access fee for the spa, which is included at other spa locations if you are a guest of the lodging facilities. Overall service is questionable at best. We requested ice after a workout and I was directed to the café to get the ice myself. All the prices we were paying were a la Carte, which was highly unacceptable, as there seemed to be an extra charge for almost everything we requested, Chicago Today,* March, 2014.

- *There were several hidden charges not included in the quoted overall price, i.e., daily required fees for the fitness center, pool, and onsite daily parking fee. Cleveland Preston,* February, 2014.

- *I booked the room with this hotel before discovering this forum and decided to take a chance. Boy!! It was it a big mistake. As one of the reviewers had said, they nickel and dime you to death. The hotel is understaffed and the service is horrible. I had to wait 30 minutes for valet parking service to retrieve my car. The carpet in the room was wet and the refrigerator in the room was not working. For $370 a night, definitely not worth the price. Travadvisor.com,* July 7, 2009.

- Other *Travadvisor* reviews stated, *Ouch. Disappointing and disgraceful,* and *I booked a day at the spa and was horrified at what I experienced...I am sick and tired of hotels riding on their laurels of a five-diamond rating...I will never return.*

- Former *Juiced* magazine editor and British journalist Jackie Ben said in a review, *How not to celebrate the Fourth (of July)...Checking in there was an exercise in eye rolling condescension because we were not only labeled cheapskate, Web bookers but only checked in for one paltry night...We were nickeled and dimed an extra $50 on the bill...The wireless in the coffee shop would not let you check email or do anything useful other than surf the Green Point Resort*

Web page...It was horrible. The delicious irony was Julio, a lonely protester employee stoically handing out fliers to guests about how Green Point treats its employees. Green Point—Cheap and Mean, it (the flier) began.

However, Green Point's renovation is almost complete and there appears to be light at the end of the tunnel.

- TogetherTravel.com selected the resort as one of their *Great Family Resorts* in March, 2014 and The New York Daily News travel correspondent Mark Metzger ended a solid review of Green Point by saying, *Overall, we're hopeful that Green Point will retain the best of its past as it updates for the future. It appears to be on track.*

- One review on Travadvisor.com gave Green Point glowing reviews, *I absolutely loved this place! Our room had one of the best bathrooms I've ever seen. (It was bigger than some hotel rooms I've stayed in!) The amenities were great...bath salts, spa quality bath gels and lotions, and herb teas...even a candle was provided. The food was incredible. We had room service twice and ate in the restaurant. Everything was fabulous. The staff was great. I couldn't have asked for more. This is my new favorite resort!*

What are some of the alternatives Green Point could consider to change its current market position and make sure that the resort again becomes a favorite vacation destination for its guests?

Possible Alternatives

1. Create a powerful and consistent marketing campaign, titled *The Green Point Life*, in which the strategic vision is extended beyond the resort's physical property and touches targeted consumers in major metropolitan areas are.

2. Improve customer service.

3. Make additional capital investments to actually make Green Point a five-diamond resort.

4. Increase prices to create an aura of greater exclusivity at the resort.

5. Endure the renovation, continue to discount and maintain current budgets, expecting more consumers will find out about the renovation and visit the resort.

Strategy

A *focused differentiation* strategy is the best direction for Green Point because the resort has a relatively narrow buyer segment and operates in a narrow market niche. Focused strategy is appropriate because the target market (individuals and families, aged 30+, with annual incomes of more than $350,000) is large enough to be profitable and offers good growth potential.

Driving the focused differentiation strategy would be Alternative #1—create a unified and renewing marketing campaign, titled, *The Green Point Life*, in which the strategic vision is extended beyond the resort's physical property and touches targeted consumers in major markets. *The Green Point Life* would convey the message that the resort is one of the world's most desirable vacation destinations.

Alternative #1 also needs to be accompanied by Alternative #2—dramatically improving customer service—for the change in perception to last.

The Green Point Life marketing campaign will communicate to consumers how the resort's attributes and capabilities live up to the perception of a five-diamond resort. The most important key to success for campaign is making sure that Green Point stays in control of the message that reaches potential guests.

Ways in which Green Point can implement *The Green Point Life*:

Branded Television Programming. Create proprietary television programming instead of just advertising. A health and wellness show, a cooking show, or a golf show allows Green Point to extend its brand with tremendous control. Branded entertainment provides Green Point with a marketing investment that can be turned into a self-liquidating or self-funding proposition.

Green Point initially would purchase relatively inexpensive, yet extremely targeted, programming time on networks, such as Discovery Health Network, the Health Network (both emphasizing Green Point health and wellness themes), the Food Network (dining emphasis), and the Travel Channel (vacation destination emphasis).

Roy Hammer, who has a golf school at Green Point, already has a show on the Golf Channel. However, Green Point may consider producing his show and giving it more of a Green Point message.

If any of the shows produce impressive ratings, Green Point, which owns them, would be in a position to capitalize on ad sales. Networks may even decide to purchase episodes from Green Point, and in turn, make money selling ad time.

The shows also can run on Green Point's in-room video systems or programming could run on airline in-flight video systems.

Branded editorial content in prominent health, wellness, and golf magazines and on related Websites.

Sponsor a golf season preview magazine that would be distributed to sports package subscribers on DirecTV. The demographics of the DirecTV's more than 4.5 million sports package subscribers are in line with the resort's target market—mostly male adults aged 30-70 with household incomes exceeding $200,000.

Have Green Point experts (Tiffany Duval and Jeffrey McMasters) produce health and wellness and golf columns for magazines (advertorials) and Websites. Green Point also could consider sponsoring existing editorial content that reflects the message of *The Green Point Life*.

Targeted magazines and Websites:

- *SELF, Health and Fitness, Prevention, Men's Health, Travel + Leisure, Conde Nast Traveler, Golf, Golf Digest, Golf Illustrated, Sports Illustrated's* Golf Plus section, *Healing Lifestyles & Spas, Spa, Resorts & Great Hotels, and Spa Finder*

- *Yahoo! Health, YourHealth.com, WebMD Health, Spotlight Health, HealthWindows.com, Healthy Ideas from Prevention Magazine, drkoop.com, Discovery Health, CBS Health Watch*

Product Development and Placement

Become more aggressive in promoting and finding distribution channels for lines of Green Point-branded spa products.

Partner with major airlines to put Green Point spa products in first-class. Spa items, such as a small bottle of Green Point spa lotion, could be placed in all first-class bathrooms or given away to first-class passengers before takeoff.

Leverage Green Point's legendary reputation in golf and tennis by hosting more Pro-Am-type events with high-profile professional golfers and tennis players, who are no longer playing on the regular professional tours. This would offer opportunities for special promotions and make guests feel as if the resort continues to be home to the stars. These pros also could offer training instruction—an experience similar to fantasy camps run by major league baseball.

Promote Green Point as the place for corporate health. No need for Red River experiences. Green Point could offer team-building challenges. Exclusive seminars could be arranged to encourage greater productivity and performance of employees. Green Point could become, *The place where executives get healthy.*

Special Events for the media

Maximize media coverage by making special events and pricing structures for local and national media.

Strengthen strategic alliances with other Ashton properties

As noted in the situation analysis, Ashton's other resorts have attained high ratings, and letting potential guests know that Green Point is part of the family of properties will raise its perception to casual vacationers and influencers within the travel industry.

Produce a quarterly corporate magazine and/or newsletter that allows guests at all of the Ashton resorts to become more familiar with each resort's marketing message. The magazine also could act as a type direct mail newsletter that is sent to previous customers in Ashton database, offering on-going contact with guests.

Production Format:

- High-quality magazine, 8 1/2" x 11", four-color.

Editorial Ideas:

- Preview all major golf and tennis events taking place at Ashton resorts.

- Feature companies that book group incentive business.

- Dramatic photography that highlights the beauty of each resort.

- History section that concentrates on the legends of each resort.

- Features on corporate partners.

- Employees of the quarter feature.

- Health and wellness columns.

- Golf instruction feature.

- Celebrity profiles and reviews of those who have stayed at the resorts.

- Home spa tips.

- Spa product reviews.

- Restaurant reviews.

Include Green Point in special packages with Tampa Queen and PGA Gainesville, creating a unique southern-Florida resort experience. Plan a mini-Ashton golf tour with six events for amateur golfers each year (2 events each at Green Point and sister properties at strategic times during the year to drive increased occupancy).

Because Ford already sponsors the PGA Tournament at Doral, there may be an opportunity to develop a relationship with Ford spokesman Phil Mickelson.

Once Green Point has executed the *Green Point Life* campaign to show that it is a resort of premium quality it needs to focus on outstanding customer service. With the renovation of the resort and expected rise in prices, people will expect even more from the hotel staff. The *Green Point Life* campaign has set the expectations; now the resort has to live up to them.

In a guest survey done for Green Point, only 53 percent of respondents rated the concierge excellent, 58 percent rated reservations excellent, and 64 percent rated the front desk excellent. Overall, the resort received an excellent rating by 51 percent of respondents and a meager 24 percent listed excellent in price/value.

If Green Point wants to be one of America's most desired vacation destination, it should shoot for excellent rating of 95 percent and higher in any guest survey.

Areas where Green Point should focus to improve guest service:

1. Increase in pay (higher selectivity of employees)
2. Better training
3. More comprehensive reward system
4. Better internal communications (employee newsletter)

The *Green Point Life* will offer a strong competitive advantage by focusing on the special attributes that appeal to the tastes of the niche target market. The campaign helps the resort achieve differentiation-based competitive advantage by *incorporating features that raise the performance a buyer gets from the product and enhance buyer satisfaction in noneconomic or intangible ways.* Green Point Life is a direct link to the consumer's desires for relaxation, rejuvenation, image, enjoyment, and health and wellness.

The *Green Point Life* and improved customer service will require a significant financial commitment and it would not be financially prudent or as influential with consumers if it was enacted all at once. The re-launch of the resort will be the most significant time to begin *Green Point Life*, and the resort's 90th Anniversary in 2017 allows for another key moment to make a big push.

Competencies

Building core competencies, resource strengths, and organizational capabilities that rivals can't match is a sound foundation for sustainable competitive advantage.

Green Point needs to focus on its core competencies of customer service (human capital), mystiques (brand), and variety of amenities in order to be successful in crafting a long-term impression on customers. This can be achieved through more selective hiring and extensive training, an increase in advertising, and developing innovative programs.

All groups at Green Point need to be of a similar mindset to develop the core competencies. The resort should drive job applicants to apply on its Website and make the application process thorough and detailed. Have a structured training program in place to develop employees. An intern program that builds future employees from the ground up would also strengthen the brand.

The physical core competencies at Green Point are its new spa, golf courses, and tennis facility. These competencies need to be featured on all sales and marketing materials that are produced.

Organization

The organization needs to be aligned to the strategy, and although staffing levels need to be increased, Green Point has made a concerted effort to build a strong management team. Green Point has in place a system to identify strategy-critical value-chain activities. This allows them to decide which value-chain activities to handle internally and which to outsource.

Cross-unit coordination and collaboration between Green Point's operating units also allows for optimum opportunity to implement strategy. However, the organization does not have a strong tool that allows it to collaborate or coordinate with its consumers.

Budgets and Controls

The proper budget and controls need to be in place for effective implementation of *Green Point Life*. The strategic planning and budgeting process at Green Point seem to be linked, however, a few changes in the budgets are recommended to effectively support a new strategy.

Green Point was forecasting revenues in 2015 to be approximately $53 million—a 34.4 percent increase from 2014. However, the resort budgeted only $1.4 million in advertising. To significantly upgrade the resort's image, Green Point may want increase its 2010 advertising budget to 5 percent of revenues (or approximately $2.7 million based on projections).

Green Point also projected a 5 percent decrease in payroll from 2014 to 2015. With the multi-million dollar capital improvement program, the resort may want to increase its 2015 forecast payroll by approximately 10 percent, which would return it to pre-capital improvement levels. Projected increases in room occupancies with the completion of renovation should more than make up for the payroll increase.

Policies/Procedures

Policies and procedures help align actions and behavior with strategy throughout the organization, channeling all the efforts in a uniformed way. The sales division at Green Point has policies and procedures in place to work toward the common goal of increasing revenue.

Green Point has its employees following a Five-Star Service Standards program that promotes the following points:

1. Acknowledging and greeting every guest with a smile, eye contact, and an appropriate greeting.

2. Creating *moments of truth* in service by anticipating the needs of our guests and being flexible in responding to them.

3. Being knowledgeable about your job and the property.

4. Taking ownership and resolving guest complaints.

5. Taking pride in your work and being passionate about your service.

One area where policies need to be refined at Green Point might include a more simplified room and package pricing structure, especially the rates that are given to the general consumer base. Guests complain about the disjointed way in which they were billed.

Practices and Continuous Improvement

The best companies know that quality isn't a destination; rather, the quest for quality is an ongoing journey.

Employees need to be held to these Five-Star Standards in order for Green Point to truly make a change in guest perception. Performance reviews should do a thorough job of emphasizing the importance of the Five Diamond Standard. The Ritz Carlton Hotels are famous for having employees carry small laminated pocket cards that list and reinforce core values. Green Point may want to institute a similar policy.

Areas of weakness at Green Point include: inconsistent employee training and a lack of vehicles providing employees feedback on performance. In order for current employees to achieve the greatest improvements in customer service the resort needs to offer more in-depth training and create a better way to monitor the results of the training.

Systems

A support system needs to be in place to continually remind employees of the strategy. The capital improvements at Green Point have taken the first step by providing a physical system to foster successful implementation of strategy. However, the system of molding the resort's human capital can still be improved. Improvements may be achieved with successful implementation:

- Adequate information systems

- An internal company newsletter

- Emails from managers to home email addresses of employees

- Offsite team building exercises

- Requiring Green Point work uniforms that signal teamwork to guests

Green Point also is developing an improved employee survey, which will be implemented at all of Ashton's properties.

Rewards

Teamwork will be a major key in changing the resort's perception, therefore, the main rewards should reflect team performance. Create a rating system by which all units are compared against each other. Allow the employees an opportunity to tell management what types of rewards would make the most impact.

Individual achievement award should still be given, and some of those may include: stock options, bonuses, or trips to other Ashton properties. Rewards also could come from partnerships and promotions with local companies, i.e., Publix's grocery stores may offer a 10 percent discount on groceries for all Green Point employees. In turn, Publix executives and employees get a preferential rate at the resort.

Culture

Green Point should encourage a culture of servicehood. The guest should always come first and is always right. By making the Green Point culture centered on the customer, the resort will be able to achieve its goals and objectives.

This culture can be perpetuated and encourage through quality internal communication vehicles such as a company newsletter that contains testimonials from Ashton employees. Employee mentoring programs may also strengthen the desired culture. A strong culture would help Green Point lower its turnover rate, which was at approximately 25 percent in 2014.

Leadership

Leadership should be everything that it expects from its employees. Management should be an additional face to the consumer, even to the point where it gets praise cards from customers. Employees will follow leaders that are willing to get their hands dirty and help in the work. Talk is not enough.

Green Point has a strong leadership in place that serves as a positive example throughout the unit. The resort showed its commitment to building an effective team by replacing four of its 10 senior management personnel in 2014.

Strategic Management Process

Green Point Resort and Spa's strategic management process follows the basic five tasks of strategic management.

Five Tasks of Strategic Management

- Task 1. The general manager and vice president of Green Point initiate the strategic management process by putting together an annual (mid-August) executive summary that includes a current fiscal summary, a market overview, a targeted competitive analysis, a SWOT analysis, and budget assumptions. The general manager provides this direction by getting information and feedback from his senior leadership team that consists of the director of sales, director of golf, chief financial officer, director of operations, director of sales and marketing, director of human resources, spa director, director of engineering, and executive chef. Green Point's corporate office, Ashton Recreation, also participates in the strategy process, but only in an advisory capacity. Once all the information has been reviewed, the general manager produces a brief strategic vision of where the company is headed. The 2014 strategic vision at Green Point: *the resort would experience a paradigm change, and will not just incrementally improve. The tremendous investment in capital dollars must be met with a tremendous sales and marketing launch of this new resort, and a significant elevation in service and attention to detail.*

- Task 2. After the strategic vision is set, the general manager establishes core objectives that are specific to Green Point. Green Point's 2014 core objectives included: Greater customer focus, a total selling culture, enhancing the property's unique assets, and employee development.

- Task 3. Each department director at Green Point (with the help of his or her team) uses the divisional core objectives to craft a departmental strategy to achieve the division's desired outcomes. Task 1 and 2 are completed annually, however, the departmental strategy initially produced in Task 3 is reviewed and can change throughout the year.

- Task 4. Implementing and executing the chosen strategy efficiently and effectively begins with Green Point's general manager identifying important divisional actions that will be taken. In 2014, those actions included hiring a nearly complete new sales team, adding two sales manager positions, adding Ashton regional office resources, getting new referral opportunities from seven other Ashton properties, constructing a new 42,000-square-foot conference center, and spending $71 million to renovate that part of the resort. With divisional actions in place to help departments implement the chosen strategy, it is then up to the director to implement and execute his departmental strategy at stages throughout the year.

- Task 5. Department directors are responsible for evaluating and monitoring the implementation process. Evaluation—of performance in meeting objectives and initiating corrective adjustments in vision, long-term direction, objectives, strategy, or execution in light of actual experience, changing conditions, new ideas, and new opportunities—is completed formally on an annual basis. However, weekly meetings are held to monitor areas such as target market and competitive positioning.

Characterization of the Strategic Management Process

All the operations of Green Point take place locally, however the operations are fast moving. And with this in mind, the general manager, with some input from the corporate office, uses a delegation approach to strategic management. The general manager allows his directors to shape large portions of the resorts strategies because they have specialized expertise of the market and competitive conditions. Examples of the delegation approach used at Green Point are evident in weekly hour-long meetings in which all managers are encouraged to participate in strategic discussions. On the first Thursday of each month a different department gives a presentation as to its progress and current status. The second Thursday of each month is for open discussion of hot issues. The third Thursday of each month is a presentation of the division's financials, and the fourth Thursday of each month is a review of Five Diamond Standards used to evaluate employee performance in relationship to objectives. Every Thursday, Green Point management discusses topics such as an 11-day forecast, the VIPs coming in, and site inspections of groups coming in. Green Point also uses weekly status email, department breakfasts, a GM round table, and a newsletter to share information. As one manager said, *Ashton and senior leadership at Green Point give you the power to do your job.*

Mission Statement

The mission statement is a starting point for the strategic vision. It tells customers who we are, what we do, and where we are now.

Green Point's mission statement mirrors that of its corporate office: Our goal is a simple one—to create an environment that allows you to relax, rejuvenate, and feel refreshed. We are committed to providing you with friendly, thoughtful service, and assisting you with all your travel needs.

Test: Green Point's mission statement makes a good attempt at addressing the customer needs (what is being satisfied), the customer groups (who is being satisfied), and how the enterprise goes about creating and delivering value to customers. The major deficiency in the mission statement is that it could be perceived as too vague, especially with how Green Point plans to deliver value. What does assisting the customer with its travel needs really mean?

Vision

The strategic vision goes further than the mission statement and offers some insight to the question where are we going?

The almost mythical Green Point Resort & Spa is making a comeback on the strength of a major renovation and expansion. The new Green Point will once again create the blueprint for recharging both body and mind.

Test: Green Point's strategic vision does a solid job of answering the questions; what customer needs should we be satisfying, what kind of company should we be trying to become, and what buyer segments should we be concentrating on (renovation and expansion reflect the desire for affluent customers)? The questions not answered by the resort's written strategic vision include: what changes are occurring in the market arenas where we operate and what implications do these changes have for the direction in which we need to move; what new geographic areas or product markets should we be pursuing, and what should the company business makeup look like in five years? (Strategic vision should incorporate a time horizon.)

Goals and Objectives

Green Point's core goals and objectives are long-term in nature and set by the general manager. The directors then establish more specific, quantifiable, and short-term objectives to ultimately satisfy the core objectives.

The experience of a majority of companies and managers teach that companies whose managers set objectives for each key result area and then press forward with actions aimed directly at achieving these performance outcomes typically outperform companies whose managers exhibit good intentions, try hard, and hope for the best.[79]

Test: Green Point has both strategic and financial objectives. Some examples follow:

Strategic

- Remind the public of its storied reputation as the first true spa resort in the country.

- We will significantly upgrade Green Point's physical property and return its service to true luxury levels.

---

79 Thompson, Arthur A., Jr. and A.J. Strickland III; "Establishing Company Direction," *Strategic Management: Concepts and Cases*, 13th ed. (New York: McGraw-Hill, 2013), 42.

- It will provide a lifestyle to which its guests aspire.

- A brand new spa will offer philosophies and treatments to relax, revitalize, and promote wellness among its guests.

Financial

- Green Point wants to be a 4-star or four-diamond resort because when considering investment, there is no significant added value in being a 5-star or five-diamond, as rated by Forbes or AAA. Certain groups (a major percentage of room revenue) have been restricted from booking five-diamond hotels because they are perceived as too expensive. Other properties (especially those which are five star or five diamond rated would argue that this is not the case—that achieving the highest AAA and Forbes ratings increases their revenues far beyond the added costs of the achievement. Perhaps the reason that Green Point does not state its interest in five-star, five-diamond status is because it cannot achieve it—and cannot at its occupancy percentage and average occupancy rate.

- Green Point wants a 58.8 percent occupancy rate.

- Green Point wants group rates to average $245-265 per room, per night.

The current strategic and financial objectives are in agreement with each other. The strategic management process at Green Point makes sure that neither group of objectives take precedent over the other. There is good indication of strategic intent in Green Point's objectives, and they provide measurable targets in both the short and long term. The objectives should not be too much of a stretch, given the money that Ashton has spent on the property in capital improvements. It depends upon a positive marketing effort as much as the dollars. Green Point has gone down over the years (it used to enjoy a high position in the market). However, the travel industry still is struggling to recover from a stagnant economy and security fears.

Grand Strategy

Green Point Resort and Spa will experience a sea change, and will not merely improve incrementally. The tremendous investment in project capital dollars must be met with a robustly successful sales and marketing launch of this new resort, and a significant elevation in service and attention to detail.

There will be two separate opportunities to launch this message, one with the completion of much of the renovation prior to the NFC playoff game to reach the *newly renovated product* state, and another as the new Spa and Ballroom open and the *New Green Point* is positioned as one of the best, if not the best, destination resort in the United States.

It is critical that this is executed well and will require adequate resources and strategic planning. In reviewing the market, the strong performance overall supports market penetration and higher occupancy levels. A jump form 44.6% occupancy to 58.8% may appear unrealistically aggressive, however compared to market conditions of mid-sixties and up, it would be conservative.

Key to this turnaround will be the reversal of group business performance.[80]

Tests of a winning strategy

- Goodness of Fit. As the U.S. economy improves and fears of travel subside, Green Point's strategy puts it in a great position to compete. By keeping costs low while making capital improvements, Green Point maintained a good fit with the external situation in the travel industry. The resort does have some unresolved internal issues, such as a revised working agreement with union members that are not addressed in the strategic plan.

- Competitive Advantage Test. Renovation will place Green Point on equal footing with its competitors in overall appearance. Some dramatic sustainable advantages of the resort: 1) more than 400 acres of property, 2) more guest rooms than its most prominent competitors, 3) an 18,000-square-foot ballroom and a new 42,000-square-foot conference center, 4) a new spa, 5) new 7,800 square-foot athletic club, and 6) two PGA championship golf courses.

- The Performance Test. Green Point's strategy thoroughly addresses the issue of performance. To keep EBITA up, Green Point has done an excellent job of controlling costs (outperforming forecasts). However, they will need to increase staffing to realize targeted gains in profitability and long-term market position.

---

80 Resort and Spa 2014 Strategic Plan

Industry Prospects

Porter's Five Forces of Competition Model provides a solid base to understand competition within an industry. In fact, the stronger the collective impact of the competitive forces, the lower the combined profitability of participating firms.[81]

Three of the five forces in the resort/hotel industry—rivalry among competing sellers, potential entry of new competitors, and competitive pressures stemming from buyer bargaining power and seller-buyer collaboration—are extremely competitive. Macroeconomic issues, such as weather, global political unrest, war, and health issues, also play a prominent role in industry fortunes. It is because of this that the resort hotel industry remains a challenging arena in which to remain profitable over long periods of time. Examples of the intense competition:

- The travel industry grew less than 2 percent in 2012, and occupancy among Green Point (-15.1 percent) and its competitors (-7.2 percent) was down

- Industry conditions encourage cost cutting and numerous promotions

- Customers have a tendency to perceive little differentiation among *luxury* resorts, so their costs to switch brands are low

Potential Entry of New Competitors

- The capital investment to get into the resort/hotel industry is very high, reflected by Ashton's renovations of Green Point

- In a U.S. Marketing research profile conducted by BitMiner.com of 3,564 resort companies surveyed only 21 were startups—and the failure rate for startups in a three-year period is more than 35 percent

- An emerging vitality index in the same survey that compares specific industry rates to overall national industry rates where the national rate equals one shows that the index for new branches (hotels) is .69

---

81 Thompson, Arthur A., Jr. and A.J. Strickland III; "Industry and Competitive Analysis," 150.

Competitive Pressures Stemming From Buyer Bargaining Power and Seller-Buyer Collaboration

- Relatively quite high in the hotel industry

- Buyers are well educated and well informed

- The costs for buyers to switch brands are relatively low

- The number of buyers is limited

- Buyers have tremendous discretion in whether or not to purchase the product

Industry Attractiveness

Despite the fact that the travel industry pie currently is smaller, the leisure portion of the travel industry continues to be the biggest bright spot. Domestic travel increased 1.7 percent in 2014, and with major conflict in Iraq waning, the summer, fall, and winter of 2015 should experience an even greater increase. The U.S. lodging industry seems to be recovering a bit faster that the airline industry as U.S. hotel room demand actually increased .8 percent in 2014. Based on a survey conducted in late January, consumers' interest in travel continues on an upward trend.[82] However, there are some other driving forces that have kept industry growth at minimal levels including: unemployment, low consumer confidence, elevated U.S. terror levels, reduced business spending, price wars.

Despite the travel industry that has sputtered and generally experienced difficulties in areas across the country for some years, prospects have consistently remained better than rest of the country. The metro area generates $5 billion per year in tourism revenues. Overall ITM occupancy for the *Luxury* market is 70.2 percent of 50,500 hotel rooms.[83] The metro area is the third most popular domestic leisure destination behind Las Vegas and Orlando.[84]

Competitive Position

Ashton's purchase of Green Point Resort and Spa in 2011 gave the resort strong financial backing that had been lacking for many years.

82 Travel Industry Association.com, March 2014 travel outlook
83 Strategic Plan
84 Strategic Plan

While the renovation will restore the resort to luxury resort standards, Green Point still remains a great value and is more affordable than its most prominent competitors. The first phase of the renovation is scheduled for completion in Fall. A second phase, which includes building new resort villas that will sell between $900,000-1.2 million, is scheduled to begin in 2017. New pricing strategy for rooms is a loose approach, allowing more flexibility and ease of understanding for the customer. The pricing strategy for golf, which drives room and spa sales, also has become more flexible.

SWOT on competitive position

- Strengths. Leadership Team, Financial Backing, Capital Improvements, Brand Identity, Base of Loyal Customers, Balance Sheet, Diverse Amenities, and Golf Course, Spa, and Tennis Reputations

- Weaknesses. Labor Issues, Perceived Underperformance, Deteriorating Physical Property, One Restaurant, Beach Access, Activities for Children, Private Condominiums in Front of Property

- Opportunities. Employee Recruitment, New Spa, New Ballroom and Meeting Space, New Fitness Center, Complete Renovated Exterior and Interior of Property

- Threats. High Cost of Living for Employees, Renovation Not Well Received by Customers, Economy, Terrorism, Other Resorts

Strategic Questions

Background. The preceding Green Point Resort article provides a comprehensive background for Green Point and its environment. It is clear that the property struggles with a myriad of strategic questions. A selected representation of those questions is provided below.

Who? If assigned, this assignment will be for students working alone or students working together in groups. Your professor will clarify his or her preference.

What? For this assignment, you will answer each of the strategic questions provided. This assignment focuses on your ability to use the facts and situations contained in the article and make creative and logical recommendations from those facts and situations that Green Point could implement. Expectations for submitting a well-thought through and complete assignment will be for you to answer each question including the bullets within the questions. As you set up your format, include each question (bolded) and each sub bullet (bolded) as presented. Begin your answer in non-bolded text immediately after each sub bullet.

Where? Your professor will provide instructions as to how this assignment will be completed—whether in class, on your own time, or a combination of both.

When? Your professor will provide you with a due date in the syllabus, which may include both a date for the written work followed by a Power Point presentation.

Why? Successful and effective leadership goes beyond the hospitality business *science* of analyzing, understanding, filtering, prioritizing, and managing of people and information. Successful and effective leadership relies on the hospitality business *art* of using sound judgment, developing creative solutions to issues, and making workable decisions that will translate into long-term organizational success. The situations and issues Green Point faces are similar to those often encountered by leaders. This assignment will challenge your ability to develop thoughtful recommendations while staying within the bounds of facts and situations presented in the article.

How? For this assignment, assume the position that you are a consultant hired by Green Point to provide creative recommendations to turn these questions into strategic recommendations that management will develop into initiatives.

Questions and sub bullets

1. Old and tired. **How can Green Point overcome the perception that the property has become old and tired and regain its place among the elite resorts and spas in the world?** Green Point mainly has developed this reputation within the industry, and travel planners have become hesitant to bring groups there. For your answer, address the following sub bullets.

   - **What is your recommendation?**

   - **What information from the article led you to make this recommendation?**

- **Why did you make this recommendation?**

- **What specific steps would Green Point take in implementing this recommendation?**

- **What positive outcome should Green Point gain by implementing this recommendation?**

2. Labor challenges. **How can Green Point best resolve current labor issues and raise the level of customer service to exceed expected standards?** Ashton currently is in talks with the labor unions at Green Point and employees wearing buttons and picketing have left a poor impression with consumers. Ongoing renovations and educating employees to the standards of new owner Ashton also have made customer service a daunting challenge. For your answer, address the following sub bullets.

- **What is your recommendation?**

- **What information from the article led you to make this recommendation?**

- **Why did you make this recommendation?**

- **What specific steps would Green Point take in implementing this recommendation?**

- **What positive outcome should Green Point gain by implementing this recommendation?**

3. Staffing. **How can Green Point increase staffing to adequately manage the increase of amenities with the new renovations?** Green Point earned $40 million in gross revenues last year and $8 million in EBITA. They have done this with a lean staff. The increased amenities will require Green Point to increase staffing without a guaranteed increase in revenues. For your answer, address the following sub bullets.

- **What is your recommendation?**

- **What information from the article led you to make this recommendation?**

- **Why did you make this recommendation?**

- **What specific steps would Green Point take in implementing** this recommendation?

- **What positive outcome should Green Point gain by implementing this recommendation?**

4. Macro issues. **How can Green Point overcome powerful macro-environmental issues, such as a volatile U.S. economy, terrorism, and other issues?** At the date of this article, vacation travel is down throughout many parts of the world. Although the wars have ebbed, the battles to defeat terrorist factions continue. Threats of terrorist attacks keep travelers on edge. For your answer, address the following sub bullets.

- **What is your recommendation?**
- **What information from the article led you to make this recommendation?**
- **Why did you make this recommendation?**
- **What specific steps would Green Point take in implementing this recommendation?**
- **What positive outcome should Green Point gain by implementing this recommendation?**

5. Condos. **How can Green Point overcome the visual issues of existing and outdated private condominiums at the front of the resort?** Different homeowners associations govern these two buildings. For your answer, address the following sub bullets.

- **What is your recommendation?**
- **What information from the article led you to make this recommendation?**
- **Why did you make this recommendation?**
- **What specific steps would Green Point take in implementing this recommendation?**
- **What positive outcome should Green Point gain by implementing this recommendation?**

6. Re-positioning. Green Point is viewed as a place for wealthy retired consumers. **How does Green Point appeal to its target market**

as couples with grown children and families with children? For your answer, address the following sub bullets.

- **What is your recommendation?**

- **What information from the article led you to make this recommendation?**

- **Why did you make this recommendation?**

- **What specific steps would Green Point take in implementing this recommendation?**

- **What positive outcome should Green Point gain by implementing this recommendation?**

7. Oceanfront proximity. Green Point is not located oceanfront (within three blocks). **How can Green Point overcome the drawback of not being located on the oceanfront?** For your answer, address the following sub bullets.

- **What is your recommendation?**

- **What information from the article led you to make this recommendation?**

- **Why did you make this recommendation?**

- **What specific steps would Green Point take in implementing this recommendation?**

- **What positive outcome should Green Point gain by implementing this recommendation?**

8. Publicity and public relations. There is no director of public relations. **How does Green Point develop interest from more writers and the news media in publicizing the property?** For your answer, address the following sub bullets.

- **What is your recommendation?**

- **What information from the article led you to make this recommendation?**

- **Why did you make this recommendation?**

- **What specific steps would Green Point take in implementing this recommendation?**

- **What positive outcome should Green Point gain by implementing this recommendation?**

9. Golf school. The golf course practice range facility currently is not conducive to golf school. **How does Green Point go about making the golf course practice range facility more appealing to teaching pros as a golf school?** For your answer, address the following sub bullets.

- **What is your recommendation?**
- **What information from the article led you to make this recommendation?**
- **Why did you make this recommendation?**
- **What specific steps would Green Point take in implementing this recommendation?**
- **What positive outcome should Green Point gain by implementing this recommendation?**

10. Data mining. Poor customer tracking existed at Green Point before Ashton purchased the property. **How does Green Point communicate more effectively with existing and potential guests?** For your answer, address the following sub bullets.

- **What is your recommendation?**
- **What information from the article led you to make this recommendation?**
- **Why did you make this recommendation?**
- **What specific steps would Green Point take in implementing this recommendation?**
- **What positive outcome should Green Point gain by implementing this recommendation?**

Assignment 01:

Next Logical Position

Who?: If assigned, each person will individually complete and submit this assignment.

What?: This assignment will take you through several steps to help ensure that you have a robust understanding of your concept of where you are headed in your career and to help focus your efforts toward success.

When?: The due date and time are posted in the syllabus. You can submit the assignment early. However, you will not be permitted to submit the assignment late.

Why?: Some say that one cannot effectively manage and lead others effectively unless he or she first has a thorough understanding of him- or herself. This assignment helps to ground your thinking—where you are now and where you are headed.

How?: Research, discover, think, re-think, reflect, have fun. Begin your answers immediately after each question. Begin your answer immediately after the question. Do not delete the instructions. If you choose, you may change the color of your ink and/or change to italics to help make your answer stand out. Plan to write about 3-5 pages or so including these instructions and questions.

1. Career progression. Using your resume as a guide, consider your background, education and experience. Do your background, education, and experience follow a more-or-less logical pattern that helps forecast where you may be headed in your career? In your answer, explain why this is or why this is not the case and how this may help or challenge you.

2. What is missing? Is there anything particularly obvious that is missing in your background, education, and experience that you could address over the next year or two to make you a stronger candidate for your next career move? Discuss.

3. Particular organization or position. Is there a particular organization or position to which you aspire to work? In short, what would you like to do when you move into your next position or organization?

4. Personal goals. Think forward into the future two to three years. What are two personal goals that you would like to have successfully achieved? Discuss why these personal goals are important to you.

   1st personal goal:

   2nd personal goal:

5. Properly written, goals are expressed using SMART format. In SMART format, ensure that your goals are Specific, Measurable, Agreeable, Realistic, and Time bound (timely). Go back and re-visit your goals in the preceding question and ensure that they include all of the SMART elements.

   Here are a few examples to help you conceptualize the concept of SMART. The word, Specific means preciseness. I want to lose 10 pounds is specific. I want to lose a lot of weight is not specific. Measurable almost always uses times or counts. I will reduce my calorie intake to 1200 calories per day is a count. I will workout for 1.5 hours each day is a time. Agreeable simply means that you want to achieve the goal, that it is agreeable to you, which is necessary for success. Realistic means that the goal is doable. A goal such as, I want to lose 10 pounds by this weekend is not realistic. Timely refers to a beginning and end and may add interim goals or objectives. I will begin my diet and exercise program tomorrow morning (a beginning), and lose five pounds by the end of the first month (an objective), and reach my goal of 10 pounds by the end of the second month (an end).

6. Think forward into the future two to three years. What are two professional goals that you would like to have successfully achieved? Discuss why these professional goals are important to you.

1st professional goal:

2nd professional goal:

7. Re-visit you goals in the preceding question and ensure that they include all of the SMART elements.

8. Now that you have taken the time to think in detail and list two personal and two professional goals, you have gained additional clarity over your goals. Before completing this assignment, go back and re-visit both your personal and professional goals and make any small changes necessary.

Assignment 02:

Lifeline

Who?: If assigned, each person will individually complete and submit this assignment.

What?: This assignment will take you through several steps to help ensure that you have a robust understanding of yourself and what is important to you personally.

When?: The due date and time are posted in the syllabus. You can submit the assignment early. However, you will not be permitted to submit the assignment late.

Why?: Some say that one cannot effectively manage and lead others effectively unless he or she first has a thorough understanding of him- or herself.

How?: Research, discover, think, re-think, reflect, have fun. Begin your answers immediately after each question. Begin your answer immediately after the question. Do not delete the instructions. If you choose, you may change the color of your ink and/or change to italics to help make your answer stand out. Plan to write about 3-5 pages or so including these instructions and questions.

1. Mark the point. Draw a line across the page. The line illustrates your lifeline –from birth (at the far left side) to midpoint (in the middle) to death (at the far right side). It has a beginning and an end. Mark the point on the line, which you think best represents where you are today in your life span. Refer to it over the weeks that come.

2. Reactions. After thinking about approximately where you fall on the lifeline, write three or four of your initial reactions to this point in your life span. One-word initial reactions is fine.

3. Your past, present, and future. Discuss briefly your past, where you are now, and where you are headed in the future. A few paragraphs is fine.

4. Turning points and lessons learned. Reflecting on your past for a moment, discuss any major turning points and/or lessons learned. Major turning points and/or lessons learned can be either positive or negative. Length is up to you.

5. Wisdom. What did you gain from these turning points and/or lessons in terms of wisdom to apply either now or in the future? Whether positive or negative at the time, turning points and/or lessons learned should provide positive guidance for the future. Writing a few sentences is fine. Guidance for the future should be condensed into short and concise statements.

Assignment 03:

10 Adjectives That Describe Me

Who?: If assigned, each person will individually complete and submit this assignment.

What?: This assignment will take you through several steps to help ensure that you have a robust understanding of yourself and what is important to you personally.

When?: The due date and time are posted in the syllabus. You can submit the assignment early. However, you will not be permitted to submit the assignment late.

Why?: Some say that one cannot effectively manage and lead others effectively unless he or she first has a thorough understanding of him- or herself.

How?: Research, discover, think, re-think, reflect, have fun. Begin your answers immediately after each question. Begin your answer immediately after the question. Do not delete the instructions. If you choose, you may change the color of your ink and/or change to italics to help make your answer stand out. Plan to write about 3-5 pages or so including these instructions and questions.

1. List. Develop a list of 10 adjectives, which describe you (i.e., *I am environmentally conscious*). It is a good idea to list both positive and negative adjectives. If you need help in getting ideas to help get you going, search these terms: *Words that describe behavior* or *words describing what kind of person I am.*

2. Rank order. Rank the list of adjectives describing you on a scale of 1-10 with 1 being the most important and/or meaningful to you.

3. Re-visit. Re-examine your list of 10 adjectives. Change any that you wish to change and rank order them once again.

4. Patterns. Look at the list overall. Do you see any patterns forming that help to accurately describe you, such as your skills, personality, tendencies, behaviors, and/or actions?

5. Negatives. Did you discover any negative adjectives that describe you? Do you see these as areas for behavior changes? If yes, what might be some of the actions that you would take to make changes? Do any of them particularly concern you?

6. New discoveries. Did you discover any new adjectives that you had not considered before now? If yes, how might that new knowledge of how you view yourself affect your behavior in the future?

Assignment 04:

Eulogy

Who?: If assigned, each person will individually complete and submit this assignment.

What?: This assignment will take you through several steps to help ensure that you have a robust understanding of yourself and what is important to you personally.

When?: The due date and time are posted in the syllabus. You can submit the assignment early. However, you will not be permitted to submit the assignment late.

Why?: Some say that one cannot effectively manage and lead others effectively unless he or she first has a thorough understanding of him- or herself.

How?: Research, discover, think, re-think, reflect, have fun. Begin your answers immediately after each question. Begin your answer immediately after the question. Do not delete the instructions. If you choose, you may change the color of your ink and/or change to italics to help make your answer stand out. Plan to write about 3-5 pages or so including these instructions and questions.

1. Write the eulogy, which you would have someone deliver at a funeral or memorial services after you die. Before you begin writing, I advise you to search the terms, *eulogies* or *how to write a eulogy* to give you ideas that will help in getting you started.

2. After writing this eulogy, reflect on what it is that you wrote. Does this eulogy accurately describe the person that you consider yourself as being?

3. Think about discussing this assignment with a loved one or trusted friend to help determine whether the eulogy that you wrote describes you as an *actual* person. Be sure that the setting is appropriate before discussing this assignment with someone else, as you want to ensure that you have time and that he or she is not surprised by the topic.

4. Because a eulogy will expose some of your most personal and private thoughts, it is important that you discuss this eulogy with someone that you can be honest and vulnerable with instead of someone that might not provide thoughtful and/or caring feedback.

5. If, when discussing this assignment with a loved one or trusted friend, that person provides feedback indicating that your eulogy describes the more ideal you (the person that you aspire to being) instead of the actual you (the real you), is there a message here? For example, might that input suggest behavior changes that you may wish to consider.

Assignment 05:

Key Individuals and Turning Points

Who?: If assigned, each person will individually complete and submit this assignment.

What?: This assignment will take you through several steps to help ensure that you have a robust understanding of yourself and what is important to you personally.

When?: The due date and time are posted in the syllabus. You can submit the assignment early. However, you will not be permitted to submit the assignment late.

Why?: Some say that one cannot effectively manage and lead others effectively unless he or she first has a thorough understanding of him- or herself.

How?: Research, discover, think, re-think, reflect, have fun. Begin your answers immediately after each question. Do not delete the instructions. If you choose, you may change the color of your ink and/or change to italics to help make your answer stand out.

Plan to write about 2-3 individuals, events, and/or turning points in your life. As an alternative, if you have one particular person or one particular event that was incredibly profound for you, you may limit your writing to one person or one turning point. Most will write about positive influences. However, do not forget that negative people and turning points can provide extremely valuable life lessons, as well. Plan to write about 2-3 pages or so including these instructions and questions.

To provide you help in getting started, I suggest that you search the terms: *Key individuals who influenced my life* and *events that have shaped my life.*

1. Write about two or three of the key individuals, events, and/or major turning point experiences in your life. How did each of these impact you?

2. Summarize three to five of the major life lessons that you have found as valuable takeaways as a result of these individuals, events, and/ or turning points?

Assignment 06:

My Primary Strengths and Areas for Improvement

Who?: If assigned, each person will individually complete and submit this assignment.

What?: This assignment will take you through several steps to help ensure that you have a robust understanding of yourself and what is important to you personally.

When?: The due date and time are posted in the syllabus. You can submit the assignment early. However, you will not be permitted to submit the assignment late.

Why?: Some say that one cannot effectively manage and lead others effectively unless he or she first has a thorough understanding of him- or herself.

How?: Research, discover, think, re-think, reflect, have fun. Begin your answers immediately after each question. Do not delete the instructions. If you choose, you may change the color of your ink and/or change to italics to help make your answer stand out. Plan to write about 2-3 pages or so including these instructions and questions.

1. Make a list of your primary strengths. What is it that you are particularly good at doing?

2. Make a list of areas where you could use improvement. What is it that you are not particularly good at doing?

3. Rank order. Now, go back in and re-order these strengths and areas for improvement in rank order. Strengths, in this sense, are positive and should be ordered in terms of 1 equaling *most strength*. Areas for improvement should be ordered in terms of 1 equaling *most need for improvement*.

4. Learning points. After reviewing both lists, discuss some of what you learned about yourself from this assignment. Did you discover

any surprises—either good or not so good? Do you have any plans for improvement in the list of things that you are not particularly good at doing?

5. Feedback. It is normal that you will complete this assignment without outside help. However, I suggest that you confide in a trusted friend, mentor, or loved one by asking him or her the same questions about you (don't show your lists until after that person provides an initial list). Try to have a positive and meaningful conversation that allows you to benefit. Now, answer this question: Reflect upon this conversation (with the trusted friend, mentor, or loved one) and discuss some of what you learned—either positive or negative.

6. Apply strengths. Is there opportunity for you to capitalize on your strengths beyond what you are already doing to increase your chances for greater personal and/or career success? Discuss.

7. Behavior changes. Can you effectively mitigate those areas where you could use improvement to become an even more effective person? Discuss.

Assignment 07:

10 Years in the Future

Who?: If assigned, each person will individually complete and submit this assignment.

What?: This assignment will take you through several steps to help ensure that you have a robust understanding of yourself and what is important to you personally.

When?: The due date and time are posted in the syllabus. You can submit the assignment early. However, you will not be permitted to submit the assignment late.

Why?: Some say that one cannot effectively manage and lead others effectively unless he or she first has a thorough understanding of him- or herself.

How?: Research, discover, think, re-think, reflect, have fun. Begin your answer immediately after the question. Do not delete the instructions. If you choose, you may change the color of your ink and/or change to italics to help make your answer stand out. Plan to write about 2 pages or so including these instructions and questions.

1. Pick a date in the future, 10 years out. Describe, in detail, the things that you would do and experience, making this an IDEAL day in your future. Plan to write enough detail to take up about 1-2 pages.

Dream big. Allow yourself to dream into the future about what you would like to be doing, where you might be living, explore relationships. Over time, refer back to this document and update it as your plans and wishes evolve.

Background: There is a concept referred to as *visualization*, which suggests that by effectively (detailed) thinking about what it is that you would like—envisioning it—that the mind can then take over and help us achieve (actualize) what it is that we envision (want, desire, wish for). If you want to read more about visualization, do a bit of online research searching that term.

Visualization. I often use visualization in my consulting practice when working with organizations in planning strategy. It is an effective method in helping executives focus on future states both personally and professionally.

Assignment 08:

What Difference Will You Make?

Who?: If assigned, each person will individually complete and submit this assignment.

What?: This assignment will take you through several steps to help ensure that you have a robust understanding of yourself and what is important to you personally.

When?: The due date and time are posted in the syllabus. You can submit the assignment early. However, you will not be permitted to submit the assignment late.

Why?: Some say that one cannot effectively manage and lead others effectively unless he or she first has a thorough understanding of him- or herself.

How?: Research, discover, think, re-think, reflect, have fun. Begin your answer immediately after the question. Do not delete the instructions. If you choose, you may change the color of your ink and/or change to italics to help make your answer stand out. Plan to write about 2 pages or so including these instructions and questions.

1. What difference will you make? What will you be remembered for? What is your possible relationship and contribution to the quality of life experienced by all in present and future generations?

Contributions. Include reflections on your possible relationship and contribution to the quality of life experienced by all in your family, organization, neighborhood and community, in this country, and beyond.

Be audacious. I hope that as you complete this assignment, you will be audacious enough to believe, and to decide to act on the belief that your life, your existence, can make a difference in the quality of context that future generations will inherit from us all.

Legacy. Sometimes this is referred to as *legacy*, which can be defined as giving back to family, friends, the community... or even this planet... with gratitude for what one has learned or received.

Your mark. What will you be remembered for? What will be your legacy?

Assignment 09:

What Would You Tell A Loved One Or A Close Friend?

Who?: If assigned, each person will individually complete and submit this assignment.

What?: This assignment will take you through several steps to help ensure that you have a robust understanding of yourself and what is important to you personally.

When?: The due date and time are posted in the syllabus. You can submit the assignment early. However, you will not be permitted to submit the assignment late.

Why?: Some say that one cannot effectively manage and lead others effectively unless he or she first has a thorough understanding of him or herself.

How?: Research, discover, think, re-think, reflect, have fun. Begin your answer immediately after the question. Do not delete the instructions. If you choose, you may change the color of your ink and/or change to italics to help make your answer stand out. Plan to write about 2-3 pages or so including these instructions and questions. To give you ideas and help you get going, I suggest that you search this term: *How to let others know how much you appreciate them.*

1. If you were to learn that you only had a few weeks left on earth, what would you say to your loved ones or close friends? (I am not referring to you telling them that you were going to die.) Instead, the focus of this question is to get you thinking about the difference that each of these people has made in your life. The purpose is to remind you not to wait until the end to tell those that you appreciate, love, and admire how much they mean to you and why. Be specific in your answers. If you want, feel free to use only initials or nicknames. Think back. I want for you to list what you would say to at least <u>five</u> individuals.

Appreciate others. One of the overriding themes of my leadership courses is letting others know how much you appreciate them as individuals. The concept refers to the importance of 1) recognizing the goodness of others' contributions and 2) letting them know how much you cherish and appreciate them. Most of us practice, at least to some extent, the recognizing part in 1. However, we truly become more evolved and effective leaders when we practice the sharing part in 2. It's a small adjustment that can make a tremendously positive difference in both our and others' lives.

Focus. While the focus of this exercise is on personal leadership, I don't want for you to miss its application to the business world and organizational leadership. We become more evolved and effective leaders when we practice the sharing part described above. While the application is adjusted appropriately from personal relationships to business relationships, the message is essentially the same. We must trust in and recognize the goodness of others' work and we must communicate that in the form of positive feedback for jobs well done.

Assignment 10:

Reactions

Who? If assigned, each person will individually complete and submit this assignment.

What? This assignment will take you through several steps to help ensure that you have a robust understanding of yourself and what is important to you personally.

When? The due date and time are posted in the syllabus. You can submit the assignment early. However, you will not be permitted to submit the assignment late.

Why? Some say that one cannot effectively manage and lead others effectively unless he or she first has a thorough understanding of him or herself.

How? Research, discover, think, re-think, reflect, have fun. Begin your answers immediately after the questions. Do not delete the instructions. If you choose, you may change the color of your ink and/or change to italics to help make your answer stand out. Plan to write about 2-3 pages or so including these instructions and questions.

In the preceding assignments, I have asked you to research, discover, think, re-think, reflect, and even have fun coming to grips with many of the questions that we often think about, but fail to delve deeply into. It is by examining ourselves that we come to understand that which is really important.

1. Learned. Reflect upon the past assignments and write about what you learned from the experience. Cover a minimum of four things that you learned about yourself.

2. Which assignment was the most enjoyable for you to write and why was it so?

3. Which assignment led to the highest number of surprise discoveries about yourself and why was it so?

4. Which assignment made you the most uncomfortable, emotional, and/or difficult to express and why was it so?

5. List and briefly discuss some of your plans for modification in ways of thinking, behavior, or attitude patterns as a result of thinking about these assignments. These changes can be considered major or minor, positive or negative, and they can be noticed by others or strictly internal.

Assignment 11:

Leadership Thought and Reflection

Overview:

- **Who?** If assigned by your professor, each student will individually complete this assignment.

- **What?** This assignment encompasses your total work for this course and takes you back through many of the various theories, subjects, assignments, or topics that we covered this term. Using, notes, the text, articles, and your overall impressions, you will complete this assignment by answering the questions and then upload to Blackboard before the cutoff date and time specified in the syllabus.

- **When?** Due by date and time are posted in your syllabus. You can submit the assignment early. However, you will not be permitted to submit the assignment late.

- **Why?** This assignment allows you to think further and reflect on the content of this course and how you might apply its principles in your work life upon graduation.

- **How?** Think, reflect, use your notes, text, Power Point slides, assignments, readings, and any other resources to help you become a more effective leader.

Expectations. Your professor expects a minimum of 8-pages (single-spaced, 12 point font) including this cover information and instructions.

- Note cutoff dates and times. No late submittals accepted.

- Use spelling, grammar check, and page numbers.

- This assignment is open book, open note.

- Uploaded copy only. Please submit this assignment to Blackboard. Do not combine multiple submittals (single submittal only).

- Do not paste into box on Blackboard. Upload the document.

- This assignment is an individual assignment. This assignment to be written by you personally. It is not a group exercise.

- Grading. I will rate your assignment based on various levels of thoughtful effort. Please ensure that you take time to demonstrate a deep understanding in your answers, a willingness to think about application in your future work life, that you have probed and reflected in order to have valuable take-aways from this course, and that what you write is purposeful. Finally, please ensure that you take care in presenting an assignment whereby the craftsmanship is solid and that you have taken time to write something that you are proud to submit. Read more about my expectations in the next bullet.

- Rubric. In grading your assignment, your professor will look for you to express yourself in a way that shows some level of mastery in understanding theory, subject, assignment, or topics. Second, your professor will look for habits of the mind. Specifically, your professor will look to your ability to express yourself by proposing creativity and, where appropriate, multiple solutions or plans. Third, your professor will look for you to go past the generalities of the theory, subject, assignment, or topic and delve into the complexities of the content and what it means to you. Fourth, and finally, your professor will look for an assignment that is professionally thought-through and presented with craftsmanship using extreme care to address each one of the questions in appropriate detail.

Here are your questions. Begin your answer immediately after each question. Do not worry about eliminating instructions or re-phrasing questions. Just keep this format as is. As an aid to your professor in navigating your submittal, please write your answers in *italic* to help them stand out.

1. **First, identify one key leadership theory, subject, assignment, or topic.** This course covered a number of key theories from different disciplines that encompass leadership. Choose one theory covered this term that will be important in helping you become a more effective leader in your work life after graduation: (A few words is plenty.)

2. **Explain this theory, subject, assignment, or topic.** Refer back to the theory, subject, or topic that you identified in the preceding

question. Go back to your text and summarize it in a way that provides thorough evidence that you understand its principles as well as how you will benefit in your work life in applying that theory. Answer these prompts to help you construct your answer:

a. **Why did you choose this particular theory, subject, assignment, or topic?** Answer what it was that appealed to you? (Write a short paragraph of three or four sentences.)

b. **Explain the basics of this theory, subject, assignment, or topic.** (Take as much space as you need, but a minimum of a few paragraphs. If you need more information about this theory to convey your synopsis of the theory basics, use an online search.)

c. **Application.** How will you benefit in your work life in applying this theory, subject, or topic? (Take as much space as you need, but a minimum of a few paragraphs. Go into detail about your plans for application. Create a scenario if you wish.)

d. **Reflection and innovation.** Before writing, think again about your application question. I want you to expand the possibilities and stretch your thinking. Thinking back on your application question, answer what in your opinion you will need to start doing, stop doing, or change the way you are doing something in order to become a more effective leader. (Take as much space as you need, but a minimum of a few paragraphs. Go into detail about your plans for innovating this theory, subject, assignment, or topic to *really* work especially well for you.)

3. **Second. Identify a second key leadership theory, subject, assignment, or topic.** This course covered a number of key theories from different disciplines that encompass leadership. Choose one theory covered this term that will be important in helping you become a more effective leader in your work life after graduation: (A few words is plenty.)

4. **Explain this theory, subject, assignment, or topic.** Refer back to the theory, subject, or topic that you identified in the preceding question. Go back to your text and summarize it in a way that provides thorough evidence that you understand its principles as well as how you will benefit in your work life in applying that theory. Answer these prompts to help you construct your answer:

a. **Why did you choose this particular theory, subject, assignment, or topic?** Answer what it was that appealed to you? (Write a short paragraph of three or four sentences.)

b. **Explain the basics of this theory, subject, assignment, or topic.** (Take as much space as you need, but a minimum of a few paragraphs. If you need more information about this theory to convey your synopsis of the theory basics, use an online search.)

c. **Application.** How will you benefit in your work life in applying this theory, subject, or topic? (Take as much space as you need, but a minimum of a few paragraphs. Go into detail about your plans for application. Create a scenario if you wish.)

d. **Reflection and innovation.** Before writing, think again about your application question. I want you to expand the possibilities and stretch your thinking. Thinking back on your application question, answer what in your opinion you will need to start doing, stop doing, or change the way you are doing something in order to become a more effective leader. (Take as much space as you need, but a minimum of a few paragraphs. Go into detail about your plans for innovating this theory, subject, assignment, or topic to *really* work especially well for you.)

5. **Third. Identify a third key leadership theory, subject, assignment, or topic.** This course covered a number of key theories from different disciplines that encompass leadership. Choose one theory covered this term that will be important in helping you become a more effective leader in your work life after graduation: (A few words is plenty.)

6. **Explain this theory, subject, assignment, or topic.** Refer back to the theory, subject, or topic that you identified in the preceding question. Go back to your text and summarize it in a way that provides thorough evidence that you understand its principles as well as how you will benefit in your work life in applying that theory. Answer these prompts to help you construct your answer:

a. **Why did you choose this particular theory, subject, assignment, or topic?** Answer what it was that appealed to you? (Write a short paragraph of three or four sentences.)

b. **Explain the basics of this theory, subject, assignment, or topic.** (Take as much space as you need, but a minimum of a few paragraphs. If you need more information about this theory to convey your synopsis of the theory basics, use an online search.)

c. **Application.** How will you benefit in your work life in applying this theory, subject, or topic? (Take as much space as you need, but a minimum of a few paragraphs. Go into detail about your plans for application. Create a scenario if you wish.)

d. **Reflection and innovation.** Before writing, think again about your application question. I want you to expand the possibilities and stretch your thinking. Thinking back on your application question, answer what in your opinion you will need to start doing, stop doing, or change the way you are doing something in order to become a more effective leader. (Take as much space as you need, but a minimum of a few paragraphs. Go into detail about your plans for innovating this theory, subject, assignment, or topic to *really* work especially well for you.)

7. **Fourth. Identify a fourth key leadership theory, subject, assignment, or topic.** This course covered a number of key theories from different disciplines that encompass leadership. Choose one theory covered this term that will be important in helping you become a more effective leader in your work life after graduation: (A few words is plenty.)

8. **Explain this theory, subject, assignment, or topic.** Refer back to the theory, subject, or topic that you identified in the preceding question. Go back to your text and summarize it in a way that provides thorough evidence that you understand its principles as well as how you will benefit in your work life in applying that theory. Answer these prompts to help you construct your answer:

a. **Why did you choose this particular theory, subject, assignment, or topic?** Answer what it was that appealed to you? (Write a short paragraph of three or four sentences.)

b. **Explain the basics of this theory, subject, assignment, or topic.** (Take as much space as you need, but a minimum of a few paragraphs. If you need more information about this theory to convey your synopsis of the theory basics, use an online search.)

c. **Application.** How will you benefit in your work life in applying this theory, subject, or topic? (Take as much space as you need, but a minimum of a few paragraphs. Go into detail about your plans for application. Create a scenario if you wish.)

d. **Reflection and innovation.** Before writing, think again about your application question. I want you to expand the possibilities and stretch your thinking. Thinking back on your application question, answer what in your opinion you will need to start doing, stop doing, or change the way you are doing something in order to become a more effective leader. (Take as much space as you need, but a minimum of a few paragraphs. Go into detail about your plans for innovating this theory, subject, assignment, or topic to *really* work especially well for you.)

9. **Fifth. Identify a fifth key leadership theory, subject, assignment, or topic.** This course covered a number of key theories from different disciplines that encompass leadership. Choose one theory covered this term that will be important in helping you become a more effective leader in your work life after graduation: (A few words is plenty.)

10. **Explain this theory, subject, assignment, or topic.** Refer back to the theory, subject, or topic that you identified in the preceding question. Go back to your text and summarize it in a way that provides thorough evidence that you understand its principles as well as how you will benefit in your work life in applying that theory. Answer these prompts to help you construct your answer:

a. **Why did you choose this particular theory, subject, assignment, or topic?** Answer what it was that appealed to you? (Write a short paragraph of three or four sentences.)

b. **Explain the basics of this theory, subject, assignment, or topic.** (Take as much space as you need, but a minimum of a few paragraphs. If you need more information about this theory to convey your synopsis of the theory basics, use an online search.)

c. **Application.** How will you benefit in your work life in applying this theory, subject, or topic? (Take as much space as you need, but a minimum of a few paragraphs. Go into detail about your plans for application. Create a scenario if you wish.)

d. **Reflection and innovation.** Before writing, think again about your application question. I want you to expand the possibilities and stretch your thinking. Thinking back on your application question, answer what in your opinion you will need to start doing, stop doing, or change the way you are doing something in order to become a more effective leader. (Take as much space as you need, but a minimum of a few paragraphs. Go into detail about your plans for innovating this theory, subject, assignment, or topic to *really* work especially well for you.)

CPSIA information can be obtained
at www.ICGtesting.com
Printed in the USA
FSHW02n1453011018
52464FS